EX LIBRIS

VINTAGE CLASSICS

SCOTT ON WATERLOO

Walter Scott was born in Edinburgh on 15 August 1777. He was educated in Edinburgh and called to the bar in 1792, succeeding his father as Writer to the Signet, then Clerk of Session. He published anonymous translations of German Romantic poetry from 1797, in which year he also married. In 1805 he published his first major work, a romantic poem called *The Lay of the Last Minstrel*, and became a partner in a printing business. Several other long poems followed, including *Marmion* (1808) and *The Lady of the Lake* (1810). These poems found acclaim and great popularity, but from 1814 and the publication of *Waverley*, Scott turned almost exclusively to novel-writing, albeit anonymously. A hugely prolific period of writing produced over twenty-five novels, including *Rob Roy* (1817), *The Heart of Midlothian* (1818), *The Bride of Lammermoor* (1819), *Kenilworth* (1821) and *Redgauntlet* (1824). Already sheriff-depute of Selkirkshire, Scott was created a baronet in 1820. The printing business in which Scott was a partner ran into financial difficulties in 1826, and Scott devoted his energies to work in order to repay the firm's creditors, publishing many more novels, dramatic works, histories and a life of Napoleon Bonaparte. Sir Walter Scott died on 21 September 1832 at Abbotsford, the home he had built on the Scottish Borders.

Paul O'Keeffe's acclaimed books include biographies of Wyndham Lewis (*Some Sort of Genius,* 2000), Gaudier Brzeska (*An Absolute Case of Genius,* 2004) and Benjamin Robert Haydon (*A Genius for Failure,* 2009). He has also edited a scholarly edition of Wyndham Lewis's first novel *Tarr: the 1918 Version* (1990). His most recent book is the critically acclaimed *Waterloo: The Aftermath* (2014). He lives in Liverpool.

ALSO BY WALTER SCOTT

WALTER SCOTT

Scott on Waterloo

EDITED, ANNOTATED AND INTRODUCED BY
Paul O'Keeffe

VINTAGE BOOKS
London

1 3 5 7 9 10 8 6 4 2

Vintage
20 Vauxhall Bridge Road,
London SW1V 2SA

Vintage Classics is part of the Penguin Random House group of
companies whose addresses can be found at
global.penguinrandomhouse.com.

Introduction, selection and notes copyright © Paul O'Keeffe 2015

Paul O'Keeffe has asserted his right to be identified as the
author of this Work in accordance with the Copyright,
Designs and Patents Act 1988

First published in Great Britain by Vintage in 2015

www.vintage-books.co.uk

A CIP catalogue record for this book is available from the British
Library

ISBN 9781784870232

Printed and bound by Clays Ltd, St Ives plc

Contents

CONTENTS

General Introduction

Anxiously awaited news of the battle arrived in Edinburgh by mail coach on the morning of Saturday 24 June 1815. It came in the form of an express letter, sent from Westminster at 1.30 a.m. on the 22nd by the Lord Provost, Sir John Marjoribanks, MP for Bute. The Duke of Wellington's dispatch, and two captured French eagle standards, had reached London only a couple of hours earlier carried by Major Henry Percy, his uniform still soiled by travel and a fellow officer's blood. 'As the feelings of those who have near relatives in the army must be on the stretch,' wrote the Lord Provost, 'I cannot help gratifying the inhabitants of the good town [of Edinburgh] with the communication... of the greatest intelligence that ever came to Britain.'[1] For the rest of that Saturday every church bell in the Scottish capital was rung by order of the Magistrates, and at six o'clock the following morning a cannon salvo from the castle battlements announced the victory to anyone still ignorant of it.

But with news of victory came awareness of the terrible

---

[1] *Caledonian Mercury*, 24 June 1815.

cost and on 27 June, at a meeting of concerned citizens in the Parliament House, a motion was proposed that a fund be established to relieve 'the wants of the Widows and Children of those who have been slain'.

The forty-three-year-old Walter Scott seconded the motion and 'trusted that the inhabitants of this city, who were never backward to calls of charity, would cheerfully contribute to alleviate the distresses occasioned by so glorious a cause'.[2] Such trust in the generosity of his fellow citizens did not, however, prevent his playing upon the emotions and pricking the conscience of his audience:

How many of the Gallant Men who have fallen…must have been soothed in the moment of death, by reflecting that those who were dependent on their lives, would now become a legacy to their grateful Country! How many more of our brave Defenders must we be prepared to see return to their native land, deprived by honourable wounds! of the means of following either a military or a peaceful profession! To the exertions of these brave men we owe the safety, the comfort, the luxuries which we here enjoy; and he who can hear unmoved the appeal now made, not to our Liberality, but to our Justice, is unworthy of sharing those advantages which their blood has purchased, and the fame which their exertions has acquired for their Country.

The four largest single donations pledged at the meeting – of a hundred guineas each – came from the City of Edinburgh, the Earl of Wemyss, the Duke of Buccleuch, and from Scott himself. As a successful author of poetry,

---

[2] Ibid., 29 June 1815.

and of two equally successful – though anonymous – novels, *Waverley*, which had appeared in 1814, and *Guy Mannering*, published only the previous February, he ascribed to the liberality of his publishers his ability to contribute such a sum. It was a sum 'far indeed below [his] wishes', he explained, 'but yet more commensurate with these than with the limitations of [his] ordinary income' as an advocate at the Scottish bar and Sheriff-Depute for Selkirkshire. He likened his case to that of an actor, enabled by the public's indulgence and appreciation of his talents to give the proceeds of a performance 'for the benefit of those sufferers in whom [that public was] so deeply and justly interested'.[3]

It was not until early July that Scott decided to make what would be the first foreign excursion of his life, and with the principal purpose of visiting the field of Waterloo. His journey would result in two books: one in prose called *Paul's Letters to His Kinsfolk* – like his novels published anonymously – the other in verse and with the author's profits from its first edition donated to the Waterloo Fund. He later claimed that his determination to visit Belgium was 'if not fixed, much quickened' by reading a letter sent from Brussels by the surgeon Charles Bell to his brother, who forwarded a copy to Scott. Reading it 'set [him] on fire'. The surgeon wrote of a city 'ornamented with the finest groups of armed men that the most romantic fancy could dream of'; he wrote of the French wounded, 'exhausted, beaten... [but] men capable of marching unopposed from the west of Europe to the east of Asia... strong, thickset, hardy veterans, brave spirits and unsubdued... their wild

---

[3] *Edinburgh Advertiser*, 30 June 1815.

glance...their black eyes...' But perhaps the passage that most fired Scott's imagination was Bell's account of a Brunswick officer, dressed entirely in black except for the silver death's head emblazoned on his shako, riding into town from the battle of Quatre Bras on 16 June:

> He was wounded, and had had his arm amputated on the field. He was among the first that came in. He rode straight and stark upon his horse – the bloody clouts about his stump – pale as death, but upright, with a stern fixed expression of feature, as if loth to lose his revenge.

It must have seemed, to the imaginative chronicler of Bannockburn, Prestonpans and Flodden, a timeless image of martial heroism; small wonder that the Romantic novelist and poet grasped the opportunity 'of seeing probably the last shadows of real warfare that his own age would afford'.[4]

Scott was enthralled by war and it has been suggested that, had he not been crippled, aged eighteen months, by a then undiagnosed fever – known later as infantile paralysis, today as poliomyelitis – he might have followed an army career like his elder brother, John. Even lame, in 1797, he was instrumental in forming the Royal Edinburgh Volunteer Light Dragoons, a body of gentlemanly amateurs with military hankerings, of which he was elected quartermaster and secretary. One of many militia groups mustered at that time in anticipation of French invasion, the Volunteers spent their time drilling, slicing turnips in half at the gallop, and charging along Portobello beach. And, doubtless,

---

[4] John Gibson Lockhart, *The Life of Sir Walter Scott* (Edinburgh: 1902) volume V, pp. 49–52.

round their campfire they chanted the 'War Song' their quartermaster and secretary had composed for them:

> To horse! To horse! The sabres gleam;
>   High sounds our bugle-call;
> Combined by honour's sacred tie,
> Our word is *Laws and Liberty!*
>   March forward, one and all![5]

The only time they were mobilised in earnest, however, was against their own countrymen. In May 1800, local militia were called out when 'starving & very tumultuously disposed' mobs attacked property in Edinburgh and its environs, protesting against the high price of oats. Scott's corps undertook patrol duty at a mill in Moredun, southeast of the city. They were 'pelted & much insulted' but provoked neither to pistol shot nor sabre stroke – though when a rioter seized his horse's reins Scott was momentarily tempted to relieve him of his fingers.[6]

He would have left Edinburgh for the Continent sooner had he not been obliged to attend a friend's wedding on 24 July, but at five in the morning of the 27th, leaving his wife and children at home in Abbotsford, he set out with three companions: his kinsman John Scott of Gala; Alexander Pringle, the future MP for Selkirkshire; and the advocate Robert Bruce.

---

[5] 'War Song of the Royal Edinburgh Light Dragoons' (1802), *The Poetical Works of Sir Walter Scott*, ed. J. Logie Robertson (London: 1894), p. 701.
[6] Scott to Richard Heber, 5 May 1800, *The Letters of Sir Walter Scott*, ed. H. J. C. Grierson (London: 1933) volume XII, p. 160.

On 31 July, before Scott and his party had even boarded the cutter at Harwich that would take them to the Dutch port of Helvoetsluys, the *Caledonian Mercury* carried an announcement:

IN THE PRESS
And speedily will be published . . .
Price 3s 6d.
THE FIELD OF WATERLOO.
A POEM.
by WALTER SCOTT Esq.

Not a word of it had thus far been written.

The travellers made a brief stop at Bergen-op-Zoom to examine the fortifications – besieged by the French in 1747 and by the English, disastrously, in 1814 – before proceeding to Antwerp on 6 August. Here they encountered British troops for the first time. At the cathedral they saw where Rubens' *Elevation of the Cross* and *Deposition* had hung prior to seizure by the French in 1794, the spaces 'still vacant to remind the citizens of their loss'.[7] John Scott of Gala spoke for many of his Presbyterian countrymen when he remarked that 'to persons . . . who had not been accustomed to see pictures in places of worship, the blank was not offensive'.[8] On 7 August they left Antwerp for Brussels and two days later made the pilgrimage for which their entire expedition might be said to have been a pretext.

---

[7] *Paul's Letters to His Kinsfolk*, Letter X, p161.
[8] John Scott, *Journal of a Tour to Waterloo and Paris, in company with Sir Walter Scott in 1815* (London, Saunders, and Otley: 1842), p. 26.

Walter Scott was the first celebrity, but by no means the first civilian, to visit the field of Waterloo. Sightseers with strong stomachs had begun arriving from Brussels on the morning after the battle, when the mangled dead and dying lay in heaps and the work of clearing the wounded had barely begun. During the remainder of June and throughout July, the curious continued to visit. Many picked up souvenirs from the ground, still strewn with debris discarded as worthless by looters. A particular fascination was the ubiquitous litter – Bible pages, playing cards, letters – turned out from dead men's pockets in the search for money and valuables. Scott took home with him a couple of crumpled leaves of a German prayer book and an example of the most commonplace item, a *livret militaire*, or account book, carried by every French soldier. It contained 'the state of his pay and equipments... the occasions on which he served and distinguished himself... the punishments, if any, which he had incurred' and 'a list of the duties of the private soldier, amongst which is that of knowing how to dress his victuals, and particularly to make good soup'.[9] More substantial trophies could be bought from the local peasantry and the back plate of a French cuirass, punctured by a musket ball, purchased for five francs was brought back to Abbotsford, along with an ornate, inlaid breastplate that had cost four times as much in Brussels.

By early August the last of the wounded had been brought in and the dead buried or burned along with the horse carcasses. But the summer's heat baked the thousands of corpses beneath their thin covering of earth and every tourist complained of the stench and the carrion flies. Scott thought it 'wonderful that a pestilential disease ha[d]

---

[9] *Paul's Letters to His Kinsfolk*, Letter IX, p. 41.

not broken out, to sum up the horrors of the campaign'.[10] Yet despite an awareness of the 'ghastly evidences', he could still find stirring parallels, in the stories told him of the battle, to more romantically distanced conflicts like Bannockburn and Flodden. 'Many of the blows dealt...seemed borrowed from the annals of knight-errantry,' his protagonist Paul writes, 'for several of the corpses exhibited heads cloven to the chine, or severed from the shoulders',[11] the occasional retention of an archaic spelling adding lustre to the carnage. Nevertheless, when *Paul's Letters to His Kinsfolk* was published in January 1816, containing a sixty-page description of the battle, Scott was flattered to be told that an officer on the General Staff, 'who...was well acquainted with the scene...considered the account...as given in that production *of an unknown author* to be the best and most correct that had yet been published'.[12]

Scott's party left Brussels the day after their tour of the battlefield and journeyed on by way of Mons, then across the French border, passing through Valenciennes, Péronne and Chantilly to Paris. They travelled in the wake of two invasion forces – Wellington's Anglo-Allied army, composed of Belgian, Brunswick, Dutch and Hanoverian, as well as British, regiments, and Blücher's Prussians. Each army displayed a markedly different attitude to the country they marched through. Acutely aware, ever since the Peninsular Campaign, of the advantages of maintaining good relations with a civilian population, Wellington had

[10] Ibid., p. 144.
[11] Ibid., Letter VIII, p. 115.
[12] Sir John Malcom to Scott, *Letters* IV, p. 78, footnote 2.

reminded the troops under his command that their war had been waged against 'the Usurper' Napoleon on behalf of the French King Louis XVIII and that, therefore, France was to be regarded, and treated, 'as a friendly country'. Plunder was forbidden and nothing was to be taken, from farms and villages, 'for which payment be not made'.[13] Prussian troops, by contrast, were under no such restriction or obligation. They had endured French occupation – following their defeat at the Battle of Jena – and so had 'greater wrongs to revenge'. As they swept towards Paris the Prussian conquerors' right of pillage was carried to vindictive lengths. Paul's account of the destruction, and the means used for breaking and entering, has a forensic precision betraying neither approval nor censure:

> As the peasants had left their cottages locked up, the soldiers as regularly broke them open, by discharging a musket through the keyhole and shattering the wards at once by the explosion. He who obtains admission by such violent preliminaries is not likely to be a peaceable or orderly guest; and accordingly furniture broken and destroyed, windows dashed in, doors torn down, and now and then a burned cottage [was seen, as well as] hamlets, deserted by such of the terrified inhabitants as were able to fly, and tenanted only by the aged and disabled.[14]

Of the French people Scott encountered, 'the few men look

---

[13] 'General Order, Nivelles', June 1815, *The Dispatches of Field Marshal the Duke of Wellington, during his various campaigns from 1799 to 1815* (London: 1838), vol. 12, p. 493.
[14] *Paul's Letters to His Kinsfolk*, Letter XI, p. 182.

very sulky', he wrote, 'and if you speak three words to a woman, she is sure to fall a-crying'.[15]

There were reckoned to be, if not quite a million foreign soldiers in occupied France, then certainly 800,000, 'an assembly of troops', observes Paul, 'scarce paralleled save in the annals of romance'. And the greatest concentration lay in Paris. This 'immense garrison'[16] afforded military splendour far surpassing that claimed by Charles Bell for Brussels. By the time Scott and his companions reached the French capital on 14 August it was occupied not only by the Anglo-Allied and Prussian forces but by those of the Austrian and Russian empires as well.

Paul confesses to an 'inherent partiality' for the society of soldiers. At a dinner given by Lord Cathcart to honour Tsar Alexander, Scott was able not only to indulge that partiality, but to participate vicariously, dressing up in the black boots, white leather breeches and scarlet coat with blue trimmings and silver lace of the Royal Edinburgh Volunteer Light Dragoons. Unfamiliar with the uniform, but noticing that Scott dragged his polio-wasted leg, the Tsar asked him in which 'affair' he had been wounded. Scott explained that he suffered from a natural infirmity.

'I thought Lord Cathcart mentioned that you had served,' the Tsar pursued.

'Oh yes,' Scott replied, 'in a certain sense I have served – that is, in the yeomanry cavalry.'

'Were you ever engaged?'

Scott was enjoying himself and would dine out on this conversation for years to come . . .

---

[15] Scott to his Grace the Duke of Buccleuch, August, *Letters* IV, p. 78.
[16] Scott to Archibald Constable, 5 September, *Letters* IV, p. 89.

'In some slight actions,' he replied, thinking of the stick-and-stone street fights of his Edinburgh boyhood and the Volunteers' riot control duty of 1800, 'slight actions such as the battle of the Cross Causeway and the affair at Moredun-Mill.'

At this point Lord Cathcart diplomatically moved the conversation in another direction.

At dinner Scott sat next to Count Platov, the Cossack commander. 'The Hetman addressed several sentences to me in his own language in a very obliging manner,' he recalled, 'to which I replied in English, taking care to make my answer nearly of the same length as his own speech; and with this I was glad to perceive he was perfectly satisfied.' Some days later the Cossack recognised his dinner companion in the street, dismounted from his horse, 'and, running up to him, kissed him on each side of the cheek with extraordinary demonstrations of affection'.[17]

On 31 August, at Platov's invitation – although not astride 'the gentlest of Ukrainian horses'[18] he had promised – Scott watched as 20,000 Russian troops passed in review before their Tsar and other heads and representatives of the Allied Powers. Rank after rank marched across the Place de la Concorde, in front of the saluting platform erected close to the site on which the last French king had been guillotined. From where he stood Scott could see the length of the Champs-Elysées, stretching back, 'like a glowing furnace',[19] as the sunlight reflected off the dense moving hedge of bayonets. It was a display of military power by

---

[17] *Life* V, p. 76.
[18] Ibid.
[19] Scott to Joanna Baillie, *Letters* IV, p. 95.

their conquerors that understandably attracted few French observers.

In common with other foreigners – civilian and military – making Paris their temporary home, Scott and his party were eager to see the Louvre and the vast collection of masterpieces that Napoleon had amassed, by force of conquest, from across Europe. They had made their first visit on the day they arrived, with a sense of urgency after being told that the plundered works were shortly to be returned to their countries of origin. Despite a quantity of statues and paintings, claimed by Prussia, having already left Paris in July, the collection that Scott saw on that first occasion remained for the time being largely intact. He was able to see Rubens' two great altar pieces, whose absence he had noted in Antwerp, as well as Raphael's *Transfiguration*, the *Apollo Belvedere* and the *Laocoön*, belonging to the Vatican. There were signs, however, that their days in France were numbered.

> The hammer and wedge have given awful note of preparation; the Venus, the Dying Gladiator, and many other statues, have been loosened from their pedestals, and stand prompt for returning to their native and appropriate places of abode.[20]

By the end of August the Austrians were making their claims. 'The pictures are disappearing fast from the Louvre,' Scott wrote to his wife, 'near three hundred have been packed off since I came here.'[21] But the more important

---

[20] *Paul's Letters to His Kinsfolk*, Letter XIII, p. 227.
[21] To Mrs Scott, late August 1815 *Letters* XII, p. 147.

and – for the Parisians – more emotive restitutions were to begin after Scott had left. He did not witness the occupation of the Louvre by British troops on 23 September, when the Duke of Wellington lent his support to the seizure of the Antwerp pictures on behalf of the King of the Netherlands; he did not see English engineers enforce the Austrian Emperor's claim by lowering the Venetian Horses from the Arc de Triomphe du Carrousel a week later; nor did he watch, in October, as the *Apollo Belvedere* and the *Medici Venus* were crated for Rome, crowning the diplomatic efforts of Sir William Hamilton and the foreign secretary, Lord Castlereagh. Such actions were to sour the comparatively good relations between the Parisians and the British, prompting one observer to declare that Wellington's laurels had been tarnished thereby and 'the glory of the battle of Waterloo ... effaced by the storming of the Louvre'.[22]

Towards the end of August Scott was feeling jaded. Just days before being dazzled by the massed weapons of the Russian army in the Place de la Concorde he had made a significant admission to his wife: 'I think I have seen enough of military doings which after all it is as well to read of as to witness.'[23] He decided not to attend the much bigger Russian review that was to take place in mid-September on the plain of Vertus to the east of Paris when no fewer than 150,000 men, including 36,000 cavalry, and 400 cannon would be on parade. 'I find going there would be attended with much difficulty,' he told

---

[22] Lady Malmesbury quoted in *Memoirs of Sir Lowry Cole*, ed. Maud Lowry Cole and Stephen Gwynn (London: 1934) p. 179.
[23] To Mrs Scott, late August, *Letters* XII, p. 147.

Charlotte, '& I have seen great shews of the kind of late so I shall cut it.'[24]

He had turned forty-four in Paris and began 'to tire to get home'.[25]

Not only had the Duke been 'most uncommonly kind' to Scott during his stay in Paris but 'so [had] all his military family'. And the valediction the author wrote for Paul on leaving the city suggested that he had felt himself under the personal protection of the British army:

> In such society, whatever secret discontents might in reality exist, Paris was to us like a frozen lake, over whose secret and fathomless gulphs we could glide without danger or apprehension...'[26]

Only four days after Scott's departure, however, he learned that for others the ice had been all too thin. 'We have left Paris in time,' he wrote from the safety of Brighton. 'They have begun to murder the English, one poor young man was stabbed on the Boulevards. Prussian men & officers are wounded or killed every now & then.'[27]

On his arrival at Abbotsford he discovered that his 'charger' – a reminder of his service with the Volunteers – had formed an inexplicable antipathy to him in his absence. This pure white stallion called Daisy 'looked askant at [Scott] like a devil' and would not allow him to mount,

[24] To Mrs Scott, 6 September, *Letters* XII, p. 149.

[25] To Mrs Scott, late August, *Letters* XII, p. 146.

[26] *Paul's Letters to His Kinsfolk*, Letter XVI, p. 303.

[27] To Mrs Scott, 13 September, *Letters* XII, p. 150.

throwing him to the ground each time he tried. After several attempts he was forced to sell the high-mettled creature to John Ballantyne. 'Wars and rumours of wars being over,' he said later, 'I resolved thenceforth to have done with such dainty blood. I now stick to a good sober cob.'[28] His journey had been a senior rite of passage. He had left Scotland a cavalryman *manqué*, his Light Dragoon's uniform carefully packed in his luggage; he returned transformed – at least in his own eyes – to the 'cross old bachelor', Paul. And of his next novel, published May 1816, he would write that 'among the numerous creatures of my Imagination the author has had a particular partiality for the Antiquary.'[29] It featured another self-portrait: the eponymous, bookish, garrulous buffer, Jonathan Oldbuck.

---

[28] *Life* V, p. 86.
[29] Scott to Basil Hall, 27 October 1831, *Letters* XII, p.37.

Paul's Letters to His Kinsfolk

Introduction

Walter Scott's tour of Holland, Belgium and France in the late July, August and early September of 1815 was to be subsidised by the account he intended writing of it. Precise business plans had been formulated before leaving Edinburgh, and, on the day he set out, his printer, John Ballantyne, wrote to three publishers – Archibald Constable, Thomas Longman and John Murray – inviting each to undertake payment of equal shares in printing costs; each to receive one-third of an initial print run of 3,000 copies, thereby taking equal shares in half the profits, of a 352-page book retailing at eight shillings a copy. Scott himself would receive the other half profit: a projected £450. The work would comprise 'a series of letters [from the Continent] on a peculiar plan, varied in matter and style, and to different supposititious correspondents'.[1]

---

[1] *Life* V, p. 54. Ballantyne underestimated the paper costs and the book was published at 460 pages.

Scott's 'peculiar plan' for what was to be published as *Paul's Letters to His Kinsfolk* was a travel book purporting to be written and addressed, thematically, to five individuals, each having a particular interest and receiving 'that species of information with which each is most gratified'. An unmarried sister, Margaret, was to be informed of all the general and personal details of her beloved brother's travels; an unnamed cousin, the retired Major, would be given details of military affairs; Peter, another cousin, was to be 'refreshed with politics'; the local Laird would be apprised of agricultural matters and 'the general state of the country'; and, finally, a Parson was to be told of the moral and religious state of post-revolutionary France. As ostensibly 'supposititious' as his correspondents, the author – 'a cross old bachelor' – was named Paul, recalling the epistolary evangelist.

With the exception of 'Cousin Peter', for whom no specific model has been identified, the correspondents were based on people known to Scott. His fifty-six-year-old maiden aunt Christian ('Chrittie') Rutherford provided the original for Paul's sister. The 'Laird' was modelled on the agriculturist John Southey, Lord Somerville, who had served as President of the Board of Agriculture in William Pitt's administration between 1798 and 1800. The 'Minister of the Gospel' was based on the Reverend Dr Robert Douglas of Galashiels, a man of 'sterling worth' and 'humorous conversation',[2] from whom Scott bought the farm – known locally as 'Clarty Hole' – that he had renamed, and was to rebuild, as Abbotsford. Finally, the 'Major' was based on Scott's elder brother John, although his career and that of Paul's kinsman were far from parallel. The 'Major' is said

---

[2] *Life* III, p. 296.

to have assisted in the defence of Bergen-op-Zoom when it was besieged by the French in 1747 during the War of the Austrian Succession, more than twenty years before John Scott was born. Similarly, John would have been only six years old when Paul's cousin is supposed to have fought at the Battle of Bunker Hill in 1775 during the American War of Independence. Little is known of John's military career but it was not distinguished. He had remained a Captain in the British army for over fifteen years during a period in which his country had been continuously at war and prospects of advancement excellent. Then, in 1809, his brother Walter pulled strings in the War Office and got him belatedly promoted to Major. Shortly thereafter he sold his commission and settled down to comfortable alcoholic retirement and declining digestive health. John Scott would survive the publication of *Paul's Letters to His Kinsfolk* by a matter of months, dying in early May 1816.

Writing of the book was intended to begin 'immediately on [Scott's] arrival in France', towards mid-August, and it was to be published 'if possible, the second week of September, when he propose[d] to return'.[3] That schedule could only have been possible if Scott had been able to write and send his finished letters from the Continent at the same rate as Paul is supposed to have done. The impression given by Scott's biographer, John Gibson Lockhart, suggests this is just what he did:

> He threw his daily letters to his wife into the form of communications meant for [the] imaginary group...These epistles, after having been devoured by the little circle at

---

[3] *Life* V, p. 54.

Abbotsford, were transmitted to Major John Scott, his mother, and Miss Rutherford, in Edinburgh; from their hands they passed to those of James Ballantyne [and] the copy ultimately sent to the press consisted in great part, of the identical sheets that had successively reached Melrose through the post.[4]

In practice, however, the writing followed an altogether different and more conventional procedure. The half-dozen or so letters he wrote to his wife Charlotte while he was away do not appear to have been 'thrown' into such a form, nor passed from hand to hand, as Lockhart describes. Instead, by the end of August, Scott had sent two packets of 'copy' directly to James Ballantyne, one of them containing the first two of *Paul's Letters*, and the other his finished poem, *The Field of Waterloo*. An earlier packet sent from Brussels – its contents unknown – had gone astray. Moreover, he had by then decided to send nothing further until he arrived home. 'There is much risque of miscarriage [and] I will not trust [Paul's] lucubrations till I get to some faithful post master.' He had, besides, found it impossible to write anything of substance during the three weeks he spent in Paris. 'There is a tumult in this town from morning till night beyond what it is possible for you to imagine,' he told Ballantyne. 'Fleet Street at noon is a dead calm to it. I am making large notes which is all I can do in the tempest.'[5] All this meant that the bulk of the book would have to be written after his return, putting the original publication date out of the question. This despite an advertisement in the *Caledonian Mercury* that had appeared on 25 August, that 'PAUL's LETTERS to HIS KINSFOLKS' [sic] was already 'In the Press'.

---

[4] *Life* V, pp. 55–6.
[5] Scott to James Ballantyne, 30 August 1815, *Letters* IV, p. 87.

It was not until 24 September that he reached Abbotsford and was able to resume his literary work: correcting proofs of *The Field of Waterloo*, writing a review of Jane Austin's latest novel *Emma*, and completing the book that Constable's advertisement had prematurely promised the public a month earlier. Other works were being published about the most celebrated event of the age and it was felt necessary to get *Paul's Letters* out before either the market was sated or the topicality faded. In November, Constable suggested increasing the initial print run from 3,000 to 6,000 and Scott readily agreed: 'It is a work of momentary interest & the more that can be made of it at first the better.'[6] By the end of the year it was finished. 'I'm done, thank God,' he told Ballantyne, 'with the long yarns of the most prosy of Apostles – Paul.'[7] Published in early January 1816, the first edition of 6,000 was exhausted in just three weeks. Second and third editions in the same year, and a fourth in 1817, comprised a further 3,000.

Although published anonymously, the book's title page did not bear the teasing attribution, 'by the author of *Waverley*', as the previous year's *Guy Mannering* had done, and as all his subsequent works of fiction would until his authorship of the 'Waverley Novels' was no longer even an open secret. Despite a 'supposititious' narrator and correspondents, it was, from the start, intended and marketed as a faithful piece of reportage. Besides, any pretence at 'cover' in this instance was comprehensively blown on publication when both the *Morning Post* and *Chronicle* of 29 January 1816 announced: 'It is known that Mr Walter Scott is the author of *Paul's Letters to His Kinsfolk*.'

---

[6] Scott to Constable, 3 November 1815, *Letters* IV, p. 115.
[7] Scott to Ballantyne, 29 December 1815, *Letters* IV, p. 147.

PAUL'S LETTERS

TO

HIS KINSFOLK.

EDINBURGH:

Printed by James Ballantyne and Co.

FOR ARCHIBALD CONSTABLE AND COMPANY,

EDINBURGH;

AND LONGMAN, HURST, REES, ORME, AND BROWN,

AND JOHN MURRAY, LONDON.

1816.

PAUL'S LETTERS TO
HIS KINSFOLK

LETTER I.

PAUL TO HIS SISTER MARGARET.

It is three long weeks since I left the old mansion-house, which, for years before, has not found me absent for three days, and yet no letter has assured its quiet inmates and neighbours whether my curiosity has met its punishment. Methinks I see the evening circle assembled, and anxiously expressing their doubts and fears on account of the adventurous traveller. The Major will talk of the dangers of outposts and free corps, and shall be somewhat disappointed, if the Major has displayed alacrity in putting his double-barrel in order for the moors; or if the Laird has shewn his usual solicitude for a seasonable sprinkling of rain to refresh the turnip-field. Peter's speculations on politics, and his walks to the bowling-green, have been darkened, doubtless, and saddened by the uncertainty of my fate; and I even suspect the Parson has spared his flock one *Seventhly*[1] of his text in his anxiety upon my account.

For you, my dear Margaret, can I doubt the interest you have given me in your affections from the earliest period of recollection, when we pulled *gowans*[2] together upon the green, until the moment when my travelling trunk, packed by your indefatigable exertions, stood ready to be locked; but, ere the key could be turned, reversing the frolics of the enchanted chest of the Merchant Abudah[3], sprung once more open, as if in derision of your labours. To you, therefore, in all justice, belong the first fruits of my correspondence; and while I dwell upon topics personal to myself, and therefore most interesting to you, do not let our kind friends believe that I have forgotten my promise, to send each of them, from foreign parts, that species of information with which each is most gratified. No! the Major shall hear of more and bloodier battles than ever were detailed to Young Norval by his tutor the Hermit.[4] The Laird shall know all I can tell him on the general state of the country. Peter shall be refreshed with politics, and the Minister with polemics; that is, if I can find any thing of the latter description worth sending; for if ever there existed a country without a sense of religion of any kind, it is that of France. The churches indeed remain, but the worship to which they are dedicated has as little effect upon the minds of the people, as that of the heathen Pantheon on the inhabitants of modern Rome. I must take Ovid's maxim, '*Tamen excute nullum*;'[5] and endeavour to describe the effects which the absence of this salutary restraint upon our corrupt and selfish passions, of this light, which extends our views beyond the bounds of a transitory world, has produced upon this unhappy country. More of this, however, hereafter. My first letter is addressed to you, my dear sister, and must therefore be personal.

Even your partiality would be little interested in my journey through England, or the circumstances attending my embarkation. And of my passage, it is enough to say, that sea-sick I was even unto the uttermost. All your fifteen infallible recipes proved unavailing. I could not brook the sight of lavender-drops; gingerbread-nuts were detestable to my eyes, and are so to my recollection even at this moment. I could as soon have swallowed the horns of the Arch-fiend himself as the dose of hartshorn; and for the great goblet of sea-water, 'too much of water had I, poor Ophelia.'[6] In short, he that would see as much misery, and as much selfishness, as can well be concentrated, without any permanent evil being either done or suffered, I invite him to hire a birth aboard a packet. Delicacy is lost; sympathy is no more; the bands of love and friendship are broken; one class of passengers eat and drink joyously, though intermingled with another, who are expressing their inward grievances, in a manner, which, in any other situation, seldom fails to excite irresistible sympathy. The captain and the mate, comforters by profession, indeed exhort you, from time to time, to be of good cheer, and recommend a glass of grog, or possibly a pipe of tobacco, or it may be a morsel of fat bacon, to allay the internal commotion; but it is unnecessary to say how ill the remedies apply to the disorder. In short, if you are sick, sick you must be; and can have little better comfort than in reflecting that the evil must be of short duration, though, were you to judge from your immediate feelings, you might conceive your life was likely to end first. As I neither met with a storm nor sea-fight, I do not know what effect they might produce upon a sea-sick patient; but such is the complete annihilation of energy; such the headache, the nausea, and depression of spirits, that I think any stimulus, short of the risque of being shot or drowned, would fail of rousing him to any exertion. The best is, that arrival on the land proves a certain remedy for the sorrows of the sea; and I do not think that even your *materia medica* could supply any other.

Suppose your brother then landed among the mynheers and yafrows of Holland and Belgium, as it is now the fashion to call what, before our portentous times, was usually named Flanders. Strange sights meet his eyes; strange voices sound in his ears; and yet, by a number of whimsical associations, he is eternally brought back to the land of his nativity. The Flemings, in particular, resemble the Scotch in the cast of their features, the sound of their language, and, apparently, in their habits of living, and of patient industry. They are, to be sure, a century at least behind in *costume* and manners; but the old chateau, consisting of two or three narrow houses, joined together by the gables, with a slender round turret ascending in the centre of the building, for the purpose of containing the staircase, is completely in the old style of Scottish dwelling-houses. Then the avenue, and the acre or two of ground, planted with fruit-trees in straight lines; the garden, with high hedges, clipped by the gardener's art into verdant walls; the intermixture of statues and vases; the fountains and artificial pieces of water, may still be seen in some of our ancient mansions; and, to my indifferent taste, are no unnatural decorations in the immediate vicinity of a dwelling-place, and infinitely superior to the meagreness of bare turf and gravel. At least they seem peculiarly appropriate to so flat a country as Belgium, which, boasting no objects of natural beauty or grandeur, and being deprived, in a great measure, even of the grace of living streams of water, must necessarily supply these deficiencies by the exertions of art. Nor does their taste appear to have changed since the days of William III. There seem to be few new houses built; and the old chateaux, and grounds around them, are maintained in the original style in which they were constructed. Indeed, an appearance of antiquity is one of the most distinguishing features which strikes the traveller in the Low Countries. Dates, as far back as the fifteenth, and even fourteenth centuries, are inscribed upon the front of many of the houses both in the country and in the towns and villages. And although I offended your national pride, my dear sister, when I happened to observe, that the Scotch, who are supposed to boast more than other nations of their ancient descent, in reality know less of their early history than any other people in Europe, yet, I think, you will allow, that our borough towns afford few visible monuments of the high claims we set up to early civilization.

Our neighbours, the English, are not much more fortunate in this respect, unless we take into the account the fortresses built for the purpose of defence on the frontiers of Wales and Scotland, or their ancient and beautiful churches. But we look in vain for antiquity in the houses of the middling ranks; for the mansions of the country gentlemen, and the opulent burghers of the fifteenth and sixteenth centuries, have, generally speaking, long since given place to the town-mansions of the earlier part of the last age, or the more fantastic structures of our own day. It is in the streets of Antwerp and Brussels that the eye still rests upon the forms of architecture which appear in the pictures of the Flemish school; those fronts, richly decorated with various ornaments, and terminating in roofs, the slope of which is concealed from the eye by windows and gables still more highly ornamented; the whole comprising a general effect, which, from its grandeur and intricacy, amuses at once and delights the spectator. In fact, this rich intermixture of towers, and battlements, and projecting windows, highly sculptured, joined to the height of the houses, and the variety of ornament upon their fronts, produce an effect as superior to those of the tame uniformity of a modern street, as the casque of the warrior exhibits over the slouched broad-brimmed beaver of a Quaker. I insist the more on this, for the benefit of those of the fireside at * * * *, who are accustomed to take their ideas of a fine street from Portland-place, or from the George's street of Edinburgh, where a long and uniform breadth of causeway extends between two rows of ordinary houses of three stories, whose appearance is rendered mean, by the disproportioned space which divides them, and tame from their unadorned uniformity.

If you talk, indeed, of comforts, I have no doubt that the internal arrangement of the last-named ranges of dwellings is infinitely superior to those of the ancient Flemings, where the windows are frequently high, narrow, and dark; where the rooms open into each other in such a manner as seems to render privacy impossible; where you sometimes pass into magnificent saloons, through the meanest and darkest of all possible entrances; and where a magnificent corridore conducts you, upon other occasions, to a room scarce worthy of being occupied as a pig-stye,—by such pigs at least, whose limbs are bred in England. It is for the exterior alone that I claim the praise of dignity and romantic character; and I cannot but think, that, without in the least neglecting the interior division necessary for domestic comfort, some of these beauties might, with great advantage, be adopted from the earlier school of architecture. That of the present day seems to me too much to resemble the pinched and pared foot of the ambitious Princess, who submitted to such severe discipline, in order to force her toes into the memorable glass-slipper.

These marks of ancient wealth, and burgher-like opulence, do indeed greatly excel what could be expected from the architecture of Scotland at the same period. But yet, to return to the point from which I set out, there is something in the height of the houses, and the mode of turning their gables toward the street, which involuntarily reminds me of what the principal street of our northern capital[7] was when I first recollect it.

If you enter one of these mansions, the likeness is far from disappearing. The owner, if a man of family, will meet you with his scraggy neck rising in shrivelled longitude out of the folds of a thinly-plaited stock. The cut of his coat, of his waistcoat, his well-preserved cocked-hat, his periwig, and camblet riding-coat, his mode of salutation, the kiss bestowed on each side of the face, all remind you of the dress and manners of the old Scotch laird. The women are not, I think, so handsome as my fair countrywomen, or my walks and visits were unfortunate in the specimens they presented of female beauty. But, then, you have the old dress, with the screen, or mantle, hanging over the head, and falling down upon each shoulder, which was formerly peculiar to Scotland. The colour of this mantle is indeed different—in Scotland it was usually tartan, and in Flanders it is uniformly black. The inhabitants say they derive the use of it from the Spaniards, of whose dominions their country was so long a principal part. The dress and features of the lower class bear also close resemblance to those of

Scotland, and favour the idea held by most antiquaries, that the lowlanders, at least, are a kindred tribe. The constant intercourse our ancestors maintained with Flanders, from which, according to contemporary accounts, they derived almost every article which required the least skill in manufacture, must have added greatly to those points of original similarity.

The Flemings are said to be inferior to their neighbours of Holland in the article of scrupulous attention to cleanliness. But their cottages are neat and comfortable, compared to those of our country; and the garden and orchard, which usually surround them, give them an air of ease and comfort, far preferable to the raw and uninviting appearance of a Scotch cottage, with its fractured windows stuffed with old hats and pieces of tattered garments, and its door beset on one side by a dunghill, on the other by a heap of coals.

These statistics, my dear Margaret, rather fall in the Laird's province than yours. But your departments border closely upon each other; for those facts, in which he is interested as a Seigneur de Village, affect you as a Lady Bountiful, and so the state of the cottages is a common topic, upon which either may be addressed with propriety.

Adieu! I say nothing of the pad nag and poor old Shock, because I am certain that whatever belongs peculiarly to Paul will be the object of special care during his absence. But I recommend to you to take some of the good advice which you lavish upon others; to remember that there are damps in Scotland as well as in Holland, and that colds and slow fevers may be caught by late evening walks in our own favoured climate, as well as in France or Belgium. Paul ever remains your affectionate Brother.

LETTER II.

PAUL TO HIS COUSIN THE MAJOR.

After all the high ideas, my dear Major, which your frequent and minute and reiterated details had given me, concerning the celebrated fortress of Bergen-op-Zoom[1], in former years the scene of your martial exploits, I must own its exterior has sadly disappointed me. I am well enough accustomed, as you know, to read the terms of modern fortification in the Gazette, and to hear them in the interesting narratives of your military experiences; and I must own, that bastions and ravelins, half-moons, curtains, and palisades, have hitherto sounded in my ears every whit as grand and poetical as donjons and barbicans and portcullisses, and other terms of ancient warfare. But I question much if I shall hereafter be able to think of them with exactly the same degree of respect.

A short reflection upon the principles of modern defence, and upon the means which it employs, might, no doubt, have saved me from the disappointment which I experienced. But I was not, as it happened, prepared to expect, that the strongest fortress in the Netherlands, or, for aught I know, in the world, the masterpiece of Coehorn[2], that prince of engineers, should, upon the first approach of a stranger, prove so utterly devoid of any thing striking or imposing in its aspect. Campbell is, I think, the only English poet who has ventured upon the appropriate terms of modern fortification, and you will not be surprised that I recollect the lines of a favourite author,—

———————— the tower
That, like, a standard-bearer, frown'd
Defiance on the roving Indian power.
Beneath, each bold and promontory mound,
With embrasure emboss'd and armour-crown'd,
And arrowy frize, and wedged ravelin,
Wove like a diadem its tracery round
The lofty summit of that mountain green.[3]

But, in order to give dignity to his arrowy frize and ravelin, the Bard has placed his works on the edge of a steepy ascent. Bergen-op-Zoom is nothing less. Through a country as level as the surface of a lake, you jolt onward in your cabriolet, passing along a paved causeway, which, as if an inundation were apprehended, is raised upon a mound considerably higher than the champaign country which it traverses. At length, you spy the top of a poor-looking spire or two, not rising proudly pre-eminent from a group of buildings, but exhibiting their slender and mean pinnacles above the surrounding glacis, as if they belonged to a subterranean city, or indicated the former situation of one which had been levelled with the ground. The truth is, that the buildings of the town, being sunk to a considerable depth beneath the sloping ramparts by which it is surrounded and protected, are completely hidden, and the defences themselves, to an inexperienced eye, present nothing but huge sloping banks of earth, cut into fanciful shapes and angles, and carefully faced with green turf. Yet the arrangement of these simple barriers, with reference to the command of each other, as well as of the neighbouring country, has been held, and, I doubt not, justly, the very perfection of military science. And, upon a nearer approach, even the picturesque traveller finds some gratification. This is chiefly experienced upon his entrance into the town. Here, turning at a short angle into a deep and narrow avenue, running through these mounds which at a distance seemed so pacific and unimportant, he finds himself still excluded by draw-bridges and ditches, while guns, placed upon the adjoining batteries, seem ready to sweep the ground which he traverses. Still moving forward, he rolls over draw-bridges, whose planks clatter under the feet of his horses, and through vaulted arches, which resound to the eternal smack of his driver's whip. He is questioned by whiskered sentinels, his passports carefully examined, and his name recorded in the orderly-book; and it is only after these precautions that a stranger, though as unwarlike as myself, is permitted to enter the town. The impression is a childish one; yet a Briton feels some degree of unpleasant restraint, not only at undergoing a scrutiny, to which he is so little accustomed, but even from the consciousness of entering a place guarded with such scrupulous minuteness. It is needless to tell you, my dear Major, how much this is a matter of general routine in fortified places on the continent, and how soon the traveller becomes used to it as a matter of course. But I conclude you would desire to have some account of my first impressions upon such an occasion. To you, who speak as familiarly of roaring cannon

As maids of fifteen do of puppy-dogs.[4]

my expectations, my disappointment, and my further sensations, will probably appear ridiculous enough.

These formidable fortifications will soon be of little consequence, and may probably be permitted to go to decay.

Bergen-op-Zoom, a frontier town of the last importance, while the Princes of Orange were only Stadtholders of the Seven United Provinces, is a central part of their dominions, since the Netherlands have been united into a single kingdom. Meantime, the town is garrisoned by a body of Land-poliz, which corresponds nearly to our local militia in the mode in which it is levied. All the disposable forces of the Netherlands have been sent forward into France, and more are still organizing to be dispatched in the same direction.

In the evening, by permission of the commandant, I walked round the scene of your former exploits. But you must forgive me, if my attention was chiefly occupied by the more recent assault under our brave countryman, Lord Lyndoch[5], which was so boldly undertaken, and so strangely disappointed, when success seemed almost certain. I was accompanied in my walk by a sensible native of the place, a man of Scotch descent, who spoke good English. He pretended to point out with accuracy the points on which the various assaults were made, and the spots where several of the gallant leaders fell. I cannot rest implicit faith in his narrative, because I know, and you know still better, how difficult it is to procure a just and minute account of such an enterprise, even from those who have been personally engaged in it, and how imperfect, consequently, must be the information derived from one who himself had it at second hand. Some circumstances, however, may be safely taken upon my guide's averment, because they are such as must have consisted with his own knowledge. But, first, it may be observed in general, that the history of war contains no example of a bolder attempt; and, if it failed of success, that failure only occurred after almost all the difficulties which could have been foreseen had been encountered and surmounted. In fact, the assailants, successful upon various points, were already in possession of the greater number of the bastions; and had they fortunately been in communication with each other, so as to have taken uniform measures for attacking the French in the town, they must have become masters of the place. It is even confidently said, that the French commandant sent his aid-de-camp to propose a capitulation; but the officer being killed in the confusion, other and more favourable intelligence induced the Frenchman to alter his purpose. It has been generally alleged, that some disorder was caused by the soldiers, who had entered the town, finding access to the wine-houses. My conductor obstinately denied this breach of discipline. He said, that one of the attacking columns destined to cross the stream which forms the harbour, had unhappily attempted it before the tide had ebbed, and were obliged to wade through when it was of considerable depth; and he allowed, that the severity of the cold, joined to the wetting, might give them the appearance of intoxication. But when the prisoners were put under his charge in the church, of which he was sexton, he declared solemnly, that he did not see among them one individual who seemed affected by liquor.

The fate of a Dutch officer in our service, who led the attack upon one of the bastions, was particularly interesting. He was a native of the town, and it was supposed had been useful in furnishing hints for the attack. He led on his party with the utmost gallantry; and although the greater number of them fled, or fell, under a heavy fire,—for the enemy were by this time upon the alert,—he descended into the main ditch, crossed it upon the ice, and forced his way, followed by a handful of men, as far as the internal defences of the place. He had already mounted the inner glacis, when he was wounded in many places, and precipitated into the ditch; and, as his followers were unable to bring him off, he remained on the ice until next morning, when, being still alive, he became a prisoner to the French. Their first purpose was to execute him as a traitor, from which they were with difficulty diverted by a letter from the British general, accompanied by documents to establish how long he had been in the English service. The unfortunate gentleman was then permitted to retire from the hospital to his own house in the town, where he did not long survive the wounds he had received.[6]

I did not, you may believe, fail to visit the unfortunate spot where Skerret, so celebrated for his gallantry in the peninsula, Gower, Mercer, Carleton, Macdonald, and other officers of rank and distinction, fell upon this unfortunate occasion. It is said that General Skerret, after receiving a severe wound by which he was disabled, gave his watch and purse to a French soldier, requesting to be carried to the hospital; but the ruffian dragged him down from the banquette only to pierce him with his bayonet.

While I listened to the details of this unhappy affair, and walked slowly and sadly with my conductor from one bastion to another, admiring the strength of the defences which British valour had so nearly surmounted, and mourning over the evil fate which rendered that valour fruitless, the hour of the evening, gradually sinking from twilight into darkness, suited well with the melancholy subject of my enquiries. Broad flashes of lambent lightning illuminated, from time to time, the bastions which we traversed; and the figure of my companion, a tall, thin, elderly man, of a grave and interesting appearance, and who seemed, from his voice and manner, deeply impressed by recollection of the melancholy events which he detailed, was such as might appear to characterize their historian. A few broad and heavy drops of rain occasionally fell and ceased. And to aid the general effect, we heard from below the hollow roll of the drums announcing the setting of the watch, and the deep and sullen WER DA[7] of the sentinels, as they challenged those who passed their station. I assure you this is no piece of imaginary scenery got up to adorn my letter, but the literal circumstances of my perambulation around the ramparts of Bergen-op-Zoom.

I presume you are now in active preparation for the moors, where I wish you much sport. Do not fail to preserve for me my due share in your friendship, notwithstanding that, on the subject of Bergen-op-Zoom, I am now qualified to give you story for story. Such are the advantages which travellers gain over their friends. My next letter to you shall contain more interesting, as well as more recent and more triumphant, military details.

I must not omit to mention, that in the church of Bergen-op-Zoom, a tablet of marble, erected by their brother officers, records the names of the brave men who fell in the valorous but ill-fated attack upon this famous fortress. For them, as for their predecessors who fell at Fontenoy[8], the imagination of the Briton will long body forth the emblematic forms of Honour and Freedom weeping by their monuments. Once more farewell, and remember me.

LETTER III.

PAUL TO HIS COUSIN PETER.

Thy politics, my dear Peter, are of the right Scottish cast. Thou knowest our old proverbial character of being *wise behind the hand*. After all, the wisdom which is rather deduced from events than formed upon predictions, is best calculated for a country politician, and smacks of the prudence as well as of the aforesaid proverbial attribute of our national character. Yet, believe me, that though a more strict seclusion of the dethroned emperor of France might have prevented his debarkment at Cannes, and although we and our allies might have spared the perilous farce of leaving him a globe and sceptre to play withal, there were, within France itself, elements sufficiently jarring to produce, sooner or later, a dreadful explosion. You daily politicians are so little in the practice of recollecting last year's news, that I may be excused recalling some leading facts to your recollection, which will serve as a text to my future lucubrations.

The first surrender of Paris had been preceded by so much doubt, and by so many difficulties, that the final victory seems to have been a matter not only of exultation, but even of surprise, to the victors themselves. This great event was regarded, rather as a gratification of the most romantic and extravagant expectations, than as a natural consequence of that course of re-action, the ebb of which brought the allies to the gates of Paris, as its tide had carried Buonaparte to those of Berlin and Vienna. Pleased and happy with themselves, and dazzled with the glory of their own exploit, the victors were in no humour to impose harsh conditions upon the vanquished; and the French, on their part, were delighted at their easy escape from the horrors of war, internal and external, of siege, pillage, and contribution. Buonaparte's government had of late become odious to the bulk of the people, by the pressure of taxation, by the recurring terrors of the proscription, but, above all, by the repeated disasters which the nation had latterly sustained. The constitutional charter, under which the Bourbon family were restored, was not only a valuable gift to those who really desired to be insured against the re-establishment of despotism, but operated as a salvo to the wounded feelings of the still more numerous class who wished that the crimes and calamities of the Revolution should not appear to be altogether thrown away, and who could now appeal to this Bill of Rights, as a proof that the French nation had not sinned and suffered in vain. The laboratory and chemical apparatus which was to have produced universal equality of rights, had indeed exploded about the ears of the philosophical experimentalists, yet they consoled themselves with the privileges, which had been assured to them by the King upon his Restoration.

> So though the Chemist his great secret miss,
> For neither it in art or nature is,
> Yet things well worth his toil he gains,
> And doth his charge and labour pay,
> With good unsought experiments by the way.[1]

All parties being thus disposed to be pleased with themselves, and with each other, the occupation of the capital was considered as the close of the disasters which France had sustained, and converted into a subject of general jubilee, in which the Parisians themselves rejoiced, or affected to rejoice, as loudly as their unbidden guests. But this desirable state of the public mind was soon overcast, and the French, left to their own reflections, began speedily to exhibit symptoms both of division and dissatisfaction.

The first, but not the most formidable of their causes of discontent, arose from the pretensions of the emigrant noblesse and clergy.

At the restoration of Charles II., (to which we almost involuntarily resort as a parallel case,) the nobility and gentry of England, who had espoused the cause of his father, were in a very different condition from the emigrant nobles of France. Many had indeed fallen in battle, and some few by the arbitrary sentence of the usurper's courts of justice; but the majority, although impoverished by fines and sequestrations, still resided upon their patrimonial estates, and exercised over their tenantry and cottagers the rights of proprietors. Their influence, though circumscribed, was therefore considerable; and had they been disposed to unite themselves into a party, separate from the other orders of the state, they had power to support the pretensions which they might form. But here the steady sense and candour, not alone of Ormond and Clarendon[2], but of all the leading Cavaliers, induced them to avoid a line of conduct so tempting yet so dangerous. The dangers of *re-action*, according to the modern phrase, were no sooner sounded into the public ear by the pamphlets and speeches of those who yet clung to a republic, than every purpose, whether of revenge, or of a selfish and separate policy, was disowned in a manifesto, subscribed by the principal Royalists, in which they professed to ascribe their past misfortunes, not to any particular class of their fellow-citizens, but to the displeasure of the Almighty, deservedly visiting upon them their own sins and those of the community. Such was the declaration of the Cavaliers at that important crisis; and though there were not wanting *royalistes purs et par excellence*, who, like Swift's correspondent, Sir Charles Wogan[3], censured the conduct of Clarendon for suffering to escape so admirable an opportunity to establish despotic authority in the crown, and vest feudal power in the nobility, I need not waste words in vindicating his moderate and accommodating measures to my discerning friend Peter.

The scattered remnants of the French noblesse, who survived to hail the restoration of the Bourbons, while they possessed no efficient power, held much more lofty pretensions than had been preferred by the aristocracy of Britain at the Restoration. It would be unjust to subscribe to the severe allegation, that they had forgot nothing, and learned nothing, during their long exile; yet it can hardly be either doubted, or wondered at, that they retained their prejudices and claims as a separate and privileged class, distinguished alike by loyalty and sufferings in the cause of the exiled family, to a point inconsistent with the more liberal ideas of a community of rights, which, in despite both of the frenzy of the Revolution and the tyranny of Buonaparte, had gradually gained ground among the people at large. And, while the once-privileged classes maintained such pretensions, they were utterly devoid of the means of effectually asserting them. Long years of banishment had broken off their connection with the soil of France, and their influence over those by whom it is cultivated. They were even divided amongst themselves into various classes;

and the original emigrants, whose object it was to restore the royal authority by the sword, looked with dislike and aversion upon the various classes of exiles of a later date, whom each successive wave of the Revolution had swept from their native land. Their own list did not appear to exhibit any remarkable degree of talent; those among them, whose exile was contemporary with their manhood, were now too old for public business, and those who were younger, had become, during their long residence abroad, strangers, in a manner, to the customs and habits of their country; while neither the aged nor the young had the benefit of practical experience in public affairs. It was not among such a party, however distinguished by birth, by loyalty, by devotion in the royal cause, that Louis XVIII. could find, or hope to find, the members of an useful, active, and popular administration. Their ranks contained many well qualified to be the grace and ornament of a court; but few, it would seem, fitted for the support and defence of a throne. Yet who can wonder, that the men who had shared the misfortunes of their sovereign, and shewn in his cause such proofs of the most devoted zeal, were called around him in his first glimpse of prosperity; and that, while ascending the throne, he entertained towards this class of his subjects, bound to him, as they were,

'By well-tried faith and friendship's holy ties,'[4]

the affections of a kind and grateful master. One distinguished emigrant, observing the suspicion and odium which so excusable a partiality awakened against the monarch, had the courage to urge, that, to ensure the stability of the throne, their sentence of banishment should have continued by the royal edict for ten years at least after the restoration of the house of Bourbon. It was in vain that the advocates of Louis called up on the people to observe, that no open steps had been taken in favour of the emigrants. Their claims were made and pleaded upon every hand; and, if little was expressly done in their favour, suspicion whispered, that the time was only waited for when ALL could be granted with safety. These suspicions, which naturally occurred even to the candid, were carefully fostered and enlarged upon by the designing; and the distant clank of the feudal fetters were sounded into the ears of the peasants and burghers, while the uncertainty of property alarmed the numerous and powerful proprietors of forfeited domains.

The dislike to the clergy, and the fear of their reviving claims upon the confiscated church-lands, excited yet greater discontent than the king's apprehended partiality to the emigrants. The system of the Gallic church had been thoroughly undermined before its fall. Its constitution had been long irretrievably shattered; the whole head was sore, and the whole heart was sick. Doctrines of infidelity, every where general among the higher ranks, were professed by none with more publicity than by the superior orders of the clergy; and respecting moral profligacy, it might be said of the church of France as of Ilion,

Intra maenia peccatur, et extra.[5]

It is no wonder, that, in a system so perverted, neither the real worth of many of the clergy, nor the enthusiastic zeal of others, was able to make a stand against the tide of popular odium, skilfully directed towards the church and its ministers by the reigning demagogues. Our catholic

Highland neighbour must also pardon us, if we account the superstitious doctrines of his church among the chief causes of her downfall. The necessity of manning outworks, which are incapable of being effectually defended, adds not a little to the perplexities of a besieged garrison. Thus the sarcasms and sneers, justified, at least in our heretical eyes, by some part of the catholic doctrines, opened the way for universal contempt of the Christian system. At any rate, nothing is more certain than that a general prejudice was, during the Revolution, successfully excited against the clergy, and that among the lower Parisians in particular it still exists with all its violence. Even on the day when the rabble of the Fauxbourgs hailed the triumphal return of Buonaparte to his throne, their respect for the hero of the hour did not prevent them from uttering the most marked expressions of dislike and contempt when Cardinal Fesch[6] appeared in the procession. The cry was general, *A bas la calotte!*[7] and the uncle of the restored emperor was obliged to dismount from his palfrey, and hide himself in a carriage.

The king and the Comte D'Artois[8] are, in their distresses, understood to have sought and found consolation in the exercise of religious duties. They continued, in gratitude, those devotions which they had commenced in humble submission, and their regard was naturally extended to the ministers of that religion which they professed and practised; Conduct in itself so estimable, was, in the unhappy state of the public mind, misrepresented to their subjects. The landholders were alarmed by fear of the re-establishment of tithes; the labouring poor, and the petty shopkeeper, regarded the enforcing the long-neglected repose of the Sabbath, as a tax upon their industry and time, amounting to the hire of one day's labour out of the seven. The proprietors of church-lands were alarmed, more especially when the rash zeal of some of the priesthood refused the offices of the church to those who had acquired its property. The protestants in the south of France remembered the former severities exercised against them by the sovereigns of the house of Bourbon, and trembled for their repetition under a dynasty of monarchs, who professed the catholic faith with sincerity and zeal. Add to these the profligate who hate the restraints of religion, and the unthinking who ridicule its abstracted doctrines, and you will have some idea how deeply this cause operated in rendering the Bourbons unpopular.

Those who dreaded, or affected to dread, the innovations which might be effected by the influence of the clergy and the nobles,—a class which included, of course, all the old partizans of democratical principles,—assumed the name of Constitutionalists, and afterwards of Liberalists. The one was derived from their great zeal for the constitutional charter; the other from their affected superiority to the prejudices of ancient standing. Their ranks afforded a convenient and decent place of refuge for all those who, having spent their lives in opposing the Bourbon interest, were now compelled to submit to a monarch of that family. They boasted, that it was not the person of the king to which they submitted, but the constitution which he had brought in his hand. Their party contained many partizans, especially among men distinguished by talent. Democracy, according to Burke, is the foodful nurse of ambition;[9] and men, who propose to rise by the mere force of their genius, naturally favour that form of government which offers fewest restraints to their career. This party was also united and strengthened by possessing many of those characters who had played the chief parts in the revolution, and were qualified, both by talents and experience, to understand and conduct the complicated ramifications of political intrigue.

Among those best qualified to 'ride on the whirlwind and direct the storm,'[10] was the celebrated Fouché, Duke of Otranto,[11] whose intimate acquaintance with every intrigue in France had been acquired when he exercised the office of minister of the police under the emperor. There is every reason to think that this person had no intention of pushing opposition into rebellion; and that it was only his purpose to storm the cabinet, not to expel the monarch. It cannot be denied, that there were among the Liberalists the materials for forming, what is called in England, a constitutional opposition, who, by assailing the ministry in the two chambers, might have compelled them to respect the charter of the constitution. And to those amongst them, who were actuated either by the love of rational liberty, or by a modified and regulated spirit of ambition, the reign of the Bourbons afforded much greater facilities than the restoration of the military despotism of Buonaparte. Even to the very last moment, Fouché is said to have looked round for some *mezzo termine*, some means of compromise, which might render unnecessary the desperate experiment of the emperor's restoration. When Napoleon had landed, and was advancing towards Lyons, Fouché demanded an audience of the king upon important business. The interview was declined, but two noblemen were appointed by Louis to receive his communication. He adverted to the perilous situation of the king; and offered even yet, provided his terms were granted, to arrest Napoleon's progress towards the capital. The ministers required to know the means which he meant to employ. He declined to state them, but professed himself confident of success. His terms he announced to be, that the Duke of Orleans[12] should be proclaimed lieutenant-general of the kingdom; and that Fouché himself and his party should immediately be called to offices of trust and power. These terms were of course rejected; but it was the opinion of the well-informed person from whom I had this remarkable anecdote, that Fouché would have been able to keep his word.

His recipe was not, however, put to the test; and he and his party immediately acceded to the conspiracy, and were forced onward by those formidable agents, of whom it may be observed, that, like fire and water, they are excellent servants, but dreadful masters; I mean the army, whose state, under the Bourbons, deserves the consideration of a separate epistle.—Ever, my dear friend, I remain sincerely yours.

LETTER IV.

TO THE SAME.

I left off in my last with some account of the Constitutionalists, Liberalists, or whatsoever they are called, who opposed, from various causes, the measures of Louis XVIII., without having originally any purpose of throwing themselves into the arms of Buonaparte. To this desperate step they were probably induced by the frank and universal adhesion of the army to the commander under whom they had so often conquered. No man ever better understood both how to gain and how to maintain himself in the hearts of his soldiers than Buonaparte. Brief and abrupt in his speech, austere and inaccessible in his manners to the rest of his subjects, he was always ready to play the *bon camarade* with his soldiers; to listen to their complaints; to redress their grievances, and even to receive their suggestions. This accessibility was limited to the privates and inferior officers. To the mareschals and generals he was even more distant and haughty than to his other subjects. Thus he connected himself intimately and personally with the main body of the army itself, but countenanced no intermediate favourite, whose popularity among the troops might interfere with his own.

To the motives of personal attachment, so deeply rooted and so industriously fostered, must be added the confidence of the soldiers in military talents so brilliantly displayed, and in the long course of victory which had identified the authority of Napoleon with the glory of the French arms.

To a train of the most uniform and splendid success, they might indeed have opposed the reverses of the peninsular war, or the disastrous retreat from Moscow and the battle of Leipsic, with all the subsequent reverses. But, as soldiers and as Frenchmen, they were little inclined to dwell upon the darker shades of the retrospect. Besides, partiality and national vanity found excuses for these misfortunes. In the peninsula, Buonaparte did not command; in Russia, the elements fought against him; at Leipsic, he was deserted by the Saxons; and in France betrayed by Marmiont[1]. Besides, a great part of the soldiers who, in 1814–15, filled the French ranks, had been prisoners of war during Buonaparte's last unfortunate campaigns, and he was only experimentally known to them as the victor of Marengo, Ulm, Austerlitz, Jena, Friedland, and Wagram. You cannot have forgotten the enthusiasm with which the prisoners on parole at ——[2] used to speak of the military renown of the emperor; nor their frank declaration at leaving us, that they might fight with their hands for the Bourbons, but would fight with hand and heart for Napoleon. Even the joy of their return seemed balanced, if not overpowered, by the reflection, that it originated in the dethronement of the emperor. To recollect the sentiments of these officers, unsuppressed even in circumstances most unfavourable for expressing them, will give you some idea of the ardour with which they glowed when they found themselves again in arms, and forming part of a large and formidable military force, actuated by the same feelings.

It was the obvious policy of the Bourbons to eradicate, if possible, this dangerous attachment, or to give it a direction towards the reigning family. For this purpose, every attention was paid to the army; they were indulged, praised, and flattered; but flattery, praise, and indulgence, were only received as the surly mastiff accepts, with growling sullenness, the food presented to him by a new master. There was no common tone of feeling to which the Bourbons could successfully appeal. It was in vain they attempted to conjure up the antiquated fame of *Henri Quatre*[3] to men who, if ever they had heard of that monarch, must have known that his martial exploits were as much beneath those of Buonaparte, as his moral character was superior to the Corsican's. In the reigning family there was no individual who possessed so decided a military character as to fill, even in appearance, the loss which the army had sustained in their formidable commander, and the moment of national difficulty was unfortunately arrived, in which the personal activity of the monarch, a circumstance which, in peaceful times, is of little consequence, was almost indispensably essential to the permanence of his authority.

Burke says somewhere, that the king of France, when restored, ought to spend six hours of the day on horseback. 'I speak,' he adds, 'according to the letter.'[4] The personal infirmities of the good old man, who has been called to wear this crown of thorns, put the required activity out of the question. But the justice of the maxim has not been the less evident. Not only the soldiers, but the idle and gaping population of Paris, despised the peaceful and meritorious tranquillity of Louis XVIII., and recalled with regret the bustling and feverish movements of Buonaparte, which alternately gave them terror and surprise and amusement. Indeed, such was the restless activity of the ex-emperor's disposition, that he contrived, as it were, to multiply himself in the eyes of the Parisians. In an incredibly short space of time, he might be seen in the most distant quarters of the city, and engaged in the most different occupations. Now he was galloping along a line of troops,—now alone, or with a single aid-de-camp, inspecting some public building,—in another quarter you beheld him in his carriage,—and again found him sauntering among the objects of the fine arts in the Louvre. With a people, so bustling, so active, and so vain-glorious as the French, this talent of ubiquity went a great way to compensate the want of those virtues which the emperor did not pretend to, and which the legitimate monarch possesses in such perfection. 'The King,' said an Englishman to a Frenchman, 'is a man of most excellent dispositions.'—'*Sans doute.*'—'Well read and well informed.'—'*Mais oui.*'—'A gentleman in his feelings and manners.'—'*Assurément, Monsieur, il est né François.*'—'Placable, merciful, moral, religious.'—'*Ah, d'accord—mais après tout*' (a mode in which a Frenchman always winds up his argument,) '*il faut avouer, qu'un Roi qui ne peut monter à cheval est un bien chetif animal.*'[5]—This opinion, in which the possession of the equestrian art was balanced against all mental qualities, is not peculiar to the person by whom it was delivered; and it is certain that the king's affairs suffered greatly by his being unable to shew himself, even in the exterior appearance, as a military commander. Ney[6], who was probably for the time sincere in his professions of zeal to the sovereign, whom he so soon afterwards deserted, recommended that he should review the regiments as they passed through Paris, even if it were in a litter. But the affecting apology of the king is best pleaded in the words of his own manifesto: 'Enfeebled by age, and twenty-five years of misfortunes, I cannot say, like my ancestor, *Rally around my white plume*; but I am willing to follow to the dangers to which I cannot lead.'[7]

None of the royal family, unfortunately, possessed

the temper and talents necessary for supplying the king's deficiencies. The Duke d'Angouleme[8], like his father Monsieur, was retired, and understood to be bigotted to the catholic observances, and much ruled by the clergy. The Duke de Berri[9], with more activity, had a fierce and ungovernable temper, which often burst out upon improper and unseemly occasions. Under their auspices, the attempts to new-model the army, by gradually introducing officers attached to the royal family, gave much offence, without producing any sensible advantage. In some instances the new officers were not received by the corps to whom they were sent; in some they were deprived of the influence which should attend their rank, by the combination of the soldiers and officers; in other cases, they were perverted by the universal principles of the corps whom they were appointed to command; and, finally, there were instances, as in the case of Labedoyere[10], in which the court were imposed upon by specious professions, and induced to promote persons the most inimical to the royal interests. The re-establishment of the household troops, in which a comparatively small body of *gardes de corps* were, at a great expence, and with peculiar privileges, established as the immediate guardians of the king's person, was resented by the army in general, but more especially by the *ci-devant* imperial, now royal, guards.

In a word, matters had gone so far, that the army, as in Cromwell's time, existed as an isolated and distinct body, not under the government of the legislature, but claiming exclusive rights and privileges, and enjoying a separate and independent political existence of its own. Whenever this separation between the civil and military orders takes place, revolution and civil war cannot be far distant.

But there was one powerful cause of irritation common to the French nation in general, though particularly affecting the army. That very people of Europe, the most ambitious of fame in arms, who so lately and so fully stood possessed of the palm of conquest, which for centuries had been the object of their national ambition, had at once lost that pre-eminence, and with it

> The earthquake-voice of victory,
> To 'them' the breath of life.[11]

The height to which their military reputation had been raised, the enormous sacrifices which had been made to attain it, the rapid extension of their empire, and the suddenness of their fall in power and in esteem, were subjects of the most embittered reflection. We in Britain vainly imagined, that the real losses which France sustained in extending her influence and her triumphs, must have disgusted her with the empty fame for which she paid so dearly. But however the French might feel under the immediate pressure of each new conscription, nothing is more certain than that their griefs, like the irritation of men impressed into our naval service, were forgotten in the eclat of the next victory, and that all the waste of blood and treasure by which it was obtained, was accounted a cheap expenditure for the glory of France.

When a people, with minds so constituted, beheld within the walls of their capital the troops of the nations whom they had so often subdued, their first effort was to disguise, even from themselves, the humiliation to which they were subjected. When they had looked so long upon a stranger as to be certain he was not laughing at them, which seemed to be their first apprehension, their usual opening was a begging of the general question, 'You know we were not conquered—our reception of the king was a voluntary act—our general and unanimous joy bears witness that this is the triumph of peace over war, not of Europe over France.' With such emollients did they endeavour to dress the surface of a wound which internally was inflamed and rankled.

These harmless subterfuges of vanity held good, until they had forgotten the late alarming and precarious state in which their country had been placed, and particularly until the departure of the allied troops (a measure most impolitically precipitate) had removed the wholesome awe which their presence necessarily imposed. Then instantly operated the principle of Tacitus—*qui timeri desierint, odisse incipient.*[12] A thousand hostile indications, trifling perhaps individually, but important from their number and reiteration, pointed out the altered state of the public mind towards the allies. The former complaisance of the French nation, founded perhaps as much upon their good opinion of themselves as in their natural disposition to oblige others, was at once overclouded, and the sight of a foreigner became odious, as reminding them of the aspect of a conqueror. Caricatures, farces, lampoons, all the *petite guerre*, by which individual malice has occasionally sought gratification, were resorted to, as the only expressions of wounded feeling now competent to the Great Nation. The equanimity with which the English in particular gave the losers leave to laugh as loudly as losers and beaten men could, rather exasperated than appeased the resentment of the French. The most unoffending foreigners were exposed to insult, and embroiled in personal quarrels with gratuitous antagonists in the public places of Paris, where, in former times, the name of a stranger was a sufficient protection even when an aggressor. All these circumstances indicated a tone of feeling, ulcerated by the sense of degradation, and which burned to regain self-opinion by wreaking vengeance on their conquerors. The nation was in the situation of losing gamblers, who reflect indeed upon their losses with mortification and regret, but without repenting the folly which caused them; and, like them also, the French only waited some favourable conjuncture again to peril the remains of their fortune upon the same precarious hazard.

The language of the government of France was gradually and insensibly tinged by the hostile passions of her population. The impatient and irritated state of the army dictated to her representative, even at the Congress, a language different from what the European republic had a right to expect from the counsellors of the monarch whom their arms had restored. It is probable the government felt that their army resembled an evoked fiend pressing for employment, and ready to tear to pieces even the wizard whom he serves, unless instantly supplied with other means of venting his malevolence. But if it was a part of the Bourbon policy, rather to encounter the risk and loss of an external war, than to leave their army in peace and at leisure to brood over their discontents and disgraces, they had no time allowed them to make the ungracious experiment. A plot was already on foot and far advanced, to ensure, as it was supposed, the recovery of the national glory, by again placing on the throne, him, under whose auspices, and by whose unparalleled military successes, it had been formerly raised to the highest pitch of military splendour.

Such was the influence of the various causes which

I have endeavoured to detail, that the reception of the insinuations of the conspirators, particularly in the army, exceeded their wishes, and nearly broke out before the time proposed. It is at least pretty certain that their zeal outwent the discretion of their principal, and that Napoleon more than once declined the invitations which he received to return from Elba. The co-operation of Murat[13] was a point of extreme moment; and until a Neapolitan army could approach the north of Italy, Buonaparte's situation must have been desperate, supposing him to have received a check in the south of France at the outset of his expedition. A series of dark intrigues, therefore, commenced between the principal conspirators and King Joachim, which ended in his winding up his courage to the perilous achievement which they recommended. In the north of Italy were many officers and soldiers who had formerly served under Eugene Beauharnois[14]. And it was reasonably believed, considering the weak state of the Austrians, that Murat's army, Neapolitans as they were, might have at least made their way so far as to have recruited their ranks by the union of these veterans.

Internally the conspiracy proceeded with the most surprising secrecy and success. The meetings of the chief leaders were held under the auspices of Madame Maret, Duchess of Bassano[15]. But subordinate agents were to be found every where, and more especially among the coffee-houses and brothels of the Palais Royale, those assemblages of every thing that is desperate and profligate. 'Buonaparte,' said a Royalist to me the other day, 'had with him all the *rogue-men* and all the *rogue-women*, and, in our country, their numbers are nineteen out of twenty.' One of these places of nocturnal rendezvous, called the Caffé Montaussier[16], was distinguished for the audacity with which its frequenters discussed national politics, and the vociferous violence with which they espoused the cause of the dethroned emperor. That the police, whose surveillance, in Buonaparte's reign, extended to the fire-side and bed-chamber of every citizen, should have either overlooked, or observed with supine indifference, those indications of treason in places open for public rendezvous, argues the incapacity of the superior directors, and the treachery of those who were employed under them. Even the partial discovery of Excelman's correspondence with Murat[17] served but to shew the imbecility of a government who could not, or durst not, bring him to punishment. The well-known symbol of the Violet, by which Buonaparte's friends intimated his return to France with the re-appearance of that flower in spring, was generally known and adopted, at least two months before the period of his landing, yet attracted no attention on the part of the police. Indeed, so gross was their negligence, that a Frenchman, finding his friend ignorant of some well-known piece of news, observed, in reply, *Vous etes apparemment de la police?* as if to belong to that body inferred a necessary ignorance of every thing of importance that was going forward in the kingdom.

With so much activity on the one side, and such supine negligence on the other, joined to a state of public feeling so favourable to his enterprise, one is scarcely surprised at Napoleon's wonderful success. The mass of the army went over to him as one man; and the superior officers, who found their influence too feeble to check the progress of the invader, took, with a few distinguished exceptions, the resolution to swim along with the stream which they could not oppose. But however discontented with the government of the Bourbons, the middling ranks in civil life were alarmed as with a clap of thunder by this momentous event. They beheld themselves once more engaged in a war with all Europe, and heard once more the Prussian trumpets at the gates of the metropolis. To dispel these alarms, Napoleon, with a versatile address, which could hardly have succeeded any where save in France, endeavoured to put such a colour upon his own views as best suited those whom he was immediately addressing. To the army, his proclamation, issued at Lyons[18], held forth immediate war, conquest, and the re-establishment of the military fame of France. But, when he reached Paris, he seemed anxious to modify this declaration. He appealed to the Treaty of Paris[19], by which he pretended to abide, and he expressed himself contented that the rights and boundaries of France should be limited according to the wishes of the allied powers as there expressed. He did more; he even alleged that his enterprise was executed with their connivance. With the assurance of a shameless charlatan, as one author expresses it[20], he asserted, that his escape was countenanced by England, otherwise, as he reasoned with apparent force, how was he permitted to leave Elba? and that his restoration had the approbation of Austria would be made manifest, he pretended, by the immediate return of Maria Louisa and her son[21] to the French territory. He even carried the farce so far as to prepare and send away state carriages to meet those valued pledges of his father-in-law's amity, conscious that the success of this gross imposition would serve his cause during the moments of general doubt and indecision, though certain to be discovered in a very few days. Meanwhile, an attempt was actually made to carry off his son from the city of Vienna, and defeated only by the want of presence of mind in one of the conspirators, who, being arrested by the police, imprudently offered a handful of gold to obtain his escape, which excited the attention and suspicion of the officer. No doubt, had the attempt succeeded, the restoration of the child would have been represented as the effects of the favour of Austria towards the father.

The declarations of the allied powers soon removed the hopes of peace, by which those who were peaceably disposed had been, for a short time, flattered. A war, of a kind altogether new, with respect to the extent of the military preparations, was now approaching and imminent, and the address of Chatterton's Sir Charles Baudin to the English might have been well applied to the people of France,—

> Say, were ye tired of godly peace,
>   And godly Henry's reign,
> That you would change your easy days
>   For those of blood and pain?
>
> Ah! fickle people, ruin'd land,
>   Thou wilt know peace noe moe;
> When Richard's sons exalt themselves,
>   Thy streets with blood shall flow.[22]

But there remained comfort to the more peaceable part of the community in the confidence of assured victory, so warmly expressed by the soldiers, and then they hoped that the short and successful war would conclude so soon as France should be restored to, what they were pleased to term, her natural boundaries. *Paix au dela du Rhin*[23] was the general wish—the soldiers affected to aim at no more remote conquest—the citizen was willing to face the burthens of a war for an object so limited, and for the re-establishment of *la gloire nationale*. And thus were the versatile people of Paris induced to look with an eye of hope, instead of terror, upon the approaching storm.

Those who were attached to the parties of the Liberalists and Royalists saw Buonaparte's successful progress with other eyes. But the Liberalists, severed from the family of Bourbon by the opinions and incidents which I have already detailed to you, were, in a manner, forced into the service of the new emperor, although, doubtless, their wishes were to substitute a government of a more popular construction. Their chiefs too, the philosophical Carnot[24] and the patriotic Fouché, did not disdain to accept, from the hand of the restored heir of the Revolution, the power, dignities, and emoluments which he artfully held out to them. And, in becoming a part of his administration, they were supposed to warrant to him the attachment of their followers, while Napoleon, by professing to embrace the constitution with some stipulations in favour of general freedom, was presumed to give a sufficient pledge that henceforth he was to regard himself only as the head of a limited monarchy. How far this good understanding would have survived his return to Paris with victory, it is scarce necessary to enquire; for not even the adhesion of Carnot and Fouché prevented some tart debates in the lower Chamber of Representatives; from which it is evident, that the Imperialists and Jacobins regarded each other with aversion and suspicion, and that their union was not likely to survive the circumstances which occasioned it.

In the meanwhile, they were embarked in a common cause; and it does not appear that the Liberalists were slack in affording assistance to Buonaparte in his preparations for external war. Like the factions in Jerusalem, during her final siege, they suspended their mutual dissensions until they should have repulsed the common enemy. There is nevertheless a rumour, which is at least countenanced by the favour which Fouché for some time held at the court of Louis XVIII., that even while that king was at Ghent[25], the wily chief of the Liberalists maintained a correspondence with his ex-monarch. But, in general, that party, comprehending the various classes of Liberalists, from the Constitutionalist to the Jacobin, may be considered as having identified themselves with the Imperialists, and undertaken the same chance of battle to which the adherents of Buonaparte had made their solemn appeal.

There was a third party in France, and a powerful one, if its real force could have been mustered and called into action. For, notwithstanding all that I have said of the various causes which divided the opinions of the nation, it must necessarily be supposed that the Bourbon family had, in many provinces, an equal, and in some, a predominating interest. Unfortunately, the Royalists being taken at unawares, remained altogether stupified and paralysed by the sudden and unanimous defection of the army. The premature or ill-conducted attempts of resistance at Marseilles and Bourdeaux were so easily subdued, as to discredit and discountenance all farther opposition. In La Vendee[26] only there was an open military resistance to Buonaparte under the banners of the king. The Royalists, in the other provinces, contented themselves with opposing a sort of *vis inertiae*[27] to the efforts which Napoleon made for calling forth the national force, and awaited with anxiety, but without any active exertion, the expected progress of the allies. This passive resistance was particularly remarkable in the departments of the north, several of which would render Napoleon no assistance, either in recruits or money, and where entreaties, threats, and even attempts at force, could not put in motion a single battalion of the national guard.

On the other hand, the eastern departments which bordered on Germany met the wishes of Buonaparte in their utmost extent. They remembered the invasion of the preceding year with all the feelings of irritation which such recollections naturally produce. Accordingly, they formed free corps of volunteers,—laboured at fortifying towns and passes,—constructed *tetes-du-pont*[28],—and multiplied all means of defence which the face of the country afforded. Thus it happened, fortunately for Buonaparte, that the part of the kingdom, whose inhabitants were most disposed to consider the war as a national quarrel, was that of which the territory was most immediately open to invasion.

I shall continue this statement, my dear Peter, in a letter to the Major, to whose department the military details properly belong, and, in the meanwhile, am ever your's.

LETTER V.

PAUL TO THE MAJOR.

I presume, my dear Major, that our political friend has communicated to you my last epistle. My next enters upon high matters, which I have some scruple to treat of to you; for who would willingly read lectures upon the art of war before Alexander the Great? But, after all, as Waterloo was a battle very different from that of Bunker's-hill[1], and from two or three other later actions with the details of which you often regale us, I conceive that even a bungling account of it from a tactician so wretched as I am, may afford some matter for your military commentaries. At any rate, active investigation has not been wanting; as I have surveyed the fields of action, and conversed familiarly with many of the distinguished officers, who there laid a claim to the eternal gratitude of their country. Your kindness will excuse my blunders, and your ingenuity will be applied to detect and supply my deficiencies.

No part of Napoleon's political life, marked as it has always been by the most rapid and extraordinary promptitude in military preparation, affords such a display of activity, as the brief interval which occurred between his resuming the imperial sceptre and resigning it, it is to be presumed, for ever. Although the conciliating the Liberalists, and para-lysing the Royalists, occupied some time; and although it was necessary to sacrifice several days to shew, and to the national love of fanfaronade, he was never an instant diverted from his purpose. While he seemed to be fully occupied with the political discussions of the various parties,—with shews, and processions, and reviews of corps of children under twelve years old, his more serious preparations for the death-struggle which he expected to encounter, were as gigantic in their character as incessant in their progress. Every effort was used to excite the population to assume arms, and to move forward corps of national guards to relieve in garrison the troops of the line now called into more active service. And while Buonaparte was convoking in the Champ de Mai, as his mock assembly of the people was fantastically entitled, a number of persons to whom the revolution had given dangerous celebrity, together with his own military adherents,—a class of men of all others most unfit for being members of a deliberative assembly,—while, I say, this political farce was rehearsing and acting, the real tragedy was in active preparation. Cannon, musquets, arms of every description, were forged and issued from the manufactories and arsenals with incredible celerity. The old corps were recruited from the conscripts of 1814; retired veterans were again called forth to their banners; new levies were instituted, under the various names of free-corps, federés, and volunteers; the martial spirit of France was again roused to hope and energy; and the whole kingdom seemed transformed at once into an immense camp, of which Napoleon was the leader and soul. One large army defiled towards Belgium, where the neighbourhood of the English and Prussian troops excited alarm; other armies were assembled in Alsace, in Lorraine, in Franche Compté, at the foot of the Alps, and on the verge of the Pyrenees. It only remained to be discovered on which side the storm was to burst.

There is little doubt, that Buonaparte, reckoning upon

the success of Murat, or hoping at least on his making a permanent diversion, had destined the north of Italy for the first scene of active and personal warfare. A threat in that quarter would have been sufficient to divert from the main struggle the whole force of Austria, already sensible, from sad experience, how vulnerable she was through her Italian frontier. Many of the Russian troops would probably have been detached to her assistance, and while a triple barrier of fortresses and garrisons of the first order, with a strong covering army, was opposed on the frontier of Flanders to the English and Prussian armies, Buonaparte himself might have taken the field on the theatre of his original triumphs, and have removed the war from the French territory, with the certainty, in case of success, that his army would be recruited among the Cisalpine veterans of Eugene Beauharnois. But Austria, on this pressing alarm, exerted herself with an activity unknown to her annals; and the troops which she rapidly hurried forward to meet Murat, exhibited, in the very first conflicts, the military superiority of the northern warriors.—'These barbarians,' said the Neapolitans, after the skirmish at Rimini[2], 'fight as if they had two lives; what chance have we against them, who pretend only to one?' And to save that single title to existence, Murat's army fled with such celerity, and so little resistance, that the campaign was ended almost as soon as begun, and with it terminated the reign of King Joachim over the delicious kingdom of Naples. No king, in a fairy tale, ever obtained a crown so easily, or lost it in a manner so simple, and at the same time so speedy. His discomfiture was attended with the most disadvantageous consequences to Buonaparte, who thus appeared hermetically sealed within the realm of France, by hostile armies advancing on all hands, and compelled to await the conflict upon his own ground.

But he neither lost courage nor slackened his preparations on account of his relative's disaster. The French grand army, already in the highest order, was still farther augmented in number and equipments. It became now obvious, that Flanders, or the adjoining French frontier, must be the scene of action. The general head-quarters were fixed at Laon; a very strong position, where some preparations were made for forming an army of reserve, in case of a disaster. The first corps occupied Valenciennes, and the second Maubeuge, communicating by their right wing with the armies assembled in the Ardennes and on the Moselle, and resting their left upon the strong fortifications of Lisle. Here they waited the numerous reinforcements of every kind which Buonaparte poured towards their position.

The deficiency of artillery was chiefly apprehended. The allies had, in 1814, carried off most of the French field-trains. But, by incredible exertions, the loss was more than supplied; for, besides the usual train attached to separate corps, each division of the army had a park of reserve, and the imperial guard, in particular, had a superb train of guns, consisting almost entirely of new pieces. It is remarkable, that in casting these fine engines of war, the old republican moulds had, in general, been employed; for I observed, that most of the guns taken at Waterloo have engraved upon them the emphatic inscriptions, Liberté, Egalité, Fraternité, and so forth; not to mention others, which, in honour of philosophy, bore the names of Voltaire, Rousseau, and other writers of deistical eminence. The army in all possessed more than three hundred guns; a quantity of artillery which has been thought rather beyond the proportion of its numbers.

Cavalry was another species of force in which Buonaparte was supposed to be peculiarly weak. But the very reverse proved to be the case. The care of Louis XVIII. had remounted several of the regiments which had suffered in the campaigns of 1813 and 1814; and the exertions of Napoleon and his officers completed their equipment, as well as the levy of others; so that a finer body of cavalry never took the field. They were upwards of twenty thousand in number; of whom the lancers were distinguished by their address, activity, and ferocity; and the cuirassiers, of whom there are said to have been nine regiments, by the excellence of their appointments, and the superior power of their horses. This last corps was composed of soldiers selected for their bravery and experience, and gave the most decisive proofs of both in the dreadful battle of Waterloo. Their cuirasses consisted of a breastplate and back, joined together by clasps, like the ancient plate-armour. Those of the soldiers were of iron, those of the officers of brass, inlaid with steel. They are proof against a musquet-ball, unless it comes in a perfectly straight direction. To these arms was added a helmet, with cheek-pieces, and their weapons of offence were a long broadsword and pistols. They carried no carabines. The horses of the cuirassiers, although, upon trial, they proved inferior to those of our heavy cavalry, were probably better than those of any other corps in Europe. They were selected with great care, and many of the carriage and saddle-horses, which Buonaparte had pressed for the equipment of the army, were assigned to mount these formidable regiments.

Of the infantry of the French, it was impossible to speak too highly, in point of bravery and discipline in the field. The *elite* of the army consisted of the imperial guards, who were at least 20,000 strong. These chosen cohorts had submitted with the most sullen reluctance to the change of sovereigns in 1814; and no indulgence nor flattery, which the members of the Bourbon family could bestow upon them, had availed to eradicate their affection to their former master, which often displayed itself at times and in a manner particularly offensive to those who were their temporary and nominal commanders. The imperial guards were pledged, therefore, as deeply as men could be, to maintain the new revolution which their partiality had accomplished, and to make good the boast, which had called France to rely 'upon their stars, their fortune, and their strength.' The other corps of infantry, all of whom participated in the same confidence in themselves and their general, might amount, including the artillery, to 110,000 men, which, with the guards and cavalry, formed a gross total of 150,000 soldiers, completely armed and equipped, and supplied, even to profusion, with every kind of ammunition. So fascinated was this brilliant army with recollection of former victories, and confidence in their present strength, that they not only heard with composure the report of the collected armies which marched against them from every quarter of Europe, but complained of the delay which did not lead them into instant battle. They were under a General who knew well how to avail himself of those feelings of confidence and ardour.

It had been supposed, as well in France and in the army, as in other parts of Europe, that Buonaparte meant to suffer the allies to commit the first hostile act, by entering the French territory. And although the reputation of being the actual aggressor was of little consequence where both parties had so fully announced their hostile intentions, it was still supposed that a defensive war, in which he could avail himself of the natural and artificial strength of French Flanders, might have worn out, as in the early war of the revolution, the armies and spirits of the allies, and exposed them to all those privations and calamities peculiar to an invading army, in a country which is resolutely defended.

But the temper of Buonaparte, ardent, furious, and impetuous, always aiming rather at attack than defence, combined, with the circumstances in which he found himself, to dictate a more daring system of operations.

His power was not yet so fully established as to ensure him the national support during a protracted war of various chances, and he needed now, more than ever, the dazzling blaze of decisive victory to renew the charm, or *prestige*, as he himself was wont to call it, once attached to his name and fortunes. Considerations peculiar to the nature of the approaching campaign, probably united with those which were personal to himself. The forces now approaching France greatly exceeded in numbers those which that exhausted kingdom could levy to oppose them, and it seemed almost impossible to protect her frontiers at every vulnerable point. If the emperor had attempted to make head against the British and Prussians in French Flanders, he must have left open to the armies of Russia and Austria the very road by which they had last year advanced to Paris. On the other hand, if, trusting to the strength of the garrison towns and fortresses on the Flanders frontiers, Napoleon had conducted his principal army against those of the Emperors of Russia and Austria, the numerous forces of the Duke of Wellington and Blucher[3] might have enabled them to mask these strong places by a covering army, and either operate upon the flank of Napoleon's forces, or strike directly at the root of his power by a rapid march upon the capital. Such were the obvious disadvantages of a defensive system.

A sudden irruption into Belgium, as it was more suited to the daring genius of Napoleon, and better calculated to encourage the ardour of his troops, afforded him also a more reasonable prospect of success. He might, by a rapid movement, direct his whole force against the army either of England or of Prussia, before its strength could be concentrated and united to that of its ally. He might thus defeat his foes in detail, as he had done upon similar occasions, with the important certainty, that one great and splendid victory would enable him to accomplish a levy *en masse*, and thus bring to the field almost every man in France capable of bearing arms; an advantage which would infinitely more than compensate any loss of lives which might be sustained in effecting it. Such an advantage, and the imposing attitude which he would be thereby entitled to assume towards the allies, might have affected the very elements upon which the coalition was founded, and afforded to Buonaparte time, means, and opportunity of intimidating the weak and seducing the stronger members of the confederacy. In Belgium, also, if successful, he might hope to recruit and extend his army by new levies, drawn from a country which had so lately been a part of his own kingdom, and which had not yet had time to attach itself to the new dynasty of powers to whom it had been assigned. For this purpose, he carried musquets with him to equip an insurrectionary army, and officers of their own nation to command them; and although the loyal Belgians were much shocked and scandalized at the hopes expressed by those preparations, it may be presumed they would not have been so confidently entertained without some degree of foundation.

The proposed advance into Belgium had the additional advantage of relieving the people of France from the presence of an army which, even upon its native soil, was a scourge of no ordinary severity. The superiority which long war and a train of success had given to the military profession in France, over every other class of society, totally reversed in that country the wholesome and pacific maxim, *Cedant arma togae*[4]. In the public walks, in the coffee-houses and theatres of Paris, the conduct of the officers towards a *Pekin*, (a cant word by which, in their arrogance, they distinguished any citizen of a peaceful profession,) was, in the highest degree, insolent and overbearing. The late events had greatly contributed to inflame the self-importance of the soldiery. Like the praetorian bands of Rome, the janizaries of Constantinople, or the strelitzes of Moscow, the army of France possessed all the real power of the state. They had altered the government of their country, deposed one monarch, and re-elevated another to the throne which he had abdicated. This gave them a consciousness of power and importance, neither favourable to moderation of conduct nor to military discipline. Even while yet in France, they did not hesitate to inflict upon their fellow-subjects many of those severities, which soldiery in general confine to the country of an enemy; and, to judge from the accounts of the peasantry, the subsequent march of the allies inflicted upon them fewer, or at least less wilful evils, than those which they had experienced at the hands of their own countrymen. These excesses were rarely checked by the officers; some of whom indulged their own rapacity under cover of that of the soldiers, while the recent events which invited soldiers to judge and act for themselves, had deprived others, who, doubtless, viewed this licence with grief and resentment, of the authority necessary to enforce a wholesome restraint upon their followers.

This looseness of discipline was naturally and necessarily followed by dissensions and quarrels among the troops themselves. The guards, proud of their fame in arms, and of their title and privileges, were objects of the jealousy of the other corps of the army, and this they repaid by contumely and arrogance, which led, in many cases, to bloody affrays. The cavalry and infantry had dissensions of old standing, which occasioned much mutiny and confusion. Above all, the licence of pillage led to perpetual quarrels, where one regiment or body of troops, who were employed in plundering a village or district, were interrupted by others who desired to share with them in the gainful task of oppression.

These feuds, and the laxity of discipline in which chiefly they originated, may be traced to Buonaparte's total disuse in this, as in his more fortunate campaigns, of the ordinary precautions for maintaining an army by the previous institution of magazines. By neglecting to make such provision, he no doubt greatly simplified his own task as a general, and accelerated, in the same degree, his preparations for a campaign, and the march of an army unincumbered with forage-carts. But he injured, in a much greater proportion, the discipline and moral qualities of his soldiery, thus turned loose upon the country to shift for their own subsistence; and,—had such a motive weighed with him,—he aggravated, in a tenfold degree, the horrors of warfare.

The evils arising from the presence of his army were

now to be removed into the territories of an enemy. The marches and combination of the various corps d'armée were marked in a distinguished manner by that high military talent which planned Buonaparte's most fortunate campaigns. In the same day, and almost at the same hour, three large armies; that from Laon, headed by the emperor himself; that of the Ardennes, commanded by the notorious Vandamme; and that of the Moselle, under the orders of General Girard[5], having broken up from their different cantonments, attained, by a simultaneous movement, an united alignement upon the extreme frontiers of Belgium. The good order and combination with which the grand and complicated movements of these large armies were executed, was much admired among the French officers, and received as the happy augury of future success.

To his army thus assembled, Buonaparte, upon the 14th of June, 1815, made one of those inflated and bombastic addresses, half riddle, half prophecy, which he had taught the French armies to admire as masterpieces of eloquence. He had not neglected his system of fortunate days; for that upon which he issued his last proclamation was the anniversary of the Marengo and Friedland victories; on which, as well as after those of Austerlitz and Wagram, he assured his troops he had fallen into the generous error of using his conquests with too much lenity. He reminded his soldiers of his victory over Prussia at Jena; and having no such advantage to boast over the English, he could only appeal to those among his ranks who had been prisoners in Britain, whether their situation had not been very uncomfortable. He assured them they had the private good wishes of the Belgians, Hanoverians, and soldiers of the confederation of the Rhine, although for the present forced into the enemy's ranks; and concluded, by asserting, that the moment was arrived, for every courageous Frenchman to conquer or to die.

This speech was received with infinite applause (*comme de raison*,) and on the morning of the subsequent day (15th June) his army was in motion to enter Belgium.

But my exhausted paper reminds me that this must be the boundary of my present epistle.—Yours, affectionately,

PAUL.

LETTER VI.

PAUL TO MAJOR ——, IN CONTINUATION.

I gave you, in my last, some account of the auspices under which Buonaparte opened the last of his fields. The bloody game was now begun; but, to understand its progress, it is necessary to mark the position of the opposite party.

Notwithstanding the fertility of Belgium, the maintenance of the numerous troops which were marched into that kingdom from Prussia, and transported thither from England, was attended with great burthens to the inhabitants. They were therefore considerably dispersed, in order to secure their being properly supplied with provisions. The British cavalry, in particular, were cantoned upon the Dender, for the convenience of forage. The Prussians held the line upon the Sambre, which might be considered as the advanced posts of the united armies.

Another obvious motive contributed to the dislocation of the allied force. The enemy having to chuse his point of attack along an extended frontier, it was impossible to concentrate their army upon any one point, leaving the other parts of the boundary exposed to the inroads of the enemy; and this is an advantage which the assailant must, in war, always possess over his antagonist, who holds a defensive position. Yet the British and Prussian divisions were so posted, with reference to each other, as to afford the means of sudden combination and mutual support; and, indeed, without such an arrangement, they could not have ultimately sustained the attack of the French, and

Buonaparte's scheme of invasion must have been successful on all points.

But though these precautions were taken, it was generally thought they would not be necessary. A strong belief prevailed among the British officers, that the campaign was to be conducted defensively on the part of the French; and when the certain tidings of the concentration of the enemy's forces, upon the extreme frontier of Belgium, threatened an immediate irruption into that kingdom, it was generally supposed, that, as upon former occasions, the road adopted by the invaders would be that of Namur, which, celebrated for the sieges it had formerly undergone, had been dismantled like the other fortified places in Flanders by the impolicy of Joseph II[1]., and is now an open town. And I have heard it warmly maintained by officers of great judgment and experience, that Buonaparte would have had considerable advantages by adopting that line of march in preference to crossing at Charleroi. Probably, however, these were compensated by the superior advantage of appearing on the point where he was least expected. In fact, his first movements seem to have partaken of a surprise.

It is not to be supposed that the Duke of Wellington had neglected, upon this important occasion, the necessary means to procure intelligence,—for skill in obtaining which, as well as for talent in availing himself of the information when gained, he was pre-eminently distinguished on the peninsula. But it has been supposed, either that the persons whom he employed as his sources of intelligence, were, upon this occasion, seduced by Buonaparte, or that false information was conveyed to the English general, leading him to believe that such had been the case, and of course inducing him to doubt the reports of his own spies. The

PAUL'S LETTERS TO HIS KINSFOLK

story is told both ways; and I need hardly add, that very possibly neither may be true. But I have understood from good authority, that a person, bearing, for Lord Wellington's information, a detailed and authentic account of Buonaparte's plan for the campaign, was actually dispatched from Paris in time to have reached Brussels before the commencement of hostilities. This communication was entrusted to a female, who was furnished with a pass from Fouché himself, and who travelled with all dispatch in order to accomplish her mission; but being stopped for two days on the frontiers of France, did not arrive till after the battle of the 16th. This fact, for such I believe it to be, seems to countenance the opinion, that Fouché maintained a correspondence with the allies, and may lead, on the other hand, to suspicion, that though he dispatched the intelligence in question, he contrived so to manage, that its arrival should be too late for the purpose which it was calculated to serve. At all events, the appearance of the French upon the Sambre was at Brussels an unexpected piece of intelligence.

The advance of Buonaparte was as bold as it was sudden. The second corps of the French attacked the out-posts of the Prussians, drove them in, and continued the pursuit to Marchienne-du-pont, carried that village, secured the bridge, and there crossing the Sambre, advanced towards a large village, called Gosselies, in order to intercept the Prussian garrison of Charleroi should it retreat in that direction. The light cavalry of the French, following the movement of the second corps as far as Marchienne, turned to their right after crossing that river, swept its left bank as far as Charleroi, which they occupied without giving the Prussians time to destroy the bridge. The third corps d'armee occupied the road to Namur, and the rest of the troops were quartered between Charleroi and Gosselies, in the numerous villages which everywhere occur in that rich and populous country. The Prussian garrison of Charleroi, with the other troops which had sustained this sudden attack, retired in good order upon Fleurus, on which point the army of Blucher was now concentrating itself.

The advantages which the French reaped by this first success, were some magazines taken at Charleroi, and a few prisoners; but, above all, it contributed to raise the spirits and confirm the confidence of their armies.

Upon the 16th, at three in the morning, the troops which had hitherto remained on the right of the Sambre, crossed that river; and now Buonaparte began to develope the daring plan which he had formed, of attacking, upon one and the same day, two such opponents as Wellington and Blucher.

The left wing of the French army, consisting of the 1st and 2d corps, and of four divisions of cavalry, was entrusted to Ney, who had been suddenly called from a sort of disgraceful retirement to receive this mark of the emperor's confidence. He was commanded to march upon Brussels by Gosselies and Frasnes, overpowering such opposition as might be offered to him in his progress by the Belgian troops, and by the British who might advance to their support.

The centre and right wing of the army, with the imperial guards, (who were kept in reserve) marched to the right towards Fleurus against Blucher and the Prussians. They were under the immediate command of Buonaparte himself.

The news of Napoleon's movements in advance, and of the preliminary actions between the French and Prussians, reached Brussels upon the evening of the 15th. The Duke of Wellington, the Prince of Orange[2], and most other officers of distinction, were attending a ball given on that evening by the Duchess of Richmond. This festivity was soon overclouded. Instant orders were issued that the garrison of Brussels, the nearest disposable force, should move out to meet the approaching enemy; similar orders were issued to the cavalry, artillery, and the guards, who were quartered at Enghien; other troops, cantoned at greater distances, received orders to move to their support.

Our two distinguished Highland corps, the 42d and 92d, were among the first to muster. They had lain in garrison in Brussels during the winter and spring, and their good behaviour had attracted the affection of the inhabitants in an unusual degree. Even while I was there, *Les petits Ecossois*, as they called them, were still the theme of affectionate praise among the Flemings. They were so domesticated in the houses where they were quartered, that it was no uncommon thing to see the Highland soldier taking care of the children, or keeping the shop, of his host. They were now to exhibit themselves in a different character. They assembled with the utmost alacrity to the sound of the well-known pibroch, '*Come to me and I will give you flesh*'[3] an invitation to the wolf and the raven, for which the next day did, in fact, spread an ample banquet at the expence of our brave countrymen as well as of their enemies. They composed part of Sir Thomas Picton's[4] division, and early in the morning of the 16th marched out together with the other troops, under the command of that distinguished and lamented officer. The Duke of Brunswick[5], also, took the field at the head of his 'black Brunswickers,' so termed from the mourning which they wore for his father, and which they continue to wear for the gallant prince who then led them. Those whose fate it was to see so many brave men take their departure on this eventful day, 'gay in the morning as for summer-sport,'[6] will not easily forget the sensations which the spectacle excited at the moment, and which were rendered permanent by the slaughter which awaited them. Fears for their own safety mingled with anxiety for their brave defenders, and the agony of suspense sustained by those who remained in Brussels to await the issue of the day, was described to me in the most lively manner by those whose lot it was to sustain such varied emotions. It has been excellently described in a small work, entitled 'Circumstantial Details of the Battle of Waterloo,'*[7] which equals, in interest and authenticity, the Account of the Battle of Leipsic by an Eye-witness[8], which we perused last year with such eager avidity.

The anxiety of the inhabitants of Brussels was increased by the frightful reports of the intended vengeance of Napoleon. It was firmly believed that he had promised to his soldiers the unlimited plunder of this beautiful city if they should be able to force their way to it. Yet, even under such apprehensions, the bulk of the population shewed no inclination to purchase mercy by submitting to the invader, and there is every reason to believe, that the friends whom he had in the city were few and of little influence. Reports, however, of treachery were in circulation, and tended to augment the horrors of this agonizing period. It is said there was afterwards found, in Buonaparte's port-folio, a list, containing the names of twenty citizens, who, as friends of France, were to be exempted from the general pillage.

---

* Published by Booth and Egerton, London.

I saw also a superb house in the Place Royale employed as a military hospital, which I was told belonged to a man of rank, who, during the battle of the 18th, believing the victory must rest with Buonaparte, had taken the ill-advised step of joining the French army. But whatever might be the case with some individuals, by far the majority of the inhabitants of every class regarded the success of the French as the most dreadful misfortune which could befal their city, and listened to the distant cannonade as to sounds upon which the crisis of their fate depended. They were doomed to remain long in uncertainty; for a struggle, on which the fate of Europe depended, was not to be decided in a single day.

Upon the 16th, as I have already mentioned, the left wing of the French under General Ney, commenced its march for Brussels by the road of Gosselies. At Frasnes they encountered and drove before them some Belgian troops who were stationed in that village. But the gallant Prince of Orange, worthy of his name, of his education under Wellington, and of the rank which he is likely to hold in Europe, was now advancing to the support of his advanced posts, and re-enforced them so as to keep the enemy in check.

It was of the utmost importance to maintain the position which was now occupied by the Belgians, being an alignement between the villages of Sart a Mouline and Quatre Bras. The latter farm-house, or village, derives its name from being the point where the highway from Charleroi to Brussels is intersected by another road at nearly right angles. These roads were both essential to the allies; by the high-road they communicated with Brussels, and by that which intersected it with the right of the Prussian army stationed at St Amand. A large and thick wood, called Le Bois de Bossu, skirted the road to Brussels on the right hand of the English position; along the edge of that wood was a hollow way, which might almost be called a ravine; and between the wood and the French position were several fields of rye, which grows in Flanders to an unusual and gigantic height.

In this situation, it became the principal object of the French to secure the wood from which they might debouche upon the Brussels road. The Prince of Orange made every effort to defend it; but, in spite of his exertions, the Belgians gave way, and the French occupied the disputed post. At this critical moment, the division of Picton, the corps of the Duke of Brunswick, and shortly after the division of the guards from Enghien, came up and entered into action. 'What soldiers are those in the wood?' said the Duke of Wellington to the Prince of Orange. 'Belgians,' answered the prince, who had not yet learned the retreat of his troops from this important point. 'Belgians!' said the Duke, whose eagle eye instantly discerned what had happened, 'they are French, and about to debouche on the road; they must instantly be driven out of the wood.' This task was committed to General Maitland, with the grenadiers of the Guards, who, after sustaining a destructive fire from an invisible enemy, rushed into the wood with the most determined resolution. The French, who were hitherto supposed unrivalled in this species of warfare, made every tree, every bush, every ditch, but more especially a small rivulet which ran through the wood, posts of determined and deadly defence, but were pushed from one point to another until they were fairly driven out of the position. Then followed a struggle of a new and singular kind, and which was maintained for a length of time. As often as the British endeavoured to advance from the skirts of the wood, in order to form in front of it, they were charged by the cavalry of the enemy, and compelled to retire. The French then advanced their columns again to force their way into the wood, but were compelled to desist by the heavy fire and threatened charge of the British. And thus there was an alternation of advance and retreat, with very great slaughter on both sides, until, after a conflict of three hours, General Maitland[9] retained undisputed possession of this important post, which commanded the road to Brussels.

Meantime the battle was equally fierce on every other point. Picton's brigade, comprehending the Scotch Royals, 92d, 42d, and 44th regiments, was stationed near the farm-house of Quatre Bras, and was the object of a most destructive fire, rendered more murderous by the French having the advantage of the rising ground; while our soldiers, sunk to the shoulders among the tall rye, could not return the vollies with the same precision of aim. They were next exposed to a desperate charge of the French heavy cavalry, which was resisted by each regiment separately throwing itself into a solid square. But the approach of the enemy being partly concealed from the British by the nature of the ground, and the height of the rye, the 42d regiment was unable to form a square in the necessary time. Two companies, which were left out of the formation, were swept off and cut to pieces by the cavalry. Their veteran colonel, Macara[10], was amongst those who fell. Some of the men stood back to back, and maintained an unyielding and desperate conflict with the horsemen who surrounded them, until they were at length cut down. Nothing could be more galling for their comrades than to witness their slaughter, without having the power of giving them assistance. But they adopted the old Highland maxim, 'Today for revenge, and tomorrow for mourning,'[11] and received the cuirassiers with so dreadful and murderous a fire, as compelled them to wheel about. These horsemen, however, displayed the most undaunted resolution. After being beaten off in one point, they made a desperate charge down the causeway leading to Brussels, with the purpose of carrying two guns, by which it was defended. But at the moment they approached the guns, a fire of grape-shot was opened upon them; and, at the same time, a body of Highlanders, posted behind the farmhouse, flanking their advance, threw in so heavy a discharge of musketry, that the regiment was in an instant nearly annihilated.

The result of these various attacks was, that the French retreated with great loss, and in great confusion; and many of the fugitives fled as far as Charleroi, spreading the news that the British were in close pursuit. But pursuit was impracticable, for the English cavalry had so far to march, that when they arrived upon the ground night was approaching, and it was impossible for them to be of service. Ney therefore re-established himself in his original position at Frasnes, and the combat died away with nightfall. The British had then leisure to contemplate the results of the day. Several regiments were reduced to skeletons by the number of killed and wounded. Many valuable officers had fallen. Among these were distinguished the gallant Duke of Brunswick, who in degenerate times had remained an unshaken model of ancient German valour and constancy. Colonel Cameron[12], so often distinguished in Lord Wellington's dispatches from Spain, fell while leading the 92d to charge a body of cavalry, supported by infantry. Many other regretted names were read on the bloody list. But if it was a day of sorrow, it was one of triumph also.

It is true, that no immediate and decisive advantage resulted from this engagement, farther than as for the present it defeated Napoleon's plan of advancing on Brussels. But it did not fail to inspire the troops engaged with confidence and hope. If, when collected from different quarters, after a toilsome march, and in numbers one half inferior to those of the enemy, they had been able to resist his utmost efforts, what had they not to hope when their forces were concentrated, and when their artillery and cavalry, the want of which had been so severely felt during the whole of that bloody day, should be brought up into line? Meanwhile they enjoyed the most decided proof of victory, for the British army bivouacked upon the ground which had been occupied by the French during the battle, with the strongest hopes that the conflict would be renewed in the morning with the most decisive success. This, however, depended upon the news they should hear from Fleurus, where a furious cannonade had been heard during the whole day, announcing a general action between Napoleon and Prince Marshal Blucher. Even the Duke of Wellington was long ere he learned the result of this engagement, upon which his own ulterior measures necessarily must be regulated. The Prussian officer sent to acquaint him with the intelligence had been made prisoner by the French light troops; and when the news arrived, they bore such a cloudy aspect as altogether destroyed the agreeable hopes which the success at Quatre Bras had induced the troops to entertain.

But pledged as I am to give you a detailed account of this brief campaign, I must reserve the battle of Ligny to another occasion. Meanwhile I am ever sincerely yours.

LETTER VII.

PAUL TO MAJOR ——, IN CONTINUATION.

When Buonaparte moved with his centre and right wing against Blucher, he certainly conceived that he left to Ney a more easy task than his own; and that the Mareschal would find no difficulty in pushing his way to Brussels, or near it, before the English army could be concentrated in sufficient force to oppose him. To himself he reserved the task of coping with Blucher, and by his overthrow cutting off all communication between the Prussian and British armies, and compelling each to seek safety in isolated and unconnected movements.

The Prussian veteran was strongly posted to receive the enemy, whom upon earth he hated most. His army occupied a line where three villages, built upon broken and unequal ground, served each as a separate redoubt, defended by infantry, and well furnished with artillery. The village of St Amand was occupied by his right wing, his centre was posted at Ligny, and his left at Sombref. All these hamlets are strongly built, and contain several houses, with large court-yards and orchards, each of which is capable of being converted into a station of defence. The ground behind these villages forms an amphitheatre of some elevation, in front of which was a deep ravine, edged by straggling thickets of trees. The villages were in front of the ravine; and masses of infantry were stationed behind each, destined to reinforce the defenders as occasion required.

In this strong position Blucher had assembled three corps

of his army, amounting to 80,000 men. But the fourth corps, commanded by Bulow[1], (a general distinguished in the campaign of 1814,) being in distant cantonments between Liege and Hannut, had not yet arrived at the point of concentration. The force of the assailants is stated in the Prussian dispatches at 130,000 men. But as Ney had at least 30,000 soldiers under him at Quatre Bras, it would appear that the troops under Buonaparte's immediate command at the battle of Ligny, even including a strong reserve, which consisted of the first entire division, could not exceed 100,000 men. The forces, therefore, actually engaged on both sides, might be nearly equal. They were equal also in courage and in mutual animosity.

The Prussians of our time will never forget, or forgive, the series of dreadful injuries inflicted by the French upon their country after the defeat of Jena. The plunder of their peaceful hamlets, with every inventive circumstance which the evil passions of lust, rapine, and cruelty could suggest; the murder of the father, or the husband, because 'the *pekin* looked dangerous,' when he beheld his property abandoned to rapine, his wife, or daughters, to violation, and his children to wanton slaughter; such were the tales which the Prussian Land-wehr told over their watch-fires to whet each other's appetite to revenge. The officers and men of rank thought of the period when Prussia had been blotted out of the book of nations, her queen martyred by studied and reiterated insult, until she carried her sorrows to the grave, and her king only permitted to retain the name of a sovereign to increase his disgrace as a bondsman.[2] The successful campaign of 1814 was too stinted a draught for their thirst of vengeance, and the hour was now come when they hoped for its amplest gratification.

The French had, also, their grounds of personal animosity not less stimulating. These very Prussians, to whom (such was their mode of stating the account) the emperor's generosity had left the name of independence, when a single word could have pronounced them a conquered province; these Prussians, admitted to be companions in arms to the victors, had been the first to lift the standard of rebellion against them, when the rage of the elements had annihilated the army with which Napoleon invaded Russia. They had done more: they had invaded the sacred territory of France; defeated her armies upon her own soil; and contributed chiefly to the hostile occupation of her capital. They were commanded by Blucher, the inveterate foe of the French name and empire, whom no defeat could ever humble, and no success could mitigate. Even when the Treaty of Paris was received by the other distinguished statesmen and commanders of the allies as a composition advantageous for all sides, it was known that this veteran had expressed his displeasure at the easy terms on which France was suffered to escape from the conflict. Amid the general joy and congratulation, he retained the manner (in the eyes of the Parisians) of a gloomy malcontent. A Frenchman, somewhat acquainted with our literature, described to me the Prussian general, as bearing upon that occasion the mien and manner of Dryden's spectre-knight:—

> Stern look'd the fiend, and frustrate of his will,
> Not half sufficed, and greedy yet to kill.[3]

And now this inveterate enemy was before them, leading troops, animated by his own sentiments, and forming the vanguard of the immense armies, which, unless checked by decisive defeat, were about to overwhelm France, and realize those scenes of vengeance which had been in the preceding year so singularly averted.

Fired by these sentiments of national hostility, the ordinary rules of war, those courtesies and acts of lenity which on other occasions afford some mitigation of its horrors, were renounced upon both sides. The Prussians declared their purpose to give and receive no quarter. Two of the French divisions hoisted the black flag, as an intimation of the same intention; and it is strongly affirmed that they gave a more sanguinary proof of their mortal hatred by mutilating and cutting off the ears of the prisoners who fell into their hands at crossing the Sambre. With such feelings towards each other, the two armies joined battle.

The engagement commenced at three in the afternoon, by a furious cannonade, under cover of which the third corps of the French army, commanded by Vandamme, attacked the village of St Amand. They were received by the Prussians with the most determined resistance, in despite of which they succeeded in carrying the village at the point of the bayonet, and established themselves in the church and church-yard. The Prussians made the most desperate efforts to recover possession of this village, which was the key of their right-wing. Blucher put himself at the head of a battalion in person, and impelled them on the French with such success, that one end of the village was again occupied; and the Prussians regained possession of that part of the heights behind it, which, in consequence of Vandamme's success, they had been obliged to abandon. The village of Ligny, attacked and defended with the same fury and inveteracy, was repeatedly lost and regained, each party being alternately reinforced from masses of infantry, disposed behind that part of the village which they respectively occupied. Several houses inclosed with court-yards, according to the Flemish fashion, formed each a separate redoubt, which was furiously assailed by the one party, and obstinately made good by the other. It is impossible to conceive the fury with which the troops on both sides were animated. Each soldier appeared to be avenging his own personal quarrel; and the slaughter was in proportion to the length and obstinacy of a five hours combat, fought hand to hand, within the crowded and narrow streets of a village. There was also a sustained cannonade on both sides through the whole of the afternoon. But in this species of warfare the Prussians sustained a much heavier loss than their antagonists, their masses being drawn up in an exposed situation upon the ridge and sides of the heights behind the villages, while those of the French were sheltered by the winding hollows of the lower grounds.

While this desperate contest continued, Buonaparte apparently began to doubt of its ultimate success. To ensure the storming of Saint Amand, he ordered the first corps of infantry, which was stationed near Frasnes, with a division of the second corps commanded by Girard[4], and designed to be a reserve either to his own army or to that of Marshal Ney, to move to the right to assist in the attack, Of this movement Ney complained heavily in a letter to Fouché, as depriving him of the means of ensuring a victory at Quatre Bras.

The reinforcement, as it happened, was unnecessary, so far as the first corps was concerned; for about seven o'clock Vandamme had, after reiterated efforts, surmounted the resistance of the Prussians at St Amand; and Girard had obtained possession of Ligny. Sombref, upon the left of the Prussian line, was still successfully defended by the Saxon general, Thielman, against Mareschal Grouchy[5], and the Prussians, though driven from the villages in front of the amphitheatre of hills, still maintained their alignement upon the heights themselves, impatiently expecting to be succoured, either by the English or by their own fourth division under Bulow. But the Duke of Wellington was himself actively engaged at Quatre Bras; and Bulow had found it impossible to surmount the difficulties attending a long march through bad roads and a difficult country. In the meanwhile Buonaparte brought this dreadful engagement to a decision, by one of those skilful and daring manoeuvres which characterize his tactics.

Being now possessed of the village of Ligny, which fronted the centre of the Prussian line, he concentrated upon that point the imperial guards, whom he had hitherto kept in reserve. Eight battalions of this veteran and distinguished infantry, formed into one formidable column, supported by four squadrons of cavalry, two regiments of cuirassiers, and the horse-grenadiers of the guard, traversed the village of Ligny at the *pas de charge*, threw themselves into the ravine which separates the village from the heights, and began to ascend them, under a dreadful fire of grape and musketry from the Prussians. They sustained this murderous discharge with great gallantry, and, advancing against the Prussian line, made such an impression upon the masses of which it consisted, as threatened to break through the centre of their army, and thus cut off the communication between the two wings; the French cavalry, at the same time, charged and drove back that of the Prussians.

In this moment of consternation, the cause of Europe had nearly suffered a momentous loss in the death or captivity of the indomitable Blucher. The gallant veteran had himself headed an unsuccessful charge against the French cavalry; and his horse being shot under him in the retreat, both the fliers and pursuers passed over him as he lay on the ground; an adjutant threw himself down beside his general, to share his fate; and the first use which the Prince-Marshal made of his recovered recollection was, to conjure his faithful attendant rather to shoot him than to permit him to fall alive into the hands of the French. Meantime, the Prussian cavalry had rallied, charged, and in their turn repulsed the French, who again galloped past the Prussian general, as he lay on the ground, covered with the cloak of the adjutant, with the same precipitation as in their advance. The general was then disengaged and remounted, and proceeded to organize the retreat, which was now become a measure of indispensable necessity.

The Prussian artillery, being dispersed along the front of an extended line, could not be easily withdrawn, and several pieces fell into the hands of the French. Blucher's official dispatch limits the number of guns thus lost to fifteen, which Buonaparte extends to fifty. But the infantry, retiring regularly, and in masses impenetrable to the cavalry of the pursuers, amply preserved that high character of discipline, which, in the campaigns of the preceding year, had repeatedly enabled them to convert retreat and disorder of one day into advance and victory upon the next. In their retreat, which they continued during the night, they took the direction of Tilly; and in the next morning were followed by General Thielman with the left wing, who, after evacuating the village of Sombref, which he had maintained during the whole preceding day, formed the rear-guard of the Prince-Marshal's army. Being at length joined by the fourth corps, under General Bulow, the Prussian army was once more concentrated in the neighbourhood of the village of Wavre, ten miles behind the scene of their former defeat; and the utmost exertions were used by Blucher, and the officers under him, to place it in a condition for renewing the conflict.

The carnage of the Prussians in this unsuccessful battle was very great. I have heard it estimated at twenty thousand men, being one-fourth part of their whole army. Buonaparte, however, only rates it at fifteen thousand *hors de combat*; an enormous loss, especially considering, that, owing to the inveteracy of the combat, and the steady valour displayed by the vanquished in their retreat, there were hardly any prisoners taken.

The events of the 16th had a material influence on the plans of the generals on either side. While the Duke of Wellington was proposing to follow up his advantage at Quatre Bras, by attacking Ney at Frasnes, he received, on the morning of the 17th, the news that Blucher had been defeated on the preceding day, and was in full retreat. This left the Duke no option but to fall back to such a corresponding position as might maintain his lateral communication with the Prussian right wing; since to have remained in advance would have given Buonaparte an opportunity either to have placed his army betwixt those of England and Prussia, or, at his choice, to have turned his whole force against the Duke's army, which was inferior in numbers. The English general accordingly resolved upon retreating towards Brussels; a movement which he accomplished in the most perfect order, the rear being protected by the cavalry under the gallant Earl of Uxbridge[6].

Meantime, Buonaparte had also taken his resolution. The defeat of the Prussians had placed it in his option to pursue them with his whole army, excepting those troops under Ney, who were in front of the Duke of Wellington. But this would have been to abandon Ney to almost certain destruction; since, if he was unable, on the preceding day, to make any impression on the van of the British army alone, it was scarce possible he could withstand them, when supported by their main body and joined by reinforcements of every kind. In the supposed event of Ney's defeat, Buonaparte's rear would have been exposed to a victorious English army, while he knew, by repeated experience, how speedily and effectually Blucher could rally his Prussians, even after a severe defeat. He made it his choice, therefore, to turn his whole force against the English, leaving only Grouchy and Vandamme, with about twenty-five thousand men, to hang upon the rear of Blucher; and, by pursuing his retreat from Sombref to Wavre, to occupy his attention, and prevent his attempting to take a share in the expected action with the British,

Napoleon probably expected to find the English army upon the ground which it had occupied during the 16th. But the movement of his own forces from St Amand and Ligny to Frasnes, had occupied a space of time which was not left unemployed by the Duke of Wellington. The retreat had already commenced, and the position at Quatre Bras was, about eleven in the forenoon, only occupied by a strong rear-guard, destined to protect the retrograde movement of the British general. Buonaparte put his troops in motion to pursue his retiring enemy. The day was stormy and rainy in the extreme; and the roads, already broken up by the English artillery in their advance and retreat, were very nearly impassable. The cavalry, whose duty it became to press upon the rear of the English, were obliged to march through fields of standing corn, which being reduced to swamps by the wetness of the season, rendered rapid movement impossible. This state of the weather and roads was of no small advantage to the British army, who had to defile through the narrow streets of the village of Genappe, and over the bridge which there crosses a small river, in the very face of the pursuing enemy. Their cavalry once or twice attacked the rear-guard, but received so severe a check from the Life Guards and Oxford Blues, that they afterwards left the march undisturbed. I am assured, that the Duke of Wellington, in passing Genappe, expressed his surprise that he had been allowed to pass through that narrow defile, unharrassed by attack and interruption, and asserted his belief, founded upon that circumstance, that Napoleon did not command in person the pursuing divisions of the French army. A French officer, to whom I mentioned this circumstance, accounted for this apparent want of activity, by alleging the heavy loss sustained upon the 16th in the battles of Quatre Bras and Ligny; the necessary disorganization of the French cavalry after two such severe actions; the stormy state of the weather upon the 17th, and the impracticability of the roads for the movements of cavalry. You, as a military critic, will be best judge how far this defence is available. I notice the same observation in an Account of the Battle of Waterloo, by a British Officer on the Staff.*[7]

With little further interruption on the part of the enemy, the British army retired upon the ever-memorable field of

---

* Published by Ridgeway, Piccadilly.

Waterloo, and there took up a position upon the road to Brussels, which I shall endeavour to describe more fully in my next Letter. The Duke had caused a plan of this and other military positions in the neighbourhood of Brussels to be made some time before by Colonel Carmichael Smith[8], the chief engineer. He now called for that sketch, and, with the assistance of the regretted Sir William de Lancey[9] and Colonel Smith, made his dispositions for the momentous events of next day. The plan itself, a relique so precious, was rendered yet more so, by being found in the breast of Sir William de Lancey's coat, when he fell, and stained with the blood of that gallant officer. It is now in the careful preservation of Colonel Carmichael Smith, by whom it was originally sketched.

When the Duke of Wellington had made his arrangements for the night, he established his head-quarters at a petty inn in the small village of Waterloo, about a mile in the rear of the position. The army slept upon their arms upon the ridge of a gentle declivity, chiefly covered with standing corn.

The French, whose forces were gradually coming up during the evening, occupied a ridge nearly opposite to the position of the English army. The villages in the rear of that rising ground were also filled with the soldiers of their numerous army. Buonaparte established his head-quarters at Planchenoit[10], a small village in the rear of the position.

Thus arranged, both generals and their respective armies waited the arrival of morning, and the events it was to bring. The night, as if the elements meant to match their fury with that which was preparing for the morning, was stormy in the extreme, accompanied by furious gusts of wind, heavy bursts of rain, continued and vivid flashes of lightning, and the loudest thunder our officers had ever heard. Both armies had to sustain this tempest in the exposed situation of an open bivouack, without means either of protection or refreshment. But though these hardships were common to both armies, yet, (as was the case previous to the battle of Agincourt,) the moral feelings of the English army were depressed below their ordinary tone, and those of the French exalted to a degree of confidence and presumption unusual even to the soldiers of that nation.

The British could not help reflecting, that the dear-bought success at Quatre Bras, while it had cost so many valuable lives, had produced, in appearance at least, no corresponding result: a toilsome advance and bloody action had been followed by a retreat equally laborious to the soldier; and the defeat of the Prussians, which was now rumoured with the usual allowance of exaggeration, had left Buonaparte at liberty to assail them separately, and with his whole force, except what small proportion might be necessary to continue the pursuit of their defeated and dispirited allies. If to this it was added, that their ranks contained many thousand foreigners, on whose faith they could not implicitly depend, it must be owned there was sufficient scope for melancholy reflections. To balance these, remained their confidence in their commander, their native undaunted courage, and a stern resolution to discharge their duty, and leave the result to Providence.

The French, on the other hand, had forgotten, in their success at Ligny, their failure at Quatre Bras, or, if they remembered it, their miscarriage was ascribed to treachery; and it was said that Bourmont and other officers[11] had been tried by a military commission and shot, for having, by their misconduct, occasioned the disaster. This rumour, which had no foundation but in the address with which Buonaparte could apply a salve to the wounded vanity of his soldiers, was joined to other exulting considerations. Admitting the partial success of Wellington, the English Duke, they said, commanded but the right wing of the Prussian army, and had, in fact, shared in Blucher's defeat, as he himself virtually acknowledged, by imitating his retreat. All was glow and triumph. No one supposed the English would halt, or make head, until they reached their vessels; no one doubted that the Belgian troops would join the emperor in a mass; it would have been disaffection to have supposed there lay any impediment in their next morning's march to Brussels; and all affected chiefly to regret the tempestuous night, as it afforded to the despairing English the means of retiring unmolested. Buonaparte himself shared, or affected to share, these sentiments; and when the slow and gloomy dawning of the morning of the 18th of June shewed him his enemies, still in possession of the heights which they occupied over-night, and apparently determined to maintain them, he could not suppress his satisfaction, but exclaimed, while he stretched his arm towards their position with a motion as if to grasp his prey, *Je les tiens donc ces Anglois*[12].

The exultation of the French was mixed, according to their custom, with many a scurril jest at the expence of their enemies. The death of the Duke of Brunswick was the subject of much pleasantry among such of the French officers as sought to make their court to Jerome, the ex-king of Westphalia[13]. To please this phantom monarch, they ridiculed the fatality which always, they said, placed these unlucky Dukes of Brunswick in concurrence with the conqueror of his states, and condemned them successively to perish as it were by his hand. The national dress of our poor Highlanders, whose bodies were found lying in the lines which they had occupied in the field of Quatre Bras, furnished more good jests than I care to record. But as I heard a Frenchman just now observe, '*Il rit bien, qui rit le dernier*[14].'

Before entering upon such particulars as I can collect of the battle of Waterloo, let me notice your criticisms upon the affairs of the 16th. You say, first, that Buonaparte ought not to have attacked both the English and Prussian armies on the same day, and you call my attention to the argument detailed in Mareschal Ney's letter to Fouché[15]. And, secondly, you are of opinion, that, having defeated the Prussians at Ligny, Napoleon should have pursued the routed army of Blucher with his whole cavalry at least, and rendered it impossible for him to rally sooner than under the walls of Maestricht. Such, you say, is the opinion of all military judges in our neighbourhood, by which I know you mean all our friends with blue coats and red collars, whether half-pay captains, ex-officers of volunteers, commanders of local militia, or deputy-lieutenants. 'Never a man's thought in the world keeps the road-way better than thine, my dear Major[16]'; but in despite of this unanimous verdict against the ex-emperor, I will venture to move for a writ of error.

Upon the first count of the indictment, be pleased to reflect, that Buonaparte's game was at best a difficult one, and that he could embrace no course which was not exposed to many hazards. It is not the ultimate success, or miscarriage, of his plan by which we ought to judge of its propriety, but the rational prospects which it held out before being carried into execution. Now be it remembered, that, upon the 16th, Blucher's army was already concentrated at Ligny, while that of Lord Wellington was only moving up in detail to Quatre Bras. Mareschal Ney would scarcely have recommended to Napoleon to move straight towards Brussels by Quatre Bras and Genappe, leaving upon his right, and eventually in his rear, an army of 80,000 Prussians, expecting hourly to be joined by Bulow with 20,000 more, altogether disengaged and unoccupied. The consequence of such a movement must necessarily have been, that, menaced by the enemy's whole force, the Duke of Wellington might have relinquished thoughts of collecting his army in a post so much in advance as Quatre Bras; but a concentration upon Waterloo would have been the obvious alternative; and if the emperor had advanced to that point and attacked the English without their receiving any assistance from the untouched army of the Prussians, we must suppose Blucher less active in behalf of his allies when at the head of an entire army, than he proved himself to be when commanding one which had sustained a recent defeat. In a word, if left unattacked, or masked only by a force inferior to their own, the Prussians were in a situation instantly to have become the assailants; and, therefore, it seems that Buonaparte acted wisely in sending the greater part of his army against that body of his enemies which had already combined its forces, while he might reasonably hope, that the divisions under Ney's command could dispose of the British troops as they came up to the field of battle wearied and in detail. In fact, his scheme had, in its material points, complete success, for Napoleon did defeat the Prussians; and, by his success against them, compelled the English to retreat, and gained an opportunity of attacking them with his whole force in a battle, where the scale more than once inclined to his side. If, in the conjoined assault of the 16th, Ney failed in success over an enemy far inferior in numbers, it can only be accounted for by the superior talents of the English general, and the greater bravery of the soldiers whom he commanded. Something like a conscious feeling of this kind seems to lurk at the bottom of the mareschal's statement, who scarce pardons the emperor for being successful upon a day on which he was himself defeated.

The manner in which Ney complains of being deprived of the assistance of the first brigade, held hitherto in reserve, between his right and the left wing of Napoleon, and withdrawn, as he alleges, to the assistance of the latter just when, on his side, 'victory was not doubtful,' savours of the same peevish criticism. Napoleon sent for these troops when their aid appeared essential to carry the village of St Amand, and thereby to turn the right flank of the Prussians, and he returned them to their original position the instant he perceived a possibility of carrying his point without them. Surely more could not have been expected in the circumstances. Of the tone the mareschal assumes to his fallen master, and the reproaches which he permits himself to cast upon him, I will only say, in the words of Wolsey,

> Within these forty hours Surrey had better
> Have burned his tongue than said so.[17]

Upon the other point of censure it is more difficult to give a satisfactory explanation. The French seem to have considered the battle of Ligny as being of a character less decisive than complete victory, and a consciousness of the unbroken force of the retiring enemy certainly checked the vivacity of the pursuit. The French carried the positions of the Prussians with great slaughter; but the precipitate retreat, and the numerous prisoners announced in Buonaparte's bulletin[18], are now universally allowed to be apocryphal. Blucher, whose open and frank avowal of the defeat he sustained claims credit for the rest of his narrative, assures us, that the Prussian army was again formed within a quarter of a league from the field of battle, and presented such a front to the enemy as deterred him from attempting a pursuit. We ought therefore to conclude, (paying always the necessary deference to Buonaparte's military skill,) that although the Prussians had been driven from their positions, yet their retreat must have been conducted with such order, that no advantage would have resulted from pursuing them with a small force, while the necessity of making a movement with his main body to the left in order to repair the disaster sustained by Ney, rendered it impossible for Napoleon to press upon them with an overwhelming superiority of numbers.

These reflections, which I hazard in profound submission to your experience, close what occurs upon the important events of the 16th and 17th days of June last. Ever, my dear Major, &c.

LETTER VIII.

TO THE SAME.

The field of battle at Waterloo is easily described. The forest of Soignies, a wood composed of beech-trees growing uncommonly close together, is traversed by the road from Brussels, a long broad causeway, which, upon issuing from the wood, reaches the small village of Waterloo. Beyond this point, the wood assumes a more straggling and dispersed appearance, until about a mile farther, where, at an extended ridge, called the heights of Mount St John, from a farm-house situated upon the Brussels road, the trees almost entirely disappear, and the country becomes quite open. Along this eminence the British forces were disposed in two lines. The second, which lay behind the brow of the hill, was, in some degree, sheltered from the enemy's fire. The first line, consisting of the *elite* of the infantry, occupied the crest of the ridge, and were on the left partly defended by a long hedge and ditch, which, running in a straight line from the hamlet of Mount St John towards the village of Ohain, gives name to two farm houses. The first, which is situated in advance of the hedge, and at the bottom of the declivity, is called La Haye Sainte, (the holy hedge,) the other, placed at the extremity of the fence, is called Ter la Haye. The ground at Ter la Haye becomes woody and broken, so that it afforded a strong point at which to terminate the British line upon the left. A road runs from Ter la Haye to Ohain and the woody passes of St Lambert, through which the Duke of Wellington kept up a communication by his left with the Prussian army. The centre of the English army occupied the village of Mount Saint John, on the middle of the ridge, just where the great causeway from Brussels divides into two roads, one of which branches off to Nivelles, and the other continues the straight line to Charleroi. A strong advanced post of Hanoverian sharp-shooters occupied the house and farm-yard of La Haye Sainte, situated in advance upon the Charleroi road, and just at the bottom of the hill. The right of the British army, extending along the same eminence, occupied and protected the Nivelles road as far as the inclosures of Hougoumont, and, turning rather backwards, rested its extreme right upon a deep ravine. Advanced posts from thence occupied the village called Braine la Leude,[*] on which point there was no engagement. The ground in front of the British position sloped easily down into lower ground, forming a sort of valley, not a level plain, but a declivity varied by many gentle sweeps and hollows, as if formed by the course of a river. The ground then ascends in the same manner to a ridge opposite to that of Mount Saint John, and running parallel to it at the distance of twelve or fourteen hundred yards. This was the position of the enemy. It is in some points nearer, and in others more distant from the heights, or ridge, of Mount Saint John, according as the valley between them is of greater or less breadth.

The valley between the two ridges is entirely open and uninclosed, and on that memorable day bore a tall and strong crop of corn. But in the centre of the valley, about half way betwixt the two ridges, and situated considerably

---

[*] Or Braine the Free, to distinguish it from Braine le Compte, or Braine belonging to the count.

to the right of the English centre, was the Chateau de Goumont, or Hougoumont. This is (or rather *was*) a gentleman's house of the old Flemish architecture, having a tower, and, as far as I can judge from its ruins, a species of battlement. It was surrounded on one side by a large farm-yard, and on the other opened to a garden divided by alleys in the Dutch taste, and fenced by a brick wall. The whole was encircled by an open grove of tall trees, covering a space of about three or four acres, without any underwood. This chateau, with the advantages afforded by its wood and gardens, formed a strong *point d'appui*[1] to the British right wing. In fact, while this point was maintained, it must have been difficult for the French to have made a serious attack upon the extremity of our right wing. On the other hand, had they succeeded in carrying Hougoumont, our line must have been confined to the heights, extending towards Merke Braine, which rather recede from the field, and would have been in consequence much limited and crowded in its movements. As far as I understand the order of battle, the British line upon this right wing at the commencement of the action, rather presented the convex segment of a circle to the enemy, but as repeated repulses obliged the French to give ground, the extreme right was thereby enabled to come gradually round, and the curve being reversed, became concave, enfilading the field of battle and the high road from Brussels to Charleroi, which intersects it.

Such was the position of the British army on this memorable morning. That of the French is less capable of distinct description. Their troops had bivouacked on the field, or occupied the villages behind the ridge of La Belle Alliance. Their general had the choice of his mode of attack upon the English position, a word which, in this case, can only be used in a general sense, as a situation for an order of battle, but not in any respect as denoting ground which was naturally strong, or easily defended.

The imperfect dawn of the 18th was attended by the same broken and tempestuous weather, by which the night had been distinguished. But the interval of rest, such as it was, had not been neglected by the British, who had gained time to clean their arms, distribute ammunition, and prepare every thing for the final shock of battle. Provisions had also been distributed to the troops, most of whom had thus the means of breakfasting with some comfort.

Early in the morning numerous bodies of French cavalry began to occupy all the ridge of La Belle Alliance, opposite to that of Mount St John, and as our horse were held in readiness to encounter them, an engagement was expected between the cavalry of both armies, which our infantry supposed they would only view in the capacity of spectators, The desertion of a French officer of cuirassiers[2], attached to the party of Lewis XVIII., conveyed other information; he assured Lord Hill[3], and subsequently the Duke of Wellington, that a general attack was intended, which would commence on our right by a combined force of infantry and cavalry.

In the meanwhile the communication between our army and the Prussians by our left flank had been uninterrupted. An officer of engineers[4], who was dispatched so early as four in the morning, accompanied Bulow's division, already on march to our assistance, struggling with the defiles of St Lambert, through roads which were rendered worse and worse by every succeeding regiment and brigade of artillery. One sentiment, this gentleman assured me, seemed unanimous among the Prussians—an eager and enthusiastic desire to press forward to obtain their share of the glories and dangers of the day, and to revenge their losses upon the 16th. The common soldiers cheered him and his companion as they passed. 'Keep your ground, brave English!' was the universal exclamation, in German, and in such broken English or French as they found to express themselves—'Only keep your ground till we come up!'— and they used every effort accordingly to get into the field. But the movement was a lateral one, made across a country naturally deep and broken, rendered more so by the late heavy rains; and, on the whole, so unfit for the passage of a large body of troops, with their cavalry, artillery, &c. that even these officers, well mounted as they were, and eager to make their report to the department from which they had been dispatched, did not reach the field of battle till after eleven o'clock.

The engagement had already commenced. It is said Buonaparte fired the first gun with his own hand, which is at least doubtful. But it is certain he was in full view of the field when the battle began, and remained upon it till no choice was left him but that of death or rapid flight. His first post was a high wooden observatory, which had been constructed when a trigonometrical survey of the country was made by order of the King of the Netherlands some weeks before. But he afterwards removed to the high grounds in front of La Belle Alliance, and finally to the foot of the slope upon the road to Brussels. He was attended by his staff, and squadrons of *service*, destined to protect his person. Soult[5], Ney, and other officers of distinction, commanded under him, but he issued all orders and received all reports in person.

The clouds of cavalry, which had mustered thicker and thicker upon the skirts of the horizon in the line of La Belle Alliance, began now to advance forward. One of our best and bravest officers confessed to me a momentary sinking of the heart when he looked round him, considered how small was the part of our force properly belonging to Britain, and recollected the disadvantageous and discouraging circumstances under which even our own soldiers laboured. A slight incident reassured him. An aid-de-camp galloped up, and, after delivering his instructions, cautioned the battalion of the Guards along whom he rode to reserve their fire till the enemy were within a short distance. 'Never mind us,' answered a veteran guards-man from the ranks,—'never mind us, sir; *we know our duty.*' From that moment my gallant friend said, that he knew the hearts of the men were in the right trim, and that though they might leave their bodies on the spot, they would never forfeit their honour. A few minutes afterwards the unparalleled conflict began.

The first attack of the French, as had been announced by the royalist officer, was directed towards our right wing, embracing the post of Hougoumont and the high road to Nivelles. A glance at any plan of this ground will show, that occupying the latter with artillery, would have enabled the French to have pushed forward to the very centre of our line, especially if Hougoumont could have been carried about the same time. On the last point they were partially successful. The fury of the attack was such, that a body of sharpshooters of Nassau Ussingen, to whom the grove of Hougoumont had been confided, abandoned that part of the post, and the chateau itself must have been carried but for the stubborn and desperate courage of a detachment of the Guards to whom the defence was intrusted. Col. M'Donell, the brother of our Highland Chief Glengarry,[6] was obliged to fight hand to hand among the assailants, and was indebted to personal strength no less than courage for his success in the perilous duty of shutting the gates of the court-yard against the enemy. The Spanish general, Don Miguel Alava[7], and his aids-de-camp, exerted themselves to rally the scattered sharpshooters of Nassau, and Don Nicholas de Mennuisir was particularly distinguished by his activity. 'What would the Spaniards have done,' said a prince distinguished for his own personal spirit and courage, as well as for his experience in the peninsular war,—'What would the Spaniards have done, Don Miguel, in a fire like that of Waterloo?'—'At least, sir,' retorted the Castilian, 'they would not, like some of your father's subjects, have fled without seeing their enemy.'—By the rout of these light troops, and the consequent occupation of the wood by the French, Hougoumont was, for great part of the action, completely an invested and besieged post, indebted for its security to the walls and deep and strong ditches with which the garden and orchard were surrounded, but much more to the valiant and indomitable spirits of those by whom these defences were maintained. It was currently reported, that, during the attack, the bailiff or steward of the proprietor fired more than once from the summit of the tower upon the British, by whom the court and garden were defended, and that he was at length discovered and shot. I cannot warrant the truth of this anecdote, and it seems inconsistent with the general spirit shown by the Belgians, which was certainly anti-gallican. At any rate, the place was most furiously assailed from without, and as resolutely defended, the garrison firing through the holes which they knocked out in the garden walls, and through the hedge of the orchard; and the assailants making the most desperate attempts to carry the post, but in vain.

Still, however, Hougoumont being in some degree insulated, and its defenders no longer in communication with the rest of the British army, the French cavalry were enabled to pour round it in great strength to the attack of the British right wing. The light troops, who were in advance of the British line, were driven in by the fury of this general charge, and the foreign cavalry, who ought to have supported them, gave way on all sides. The first forces who offered a steady resistance were the Black Brunswick infantry. They were drawn up in squares, as most of the British forces were, during this memorable action, each regiment forming a square by itself, not quite solid, but nearly so, the men being drawn up several files deep. The distance between these masses afforded space enough to draw up the battalions in line when they should be ordered to deploy, and the regiments were posted with reference to each other much like the alternate squares upon a chess-board. It was therefore impossible for a squadron of cavalry to push between two of these squares, without finding themselves at once assailed by a fire in front from that which was to the rear, and on both flanks from those betwixt which it had moved forward. Often and often during that day was the murderous experiment resorted to, and almost always with the same bad success.

Yet, although this order of battle possesses every efficient power of combination for defence against cavalry, its exterior is far from imposing. The men thus drawn up occupy the least possible space of ground, and a distinguished officer, who was destined to support the Brunswickers, informed me, that when he saw the furious onset of the French cavalry, with a noise and clamour that seemed to unsettle the firm earth over which they galloped, and beheld the small detached black masses which, separated from each other, stood each individually exposed to be overwhelmed by the torrent, he almost trembled for the event. But when the Brunswick troops opened their fire with coolness, readiness, and rapidity, the event seemed no longer doubtful. The artillery also, which was never in higher order, or more distinguished for excellent practice, made dreadful gaps in the squadrons of cavalry, and strewed the ground with men and horses, who were advancing to the charge. Still this was far from repressing the courage of the French, who pressed on in defiance of every obstacle, and of the continued and immense slaughter which was made among their ranks. Or if the attack of the cavalry was suspended for a space, it was but to give room for the operation of their artillery, which, within the distance of one hundred and fifty yards, played upon so obvious a mark as our solid squares afforded with the most destructive effect. 'One fire,' said a general officer, whom I have already quoted, 'struck down seven men of the square with whom I was for the moment; the next was less deadly—it only killed three.' Yet under such a fire, and in full view of these clouds of cavalry, waiting like birds of prey to dash upon them where the slaughter should afford the slightest opening, did these gallant troops close their files over the bodies of their dead and dying comrades, and resume with stern composure that close array of battle, which their discipline and experience taught them afforded the surest means of defence. After the most desperate efforts on the part of the French to push back our right wing, and particularly to establish themselves on the road to Nivelles, and after a defence on the part of the British which rendered these efforts totally unavailing, the battle slackened in some degree in this quarter, to rage with greater fury, if possible, towards the left and centre of the British line.

It was now upon the village of Mount St John, and making use of the causeway or high-road between that hamlet and La Belle Alliance, that Buonaparte precipitated his columns, both of infantry and cavalry, under a tremendous fire of artillery, that was calculated to sweep every obstacle from their course. The ridge of the hill was upon this occasion very serviceable to the British, whose second line was posted behind it, and thus protected, in some degree, from the direct fire, though not from the showers of shells which were thrown on purpose to annoy the troops, whom the enemy with reason supposed to be thus sheltered. The first line derived some advantage from a straggling hedge, (the same which, as already mentioned, gives the name of La Haye Sainte to the farm,) extending along their centre and left, and partly masking it, though, so far from being strong enough to serve as an entrenchment or breastwork, it could be penetrated by cavalry in almost every direction. Such as it was, however, its line of defence, or rather the troops by whom it was occupied, struck awe into the assailants; and while they hesitated to advance to charge it, they were themselves in their turn charged and overwhelmed by the British cavalry, who, dashing through the fence at the intervals which admitted of it, formed, charged, and dispersed the battalions which were advancing upon their line. The French cavalry came up to support their infantry, and where the British were in the least dispersed, which, from the impetuosity of the men and horses, was frequently unavoidable, our troops suffered severely. This was particularly experienced by some distinguished regiments, whom the military fashion of the times has converted into hussars, from that excellent old English establishment formerly called Light-Dragoons, which combined with much activity a degree of weight that cannot belong to troopers more slightly mounted. You, who remember one or two of the picked regiments of 1795[8], cannot but recollect at once the sort of corps which is now in some degree superseded by those mounted on light blood horses. It is at least certain, that after the most undaunted exertions on the part of the officers, seconding those of the Earl of Uxbridge, our light cavalry were found to suffer cruelly in their unequal encounter with the ponderous and sword-proof cuirassiers, and even with the lancers. Many were killed, and several made prisoners, some of whom the French afterwards massacred in cold blood. Even the German Legion[9], so distinguished for discipline and courage during the peninsular conflicts, were unequal, on this occasion, to sustain the shock of the French cavalry. And thus, such had been Buonaparte's dexterity in finding resources and in applying them, the French seemed to have a temporary superiority in that very description of force, with which it was supposed altogether impossible he could be adequately provided. It was upon this occasion that Sir John Elley[10], now quarter-master-general, requested and obtained permission to bring up the heavy brigade, consisting of the Life Guards, the Oxford Blues, and Scotch Greys, and made a charge, the effect of which was tremendous. Notwithstanding the weight and armour of the cuirassiers, and the power of their horses, they proved altogether unable to withstand the shock of the heavy brigade, being literally rode down, both horse and man, while the strength of the British soldiers was no less pre-eminent when they mingled and fought hand to hand. Several hundreds of French were forced headlong over a sort of quarry or gravel pit, where they rolled a confused and undistinguishable mass of men and horses, exposed to a fire which, being poured closely into them, soon put a period to their struggles. Amidst the fury of the conflict some traces occurred of military indifference which merit being recorded. The Life Guards, coming up in the rear of the ninety-fifth, which distinguished regiment acted as sharpshooters in front of the line, sustaining and repelling a most formidable onset of the French, called out to them, as if it had been on the parade in the Park, 'Bravo, ninety-fifth! do you *lather* them and we'll *shave* them!'—Amid the confusion presented by the fiercest and closest cavalry fight which had ever been seen, many individuals distinguished themselves by feats of personal strength and valour. Among these should not be forgotten Shaw, a corporal of the Life-Guards[11], well known as a pugilistic champion, and equally formidable as a swordsman. He is supposed to have slain or disabled ten Frenchmen with his own hand, before he was killed by a musquet or pistol-shot. But officers, also, of rank and distinction, whom the usual habits of modern war render rather the directors than the actual agents of slaughter, were in this desperate action seen fighting hand to hand like common soldiers. 'You are uncommonly savage today,' said an officer to his friend, a young man of rank, who was arming himself with a third sabre, after two had been broken in his grasp: 'What would you have me do,' answered the other, by nature one of the most gentle and humane men breathing, 'we are here to kill the French, and he is the best man today who can kill most of them;'—

and he again threw himself into the midst of the combat. Sir John Elley, who led the charge of the heavy brigade, was himself distinguished for personal prowess. He was at one time surrounded by several of the cuirassiers; but, being a tall and uncommonly powerful man, completely master of his sword and horse, he cut his way out, leaving several of his assailants on the ground, marked with wounds, indicating the unusual strength of the arm which inflicted them. Indeed, had not the ghastly evidences remained on the field, many of the blows dealt upon this occasion would have seemed borrowed from the annals of knight-errantry, for several of the corpses exhibited heads cloven to the chine, or severed from the shoulders. The issue of this conflict was, that the French cavalry was completely beaten off, and a great proportion of their attacking columns of infantry, amounting to about 3000 men, threw down their arms, and were sent off to Brussels as prisoners. Their arrival there added to the terrors of that distracted city; for a vague rumour having preceded their march, announcing the arrival of a column of French, they were for a long time expected as conquerors, not as prisoners. Even when they entered as captives, the sight of the procession did not relieve the terrors of the citizens; the continued thunder of the cannon still announced that the battle was undecided, and the manner of the prisoners themselves was that of men who expected speedy freedom and vengeance. One officer of cuirassiers was particularly remarked for his fine martial appearance, and the smile of stern contempt with which he heard the shouts of the exulting populace. 'The emperor,' he said, 'the *emperor* will shortly be here;' and the menace of his frowning brow and clenched hand indicated the fatal consequences which would attend his arrival.

The contest was indeed so far from being decided, that it raged with the most uninterrupted fury; it had paused in some degree upon the centre and left, but only to be renewed with double ferocity in the right wing. The attack was commenced by successive columns of cavalry, rolling after each other like waves of the sea. The Belgian horse, who were destined to oppose them, again gave way, and galloped from the field in great disorder. Our advanced line of guns was stormed by the French, the artillery-men receiving orders to leave them, and retire within the squares of the infantry. Thus, at least, thirty pieces of artillery were for the time abandoned; but, to an enemy who could not either use them or carry them off. The scene now assumed the most extraordinary and unparalleled appearance. The large bodies of French cavalry rode furiously up and down amongst our small squares of infantry, seeking with desperate courage some point where they might break in upon them, but in vain, though many in the attempt fell at the very point of the bayonets.

In the meantime a brigade of horse-artillery, commanded by the lamented Major Norman Ramsay[12], opened its fire upon the columns. They retreated repeatedly, but it was only to advance with new fury, and to renew attempts which it seemed impossible for human strength and courage ultimately to withstand. As frequently as the cavalry retreated, our artillery-men rushing out of the squares in which they had found shelter, began again to work their pieces, and made a destructive fire on the retiring squadrons. Two officers of artillery were particularly noticed, who, being in a square which was repeatedly charged, rushed out of it the instant the cavalry retreated, loaded one of the deserted guns which stood near, and fired it upon the horsemen. A French officer observed that this manoeuvre was repeated more than once, and cost his troop many lives. At the next retreat of his squadron, he stationed himself by the gun, waving his sword, as if defying the British officers again to approach it. He was instantly shot by a grenadier, but prevented by his self-devotion a considerable loss to his countrymen. Other French officers and men evinced the same desperate and devoted zeal in the cause which they had so rashly and unhappily espoused. One officer of rank, after leading his men as far as they would follow him towards one of the squares of infantry, found himself deserted by them, when the British fire opened, and instantly rode upon the bayonets, throwing open his arms as if to welcome the bullet which should bring him down. He was immediately shot, for the moment admitted of no alternative. On our part, the coolness of the soldiers was so striking as almost to appear miraculous. Amid the infernal noise, hurry, and clamour of the bloodiest action ever fought, the officers were obeyed as if on the parade; and such was the precision with which the men gave their fire, that the aid-de-camp could ride round each square with perfect safety, being sure that the discharge would be reserved till the precise moment when it ought regularly to be made. The fire was rolling or alternate, keeping up that constant and uninterrupted blaze, upon which, I presume, it is impossible to force a concentrated and effective charge of cavalry. Thus, each little phalanx stood by itself, like an impregnable fortress, while their crossing fires supported each other, and dealt destruction among the enemy, who frequently attempted to penetrate through the intervals, and to gain the flank, and even the rear of these detached masses. The Dutch, Hanoverian, and Brunswick troops, maintained the same solid order, and the same ready, sustained, and destructive fire, as the British regiments with whom they were intermingled.

Notwithstanding this well-supported and undaunted defence, the situation of our army became critical. The Duke of Wellington had placed his best troops in the first line; they had already suffered severely, and the quality of those who were brought up to support them was in some instances found unequal to the task. He himself saw a Belgian regiment give way at the instant it crossed the ridge of the hill, in the act of advancing from the second into the first line. The Duke rode up to them in person, halted the regiment, and again formed it, intending to bring them into the fire himself. They accordingly shouted *En avant! en avant!* and, with much of the manner which they had acquired by serving with the French, marched up, dressing their ranks with great accuracy, and holding up their heads with military precision. But as soon as they crossed the ridge of the hill, and again encountered the storm of balls and shells, from which they had formerly retreated, they went to the right about once more, and fairly left the Duke to seek more resolved followers where he could find them. He accordingly brought up a Brunswick regiment, which advanced with less apparent enthusiasm than *Les braves Belges*, but kept their ground with more steadiness, and behaved very well. In another part of the field, the Hanoverian hussars of Cumberland, as they were called, a corps distinguished for their handsome appearance and complete equipments, were ordered to support a charge made by the British. Their gallant commanding officer shewed no alacrity in obeying this order, and indeed observed so much ceremony, that, after having been once and again ordered to advance, an aid-de-camp of the Duke of

Wellington informed him of his Grace's command, that he should either advance or draw off his men entirely, and not remain there to show a bad example and discourage others. The gallant officer of hussars considering this as a serious option, submitted to his own decision, was not long in making his choice, and having expressed to the aid-de-camp his sense of the Duke's kindness, and of the consideration which he had for raw troops, under a fire of such unexampled severity, he said he would embrace the alternative of drawing his men off, and posting them behind the hamlet of Saint John. This he accordingly did in spite of the reproaches of the aid-de-camp, who loaded him with every epithet that is most disgraceful to a soldier. The incident, although sufficiently mortifying in itself, and attended, as may be supposed, with no little inconvenience at such a moment, had something in it so comic, that neither the General nor any of his attendants were able to resist laughing when it was communicated by the incensed aid-de-camp. I have been told many of the officers and soldiers of this unlucky regiment left it in shame, joined themselves to other bodies of cavalry, and behaved well in the action. But the valiant commander not finding himself comfortable in the place of refuge which he had himself chosen, fled to Brussels, and alarmed the town with a report that the French were at his heels. His regiment was afterwards in a manner disbanded, or attached to the service of the commissariat.

These circumstances I communicate to you, not in the least as reflecting upon the national character, either of the Hanoverians or Belgians, both of whom had troops in the field, by whom it was gloriously sustained; but, as an answer to those who have remarked, that the armies not being greatly disproportioned in point of numbers, the contest ought to have been sooner decided in favour of the Duke of Wellington. The truth is, that the Duke's first line *alone*, with occasional reinforcements from the second, sustained the whole brunt of the action; and, it would have been in the highest degree imprudent to have made any movement in advance, even to secure advantages which were frequently gained, since implicit reliance could not be placed upon the raw troops and militia, of whom the support was chiefly composed. With 80,000 British troops, it is probable the battle would not have lasted two hours, though it is impossible it could in that event have been so entirely decisive, since the French, less completely exhausted, would probably have been able to take better measures for covering their retreat.

Meanwhile the battle raged in every point. The centre and left were again assaulted; and, if possible, more furiously than before. The farm-house of La Haye Sainte, lying under the centre of the British line, was at last stormed by the French troops, who put the gallant defenders to the sword. They were Hanoverian sharp-shooters, who had made good the post with the most undaunted courage, whilst they had a cartridge remaining, and afterwards maintained an unequal contest with their bayonets through the windows and embrazures. As the entrance of the farm fronted the high-road, and was in the very focus of the enemy's fire, it was impossible to send supplies of ammunition by that way; and the commanding officer unfortunately had not presence of mind to make a breach through the back part of the wall, for the purpose of introducing them. 'I ought to have thought of it,' said the Duke of Wellington, who seems to have considered it as his duty to superintend and direct even the most minute details of that complicated action; 'but,' as he added, with a very unnecessary apology, 'my mind could not embrace every thing at once.'[13] The post meanwhile, though long maintained by the enemy, was of little use to them, as our artillery on the ridge were brought to plunge into it, and the attempt to defend it as a point of support for his future attacks, cost Buonaparte more men than he had lost in carrying it. On the right, Hougoumont continued to be as fiercely assailed, but more successfully defended. The carnage in that point was dreadful; the French at length had recourse to shells, by which they set on fire, first, a large stack of hay in the farm-yard, and then the chateau itself. Both continued to blaze high in the air, spreading a thick black smoke, which ascended far over that of the cannonade, and seemed to announce that some dreadful catastrophe had befallen the little garrison. Many of the wounded had been indeed carried into the chateau for shelter, and, horrible to relate, could not be withdrawn from it when it took fire. But the Guards continued to make good the garden and the court-yard, and the enemy's utmost efforts proved unable to dispossess them. The various repulses which the French had met with in this part of the field, seemed by degrees to render their efforts less furious, and the right wing re-established its complete communication with this *point d'appui*, or key of the position, and reinforced its defenders as occasion demanded.

During this scene of tumult and carnage, the Duke of Wellington exposed his person with a freedom which, while the position of the armies, and the nature of the ground, rendered it inevitably necessary, made all around him tremble for that life on which it was obvious that the fate of the battle depended. There was scarcely a square but he visited in person, encouraging the men by his presence, and the officers by his directions. Many of his short phrases are repeated by them, as if they were possessed of talismanic effect. While he stood on the centre of the high-road in front of Mount St John, several guns were levelled against him, distinguished as he was by his suite, and the movements of the officers who came and went with orders. The balls repeatedly grazed a tree on the right-hand of the road, which tree now bears his name. 'That's good practice,' observed the Duke to one of his suite, 'I think they fire better than in Spain.' Riding up to the 95th, when in front of the line, and even then expecting a formidable charge of cavalry, he said, 'Stand fast, 95th—we must not be beat—what will they say in England?' On another occasion, when many of the best and bravest men had fallen, and the event of the action seemed doubtful even to those who remained, he said, with the coolness of a spectator, who was beholding some well-contested sport—'Never mind, we'll win this battle yet.' To another regiment, then closely engaged, he used a common sporting expression; 'Hard pounding this, gentlemen; let's see who will pound longest.' All who heard him issue orders took confidence from his quick and decisive intellect, all who saw him caught metal from his undaunted composure. His staff, who had shared so many glories and dangers by his side, fell man by man around him, yet seemed in their own agony only to regard his safety. Sir William Delancey, struck by a spent ball, fell from his horse—'Leave me to die,' he said to those who came to assist him, 'attend to the Duke.' The lamented Sir Alexander Gordon[14], whose early experience and high talents had already rendered him the object of so much hope and expectation, received his mortal wound while expostulating with the General on the personal danger to which he was exposing himself. Lieutenant-Colonel Canning[15], and many of our lost heroes, died with the Duke's name on their expiring lips. Amid the havoc which had been made among his immediate attendants, his Grace sent off a young gentleman, acting as aid-de-camp, to a general of brigade in another part of the field; with a message of importance. In returning he was shot through the lungs, but, as if supported by the resolution to do his duty, he rode up to the Duke of Wellington, delivered the answer to his message, and then dropped from his horse, to all appearance a dying man. In a word, if the most devoted attachment on the part of all who approached him, can add to the honours of a hero, never did a general receive so many and such affecting proofs of it; and their devotion was repaid by his sense of its value and sorrow for their loss. 'Believe me,' he afterwards said, 'that nothing, excepting a battle lost, can be half so melancholy as a battle won. The bravery of my troops has hitherto saved me from that greater evil; but, to win even such a battle as this of Waterloo, at the expence of the lives of so many gallant friends, could only be termed a heavy misfortune, were it not for its results to the public benefit.'

In the meanwhile it seemed still doubtful whether these sacrifices had not been made in vain; for the French, though repulsed in every point, continued their incessant attacks with a perseverance of which they were formerly deemed incapable; and the line of chequered squares, hitherto successfully opposed to them, was gradually, from the great reduction of numbers, presenting a diminished and less formidable appearance. One general officer was under the necessity of stating, that his brigade was reduced to one-third of its numbers, that those who remained were exhausted with fatigue, and that a temporary relief, of however short duration, seemed a measure of peremptory necessity. 'Tell him,' said the Duke, 'what he proposes is impossible. He, I, and every Englishman in the field, must die on the spot which we now occupy.' 'It is enough,' returned the general; 'I and every man under my command are determined to share his fate.' A friend of ours had the courage to ask the Duke of Wellington, whether in that conjuncture he looked often to the woods from which the Prussians were expected to issue.—'No,' was the answer; 'I looked oftener at my watch than at any thing else. I knew if my troops could keep their position till night, that I must be joined by Blucher before morning, and we would not have left Buonaparte an army next day. But,' continued he, 'I own I was glad as one hour of day-light slipped away after another, and our position was still maintained.'—'And if,' continued the querist, 'by misfortune the position had been carried?'—'We had the wood behind to retreat into'—'And if the wood also was forced?'—'No, no; they could never have so beaten us but we could have made good the wood against them.'—From this brief conversation it is evident that in his opinion, whose judgment is least competent to challenge, even the retreat of the English on this awful day would have afforded but temporary success to Buonaparte.

While this furious conflict lasted, the Prussian general, with the faith and intrepidity which characterises him, was pressing forward to the assistance of his allies. So early as between three and four o'clock, the division of Bulow appeared menacing the right flank of the French, chiefly with light troops and cavalry. But this movement was foreseen and provided against by Buonaparte. Besides the immense force with which he sustained the main conflict, he had kept in reserve a large body of troops, under Count Lobau[16], who were opposed to those of Bulow with a promptitude which appeared like magic; our officers being at a loss almost to conjecture whence the forces came, which appeared as it were to rise out of the earth to oppose this new adversary. The engagement (which consisted chiefly in sharp-shooting) continued in this quarter, but with no great energy, as the Prussian general waited the coming up of the main body of Blucher's army. This was retarded by many circumstances. We have already noticed the state of the cross-roads, or rather tracks, through which a numerous army had to accomplish their passage. But besides, the effects of the battle of Ligny were still felt, and it was not only natural but proper that Blucher, before involving himself in defiles from which retreat became impossible, should take some time to ascertain whether the English were able to maintain their ground until he should come up to their assistance. For, in the event of their being routed, with the usual circumstances of defeat, before the Prussians came up, Blucher must have found himself in a most critical situation, engaged in the defiles of St Lambert, with one victorious French army in front, and another pressing upon his rear at Wavre. Such at least is the opinion of our best and most judicious officers. But the loyalty of the Prince-Marshal's character did not permit him long to hesitate upon advancing to the support of his illustrious ally.

Grouchy and Vandamme, with their combined forces, had followed the Prussian rear (commanded by Tauenzein)[17] as far as Wavre, less, it would seem, with the purpose of actual fight, than of precipitating the retreat, which they supposed Blucher to have commenced with his whole army. At length Tauenzein halted upon the villages of Wavre and Bielge, on the river Dyle, and there prepared to defend himself. It is probable that, about this time, the appearance of Bulow's corps on Buonaparte's right flank made the French general desirous the Prussians should be attacked in a different and distant point, in such a serious manner as might effectually engage their attention, and prevent their detaching more forces to the support of Wellington. Accordingly orders were dispatched to Grouchy to make a serious attack upon that part of the Prussian army which was opposed to him. But Buonaparte was not aware, nor does Grouchy seem to have discovered, that the forces he was thus to engage only consisted of a strong rear-guard, which occupied the villages and position upon the Dyle to mask the march of the main army under the Prince-Marshal himself, which was already defiling to the right through the passes of St Lambert, and in full march to unite itself with Wellington and Bulow. The resistance of Tauenzein, however, was so obstinate as to confirm Grouchy in the belief that he was engaged with a great proportion of the Prussian army. The bridge at Wavre, particularly, was repeatedly lost and gained before the French were able to make their footing good beyond it. At length a French colonel snatched the eagle of his regiment, and rushing forward, crossed the bridge and struck it into the ground on the other side. His corps followed with an unanimous shout of *Vive l'Empereur!* and although the gallant officer who thus led them on was himself slain on the spot, his followers succeeded in carrying the village. That of Bielge at the same time fell into their hands, and Grouchy anxiously expected from his Emperor orders to improve his success. But no such orders arrived; the sound of the cannon in that direction slackened, and at length died away; and it was next morning before Grouchy heard the portentous news that awaited him, announcing the fate of Napoleon and his army.

Meantime Blucher pressed the march of his forces through the defiles which separated him and Wellington. Notwithstanding the consequences of his fall upon the 16th, the veteran insisted upon leaving his carriage and being placed on horseback, that he might expedite the march by precept and example. The sun was, however, near setting before his forces appeared in strength issuing from the woods upon the flank of the contending armies. It seems to have been one of Buonaparte's leading errors to miscalculate the moral force of the Prussian character, and especially that of Blucher. Though it was now obvious that the army of the Prince-Marshal was appearing on the field, Napoleon deluded himself to the last by a belief that they were followed by Grouchy, and either retreating, or moving laterally in the same line with him. In this mistake he obstinately persisted until the consequences proved fatal to the very last chance which he had of covering his own retreat. It was for some time supposed, that he mistook the Prussians for his own forces under Grouchy. This was not the case, nor was it possible it could be so. His real error was sufficient for his destruction, without exaggerating it into one that would indicate insanity. But, as appears from Mareschal Ney's letter, Buonaparte spread among the soldiers, by means of the unfortunate Labedoyere, his own belief that Grouchy was advancing to their support. He imagined, in short, that, at the very worst, his own general had made a lateral movement, corresponding to that of Blucher, and was as near to support as the other was to attack him. In this belief, all the slaughter and all the repulses of that bloody day did not prevent his risking a final and desperate effort.

Notwithstanding the perseverance with which Buonaparte had renewed his attacks upon the English position, and the vast number of his best cavalry and infantry who had fallen in the struggle, he had still in reserve nearly 15,000 men of his own guard, who, remaining on the ridge of La Belle Alliance, or behind it, had scarcely drawn a trigger during the action. But about seven o'clock at night their emperor determined to devote this proved and faithful reserve, as his last stake, to the chance of one of those desperate games in which he had been frequently successful. For this purpose he left the more distant point of observation, which he had for some time occupied upon the heights in the rear of the line, and descending from the hill, placed himself in the midst of the high-way fronting Mount St John, and within about a quarter of a mile of the English line. The banks, which rise high on each side, protected him from such balls as did not come in a direct line. Here he caused his guards to defile before him, and acquainting them that the English cavalry and infantry were entirely destroyed, and that to carry their position they had only to sustain with bravery a heavy fire of their artillery: he concluded by pointing to the causeway, and exclaiming, 'There, gentlemen, is the road to Brussels!' The prodigious shouts of *Vive l'Empereur*, with which the Guard answered this appeal, led our troops, and the Duke of Wellington himself, to expect an instant renewal of the attack, with Napoleon as the leader. Many an eye was eagerly bent to the quarter from whence the clamour proceeded; but the mist, as well as the clouds of smoke, rendered it impossible to see any object distinctly. None listened to the shout with more eager hope than our own great General, who probably thought, like the Avenger in Shakespeare,

―――― There thou shouldst be:
By this great clatter one of greatest note
Seems bruited.―――[18]

All indeed expected an attack headed by Buonaparte in person; and in failing upon this instant and final crisis to take the command of his Guards, whom he destined to try the last cast of his fortune, he disappointed both his friends and enemies.

The Imperial Guard, however, rallying in their progress such of the broken cavalry and infantry of the line as yet maintained the combat, advanced dauntlessly. But the repeated repulses of the French had not been left unimproved by the British. The extreme right of the line, commanded by General Frederick Adam[19], under Lord Hill, had gradually and almost imperceptibly gained ground after each unsuccessful charge, until the space between Hougoumont and Braine la Leude being completely cleared of the enemy, the British right wing, with its artillery and sharp-shooters, was brought round from a convex to a concave position, so that our guns raked the French columns as soon as they debouched upon the causeway for their final attack. Our artillery had orders during the whole action to fire only upon the infantry and cavalry of the French, and not to waste their ammunition and energy in the less decisive exchange of shot with the French guns. The service of the artillery was upon this occasion so accurate, and at the same time so destructive, that the heads of the French attacking columns were enfiladed, and in a manner annihilated, before they could advance upon the high road. Those who witnessed the fire and its effects, describe it to me as if the enemy's columns kept perpetually advancing from the hollow way without ever gaining ground on the plain, so speedily were the files annihilated as they came into the line of the fire. Enthusiasm, however, joined to the impulse of those in the rear, who forced forward the front into the scene of danger, at length carried the whole attacking force into the plain. But their courage was obviously damped. They advanced indeed against every obstacle till they attained the ridge, where the British soldiers lay on the ground to avoid the destructive fire of artillery, by which the assault was covered: but this was their final effort. 'Up, Guards, and at them,' cried the Duke of Wellington, who was then with a brigade of the Guards. In an instant they sprung up, and, assuming the offensive, rushed upon the attacking columns with the bayonet. This body of the Guards had been previously disposed in line, instead of the squares which they had hitherto occupied. But the line was of unusual depth, consisting of four ranks instead of two. 'You have stood cavalry in this order,' said the General, 'and can therefore find no difficulty in charging infantry.' The effect of their three fatal cheers, and of the rapid advance which followed, was decisive. The Guards of Napoleon were within twenty yards of those of our sovereign, but not one staid to cross bayonets with a British soldier. The consciousness that no support or reserve remained to them added confusion to their retreat. This was observed by both generals with suitable emotion. The Duke of Wellington perceived the disorder of the French retreat, and the advance of the Prussians on their right flank, where they were already driving in all that was opposed to them. He immediately commanded the British troops to form line, and assume the offensive. The whole line formed four deep, and, supported by the cavalry and artillery, rushed down the slopes and up the corresponding bank, driving before them the flying French, whose confusion became each moment more irretrievable. The tirailleurs of the Imperial Guard gallantly attempted to cover the retreat. They were charged by the British cavalry, and literally cut to pieces.

Buonaparte saw the issue of the fight with the same accuracy as the English General, but with far different feelings. He had shown the utmost coolness and indifference during the whole day, and while he praised the discipline and conduct of particular corps of the British army, whose gallantry he witnessed, he affected to lament their necessary and inevitable destruction. Even to reports which were incessantly brought to him of the increasing strength and progress of the Prussians upon his right flank, he turned an indifferent ear, bending his whole attention, and apparently resting his final hope, upon the success of the ultimate attack by the Imperial Guards. When he observed them recoil in disorder, the cavalry intermixed with the foot, and trampling them down, he said to his aid-de-camp, '*Ils sont meleés ensemble!*'[20] then looked down, shook his head, and became, according to the expression of his guide, pale as a corpse. Immediately afterwards two large bodies of British cavalry appeared in rapid advance on each flank; and as the operations of the Prussians had extended along his right flank, and were rapidly gaining his rear, Buonaparte was in great danger of being made prisoner. He then pronounced the fatal words, 'It is time to save ourselves,' and left to their fate the army which that day had shed their blood for him with such profusion. His immediate attendants, about ten or twelve in number, scrambled along with him out of the hollow way, and gaining the open plain, all fled as fast as their horses could carry them, or the general confusion would admit, without a single attempt, on Buonaparte's part, to rally his army or cover their retreat. Whatever may be thought of Buonaparte's behaviour on former occasions, it would appear, either that prosperity had clouded his energy of mind, or that he was in some degree wanting to himself on the conclusion of this memorable day. For, after having shown, during the progress of the battle, great judgment, composure, and presence of mind, the mode of his retreat was much less than honourable to a soldier, who had risen by personal courage and conduct to the greatest pitch of power which was ever enjoyed by an individual.

Meanwhile the front attack of the English, and that of the Prussians upon the flank, met with slight opposition. Just as the English army had deployed into line for the general charge, the sun streamed out, as if to shed his setting glories upon the conquerors of that dreadful day. Fatigue and diminution of numbers, even wounds, were forgotten, when the animating command was given to assume the offensive. Headed by the Duke of Wellington himself, with his hat in his hand, the line advanced with the utmost spirit and rapidity. The fire of the enemy from one hundred and fifty pieces of artillery did not stop them for a single moment, and in a short time the French artillery-men deserted their guns, cut loose their traces, and mingled in the flight, now altogether confused and universal, the fugitives trampling down those who yet endeavoured to keep their ranks. The first line had hardly, the vestige of military order when it was flung back on the second, and both became then united in one tide of general and undistinguished flight. Baggage-waggons, artillery-carts, guns overthrown, and all the impediments of a hurried flight, cumbered the open field as well as the causeway, without mentioning the thick-strewn corpses of the slain, and the bodies of the still more miserable wounded, who in vain shrieked and implored compassion, as fliers and pursuers drove headlong over them in the agony of fear or the ecstacy of triumph. All the guns which were in line along the French position, to the number of one hundred and fifty, fell into the immediate possession of the British. The last gun fired was a howitzer, which the French had left upon the road. It was turned upon their retreat, and discharged by Captain Campbell[21], aid-de-camp to General Adam, with his own hand, who had thus the honour of concluding the battle of Waterloo, which, it has been said, Buonaparte himself commenced.

There remained, however, for the unhappy fugitives a flight and pursuit of no ordinary description. And here the timely junction of the Prussians was of the last consequence to the common cause of Europe. The British cavalry were completely wearied with the exertions of the day, and utterly incapable of following the chase. Even the horses of the officers were altogether unable to strike a trot for any length of way, so that the arrival of the Prussians, with all their cavalry fit for instant and rapid operation, and organized by so active a quarter-master-general as Gneisenau[22], was essential to gathering in the harvest, which was already dearly won and fairly reaped.

The march and advance of the Prussians crossed the van of the British army, after they had attacked the French position, about the farm-house of La Belle Alliance, and there, or near to that spot, the Duke of Wellington and Prince-Marshal Blucher, met to congratulate each other upon their joint success and its important consequences.

The hamlet, which is said to have taken its name from a little circumstance of village scandal,* came to bear an unexpected and extraordinary coincidence with the situation of the combined armies, which inclines many foreigners even now to give the fight the name of the Battle of La Belle Alliance. Here, too, the victorious allies of both countries exchanged military greeting,—the Prussians halting their regimental band to play 'God save the King,' while the British returned the compliment with three cheers to the honour of Prussia. The Prince-Marshal immediately gave orders that every man and horse in his army capable of action should press upon the rear of the fugitives, without giving them a moment's time to rally. The night was illuminated by a bright moon, so that the fliers found no refuge, and experienced as little mercy.

To the last, indeed, the French had forfeited all claim; for their cruelty towards the Prussians, taken upon the 16th, and towards the British wounded and prisoners made during the battle of the 18th, was such as to exclude them from the benefit of the ordinary rules of war. Their lancers, in particular, rode over the field during the action, dispatching with their weapons the wounded British, with the most inveterate rancour, and many of the officers who have recovered from the wounds they received on that glorious day, sustained the greatest danger and most lasting inconvenience from such as were inflicted by those savages,

---

* A woman who resided here, after marrying two husbands in her own station of creditable yeomanry, chose to unite herself, upon her becoming a second time a widow, to her own hind or ploughman; and the name of La Belle Alliance was bestowed on her place of residence in ridicule of this match.

when they were in no condition either to offend others or defend themselves. The *Quoi! tu n'es pas mort?*[23] of the spearman was usually accompanied with a thrust of his lance, dealt with an inveteracy which gives great countenance to the general opinion, that their orders were to give no quarter. Even the British officers who were carried before Buonaparte, although civilly treated while he spoke to them, and dismissed with assurances that they should have surgical assistance and proper attendance, were no sooner out of his presence than they were stripped, beaten, and abused. Most of the prisoners whom the French took from our light cavalry were put to death in cold blood, or owed their safety to concealment or a speedy escape. In short, it seemed as if the French army, when they commenced this desperate game, had, like Buccaneers setting forth upon a cruise, renounced the common rules of war, and bonds of social amity, and become ambitious of distinguishing themselves as enemies to the human species. This unnatural hatred, rashly announced and cruelly acted upon, was as fearfully avenged. The Prussians listened not, and they had no reason to listen, to cries for mercy from those who had thus abused their momentary advantages over themselves and their allies; and their light horse, always formidable on such occasions, made a fearful and indiscriminate slaughter, scarce interrupted even by the temptation of plundering the baggage with which the roads were choaked, and unchecked by an attempt at resistance. Those soldiers who had begun the morning with such hopes, and whose conduct during the battle vindicated their having done so, were now so broken in heart and spirits, that scores of them fled at sight of a single Prussian hussar.

Yet it is remarkable that, amid the countless number who

fell, both of privates and officers, we do not notice many of those names distinguished in the bulletins of Buonaparte's former campaigns. Whether the marshals, doubting the success of their old master, hazarded themselves less frankly in his cause, or did so with better fortune than belonged to our distinguished and undaunted Picton, Ponsonby[24], and other officers of high rank whose loss we lament, it. is not for me to conjecture. But, except Duhesme[25] and Friant[26], neither of whose names were very much distinguished, we hear of no general officers among the French list of the slain. The latter was killed by a ball close to the turncoat Ney, who commanded the imperial guards in the last attack. The death of Duhesme had something in it which was Homeric. He was overtaken in the village of Genappe by one of the Duke of Brunswick's black hussars, of whom he begged quarter. The soldier regarded him sternly, with his sabre uplifted, and then briefly saying, 'The Duke of Brunswick died yesterday,' bestowed on him his death's wound.

κάτθανε καὶ Πάτροκλος, ὅ περ σέο πολλὸν ἀμείνων.[27]

General Cambrone[28] was said also to have fallen after refusing quarter, and announcing to the British, by whom it was offered, 'The Imperial Guard can die but never surrender.' The speech and the devotion of the general received honourable mention in the Minutes of the Chamber of Representatives. But the passage was ordered to be erased next day, it being discovered that General Cambrone was a prisoner in Lord Wellington's camp.

The French retreat was utter rout and confusion, the men deserting their officers, the officers the men, all discipline neglected, and every thing thrown away which could for a moment impede the rapidity of their panic flight. A slight attempt was made to halt at the village of Genappe, but there and at Charleroi, and wherever else the terrified fugitives attempted to pause, a cannon-shot or two, or the mere sound of a Prussian drum or trumpet, was sufficient to put them again to the rout.

The English remained on the field of battle and the villages adjacent. Be it not forgotten, that, after such attention to their wounded companions, as the moment permitted, they carried their succours to the disabled French, without deigning to remember that the defenceless and groaning wretches who encumbered the field of battle in heaps, were the same men who had displayed the most relentless cruelty on every temporary advantage which they obtained during this brief campaign. They erected huts over them to protect them from the weather, brought them water, and shared with them their refreshments, shewing in this the upright nobleness of their own dispositions, and giving the most vivid testimony of their deserving that victory with which Providence had crowned them—a victory as unparalleled in its consequences, as the battle itself was in its length, obstinacy, and importance. Adieu! my dear Major. Excuse a long letter, which contains much which you may have heard better told, mixed with some things with which you are probably not yet acquainted. The details which I have ventured to put into writing, are most of them from the authority of officers high in command upon that memorable day, and I may therefore be allowed to hope that even repetitions will be pardoned for the sake of giving more authenticity to the facts which I have narrated, Your's, &c.

PAUL.

LETTER IX.

PAUL TO HIS SISTER MARGARET.

I should now, my dear sister, give you some description of the celebrated field of Waterloo. But although I visited it with unusual advantages, it is necessary that I should recollect how many descriptions have already appeared[1] of this celebrated scene of the greatest event of modern times, and that I must not weary your patience with a twice-told tale. Such and so numerous have been the visits of English families and tourists, as to enrich the peasants of the vicinity by the consequences of an event which menaced them with total ruin. The good old Flemish housewife, who keeps the principal cabaret at Waterloo, even when I was there, had learnt the value of her situation, and charged three prices for our coffee, because she could gratify us by showing the very bed in which the *Grand Lord* slept the night preceding the action. To what extremities she may have since proceeded in taxing English curiosity, it is difficult to conjecture. To say truth, the honest Flemings were at first altogether at a loss to comprehend the eagerness and enthusiasm by which their English visitors were influenced in their pilgrimages to this classic spot. Their country has been long the scene of military operations, in which the inhabitants themselves have seldom felt much personal interest. With them a battle fought and won is a battle forgotten, and the peasant resumes his ordinary labours after the armies have left his district, with as little interest in recollecting the conflict, as if it had been a thunder-storm which had passed away.

You may conceive, therefore, the grave surprise with which these honest pococurantés[2] viewed the number of British travellers of every possible description, who hastened to visit the field of Waterloo.

I was early in making my pilgrimage, yet there were half a dozen of parties upon the ground at the same time with that to which I belonged. Honest John Lacoste[3], the Flemish peasant, whom Buonaparte has made immortal by pressing into his service as a guide, was the person in most general request, and he repeated with great accuracy the same simple tale to all who desired to hear him. I questioned him long and particularly, but I cannot pretend to have extracted any information in addition to what has been long ago very accurately published in the newspapers. For I presume you would be little interested in knowing that, upon this memorable occasion, the ex-emperor rode a dappled horse, and wore a grey surtout with a green uniform coat; and, in memory of his party's badge, as I suppose, a violet-coloured waistcoat and pantaloons of the same. It was, however, with no little emotion that I walked with Lacoste from one place to another, making him, as nearly as possible, show me the precise stations which had been successively occupied by the fallen monarch on that eventful day. There was a deep and inexpressible feeling of awe in the reflection, that the last of these was the identical place from which he, who had so long held the highest place in Europe, beheld his hopes crushed and his power destroyed. To recollect, that within a short month, the man whose name had been the terror of Europe, stood on the very ground which I now occupied, that right opposite was placed that commander whom the event of the day hailed, *Vainqueur de Vainqueur de la terre*[4] —that the landscape, now solitary and peaceful around me,

presented so lately a scene of such horrid magnificence—
that the very individual who was now at my side, had then
stood by that of Napoleon, and witnessed every change in
his countenance, from hope to anxiety, from anxiety to
fear and to despair,—to recollect all this, oppressed me with
sensations which I find it impossible to describe. The scene
seemed to have shifted so rapidly, that even while I stood on
the very stage where it was exhibited, I felt an inclination to
doubt the reality of what had passed.

Lacoste himself seems a sensible, shrewd peasant. He
complained that the curiosity of the visitors who came to
hear his little tale, interfered a good deal with his ordinary
and necessary occupations: I advised him to make each
party, who insisted upon seeing and questioning him, a
regular charge of five francs, and assured him that if he did
so, he would find that Buonaparte had kept his promise of
making his fortune[5], though in a way he neither wished nor
intended. Pere Lacoste said he was obliged to me for the
hint, and I dare say has not failed to profit by it.

The field of battle plainly told the history of the fight, as
soon as the positions of the hostile armies were pointed out.
The extent was so limited[6], and the interval between them
so easily seen and commanded, that the various manoeuvres
could be traced with the eye upon the field itself, as upon
a military plan of a foot square. All ghastly remains of the
carnage had been either burned or buried, and the reliques
of the fray which yet remained were not in themselves of a
very imposing kind. Bones of horses, quantities of old hats,
rags of clothes, scraps of leather, and fragments of books
and papers strewed the ground in great profusion, especially
where the action had been most bloody. Among the last,
those of most frequent occurrence were the military *livrets*,

or memorandum-books of the French soldiers. I picked up one of these, which shows, by its order and arrangement, the strict discipline which at one time was maintained in the French army, when the soldier was obliged to enter in such an accompt-book, not only the state of his pay and equipments, but the occasions on which he served and distinguished himself, and the punishments, if any, which he had incurred. At the conclusion is a list of the duties of the private soldier, amongst which is that of knowing how to dress his victuals, and particularly to make good soup. The *livret* in my possession appears to have belonged to the Sieur Mallet, of the 2d battalion of the 8th regiment of the line: he had been in the service since the year 1791, until the 18th of June, 1815, which day probably closed his account, and with it all his earthly hopes and prospects. The fragments of German prayer-books were so numerous, that I have little doubt a large edition had been pressed into the military service of one or other party, to be used as cartridge-paper. Letters, and other papers, memorandums of business, or pledges of friendship and affection, lay scattered about on the field—few of them were now legible. Quack advertisements were also to be found where English soldiers had fallen. Among the universal remedies announced by these empirics, there was none against the dangers of such a field.

Besides these fragments, the surface of the field shewed evident marks of the battle. The tall crops of maize and rye were trampled into a thick black paste, under the feet of men and horses, the ground was torn in many places by the explosion of shells, and in others strangely broken up and rutted by the wheels of the artillery. Such signs of violent and rapid motion recorded, that

Rank rush'd on rank, with squadron squadron closed,
The thunder ceased not, nor the fire reposed.[7]

Yet, abstracting from our actual knowledge of the dreadful cause of such appearances, they reminded me not a little of those which are seen upon a common a few days after a great fair has been held there. These transitory memorials were in a rapid course of disappearing, for the plough was already at work in several parts of the field. There is, perhaps, more feeling than wisdom in the wish, yet I own I should have been better pleased, if, for one season at least, the field where, in imagination, the ploughshare was coming in frequent contact with the corpses of the gallant dead, had been suffered to remain fallow. But the corn which must soon wave there will be itself a temporary protection to their humble graves, while it will speedily remove from the face of nature the melancholy traces of the strife of man.

The houses and hamlets which were exposed to the line of fire have of course suffered very much, being perforated by cannon-balls in every direction. This was particularly the case at La Haye Sainte. The inhabitants of these peaceful cottages might then exclaim, in the words of our admired friend,

'Around them, in them, the loud battle clangs;
Within our very walls fierce spearmen push,
And armed warriors cross their clashing blades:
Ah, woe is me! our warm and cheerful hearths,
And rushed floors, on which our children play'd,
Must be the bloody lair of dying men.'[8]

There was not indeed a cottage in the vicinity but what, ere the eve of the fight, was crowded with the wounded, many of whom had only strength to creep to the next place of cover, that they might lay them down to die.

The village of Saint John, and others within the English position, had escaped with the demolition of the windows, and the breaches of the walls from without. The hamlets lying on the opposite heights, within the French line of bivouack, having been plundered to the bare walls, had sustained internal as well as external damage. Among other claims upon English generosity, and which may serve to illustrate the idea which foreigners have formed of its illimitable extent, one was made by a proprietor of this district for a considerable sum, stated to be the damage which his property had sustained in and through the battle of Waterloo. He was asked, why he thought a claim so unprecedented in the usual course of warfare would be listened to. He said, he understood the British had made compensation in Spain to sufferers under similar circumstances. It was next pointed out to him that no English soldier had or could have been accessary to the damage which he had sustained, since the hamlets and houses plundered lay within Buonaparte's position. The Fleming, without having studied at Leyden[9], understood the doctrine of consequential damages. He could not see that the circumstance alleged made much difference, since, he argued, if the English had not obstinately placed themselves in the way, the French would have marched quietly on to Brussels, without doing him any material damage; and it was not until he was positively informed that his demand would not be granted that he remained silenced, but not satisfied.

Hougoumont (a name bestowed, I believe, by a mistake of our great commander, but which will certainly supersede the more proper one of Chateau-Goumont,) is the only place of consideration which was totally destroyed. The shattered and blackened ruins of this little chateau remain among the wreck of its garden, while the fruit-trees, half torn down, half fastened to the walls, give some idea of the Dutch neatness with which it had been kept ere the storm of war approached it. Most visitors bought peaches, and gathered hazel-nuts and filberds in the garden, with the pious purpose of planting, when they returned to England, trees, which might remind them and their posterity of this remarkable spot. The grove of trees around Hougoumont was shattered by grape-shot and musquetry in a most extraordinary manner. I counted one which had been struck in twenty different places, and I think there was scarce any which had totally escaped. I understand the gentleman to whom this ravaged domain belongs is to receive full compensation from the government of the Netherlands.

I must not omit to mention, that notwithstanding the care which had been bestowed in burying or burning the dead, the stench in several places of the field, and particularly at La Haye Sainte and Hougoumont, was such as to indicate that the former operation had been but hastily and imperfectly performed. It was impossible, of course, to attempt to ascertain the numbers of the slain; but, including those who fell on both sides before the retreat commenced, the sum of forty thousand will probably be found considerably within the mark, and I have seen officers of experience who compute it much higher[10]. When it is considered, therefore, that so many human corpses, besides those of many thousand horses, were piled upon a field scarcely two miles long, and not above half a mile in breadth, it is wonderful that a pestilential disease has not broken out, to sum up the horrors of the campaign.

If the peasants in the neighbourhood of Waterloo suffered great alarm and considerable damage in the course of this tremendous conflict, it must be acknowledged they have had peculiar and ample means of indemnification. They had, in the first place, the greatest share of the spoils of the field of battle, for our soldiers were too much exhausted to anticipate them in this particular. Many country people were at once enriched by the plunder of the French baggage, and not a few by that of the British, which, having been ordered to retreat during the action, became embarrassed on the narrow causeway leading through the great forest of Soignies, and was there fairly sacked and pillaged by the runaway Belgians and the peasantry; a disgraceful scene, which nothing but the brilliancy of the great victory, and the consequent enthusiasm of joy, could have allowed to be passed over without strict enquiry. Many of our officers, and some but ill able to afford such a loss, were in this manner deprived of all their clothes and baggage, at the moment of their advance into the territories of France.

A more innocent source of profit has opened to many of the poor people about Waterloo, by the sale of such trinkets and arms as they collect daily from the field of battle; things of no intrinsic value, but upon which curiosity sets a daily increasing estimate. These memorials, like the books of the Sybils, rise in value as they decrease in number. Almost every hamlet opens a mart of them as soon as English visitors appear. Men, women, and children rushed out upon us, holding up swords, pistols, carabines, and holsters, all of which were sold when I was there *a prix juste*, at least to those who knew how to drive a bargain. I saw a tolerably good carabine bought for five francs; to be sure there went many words to the bargain, for the old woman to whom it belonged had the conscience at first to ask a gold Napoleon for it, being about the value it would have borne in Birmingham. Crosses of the Legion of Honour were in great request, and already stood high in the market. I bought one of the ordinary sort for forty francs. The eagles which the French soldiers wore in front of their caps, especially the more solid ornament of that description which belonged to the Imperial Guards, were sought after, but might be had for a few sous. But the great object of ambition was to possess the armour of a cuirassier, which at first might have been bought in great quantity, almost all the wearers having fallen in that bloody battle. The victors had indeed carried off some of these cuirasses to serve as culinary utensils, and I myself have seen the Highlanders frying their rations of beef or mutton upon the breast-plates and back-pieces of their discomfited adversaries. But enough remained to make the fortunes of the people of St John, Waterloo, Planchenoit, &c. When I was at La Belle Alliance I bought the cuirass of a common soldier for about six francs; but a very handsome inlaid one, once the property of a French officer of distinction, which was for sale in Brussels, cost me four times the sum. As for the casques, or head pieces, which by the way are remarkably handsome, they are almost *introuvable*, for the peasants immediately sold them to be beat out for old copper, and the purchasers, needlessly afraid of their being reclaimed, destroyed them as fast as possible.

The eagerness with which we entered into these negociations, and still more the zeal with which we picked up every trifle we could find upon the field, rather scandalized one of the heroes of the day[11], who did me the favour to guide me over the field of battle, and who considered the interest I took in things which he was accustomed to see scattered as mere trumpery upon many a field of victory, with a feeling that I believe made him for the moment heartily ashamed of his company. I was obliged to remind him that as he had himself gathered laurels on the same spot, he should have sympathy, or patience at least, with our more humble harvest of peach-stones, filberds, and trinkets. Fortunately the enthusiasm of a visitor, who went a bow-shot beyond us, by carrying off a brick from the house of La Belle Alliance, with that of a more wholesale amateur, who actually purchased the door of the said mansion for two gold Napoleons, a little mitigated my military friend's censure of our folly, by showing it was possible to exceed it. I own I was myself somewhat curious respecting the use which could be made of the door of La Belle Alliance, unless upon a speculation of cutting it up into trinkets, like Shakspeare's mulberry-tree[12].

A relique of greater moral interest was given me by a lady,[13] whose father had found it upon the field of battle. It is a manuscript collection of French songs, bearing stains of clay and blood, which probably indicate the fate of the proprietor. One or two of these romances I thought pretty, and have since had an opportunity of having them translated into English, by meeting at Paris with one of our Scottish men of rhyme[14].

ROMANCE OF DUNOIS.

It was Dunois, the young and brave, was bound for
    Palestine,
But first he made his orisons before Saint Mary's shrine:
'And grant, immortal Queen of Heaven,' was still the
    soldier's prayer,

'That I may prove the bravest knight, and love the fairest
   fair.'

His oath of honour on the shrine he graved it with his
   sword,
And follow'd to the Holy Land the banner of his Lord;
Where, faithful to his noble vow, his war-cry fill'd the air,—
'Be honour'd aye the bravest knight, beloved the fairest
   fair.'

They owed the conquest to his arm, and then his liege-
   lord said,
'The heart that has for honour beat by bliss must be
   repaid,—
My daughter Isabel and thou shall be a wedded pair,
For thou art bravest of the brave, she fairest of the fair.'

And then they bound the holy knot before Saint Mary's
   shrine,
That makes a paradise on earth if hearts and hands
   combine;
And every lord and lady bright that were in chapel there,
Cried, 'Honour'd be the bravest knight, beloved the
   fairest fair!'

THE TROUBADOUR.

Glowing with love, on fire for fame,
   A Troubadour that hated sorrow,
Beneath his Lady's window came,
   And thus he sung his last good-morrow:
'My arm it is my country's right,
   My heart is in my true love's bower;

Gaily for love and fame to fight
   Befits the gallant Troubadour.'

And while he march'd with helm on head
   And harp in hand, the descant rung,
As faithful to his favourite maid,
   The minstrel-burthen still he sung:
'My arm it is my country's right,
   My heart is in my lady's bower;
Resolved for love and fame to fight,
   I come, a gallant Troubadour.'

Even when the battle-roar was deep,
   With dauntless heart he hewed his way,
Mid splintering lance and falchion-sweep,
   And still was heard his warrior-lay;
'My life it is my country's right,
   My heart is in my lady's bower;
For love to die, for fame to fight,
   Becomes the valiant Troubadour.'

Alas! upon the bloody field
   He fell beneath the foeman's glaive,
But still, reclining on his shield,
   Expiring sung the exulting stave:
'My life it is my country's right,
   My heart is in my lady's bower;
For love and fame to fall in fight
   Becomes the valiant Troubadour.'

The tone of these two romances chimes in not unhappily
with the circumstances in which the manuscript was

found, although I do not pretend to have discovered the real effusions of a military bard, since the first of them, to my certain knowledge, and I have no doubt the other also, is a common and popular song in France. The following Anacreontic is somewhat of a different kind, and less connected with the tone of feeling excited by the recollection, that the manuscript in which it occurs was the relique of a field of battle:—

> It chanced that Cupid on a season,
>   By Fancy urged, resolved to wed,
> But could not settle whether Reason
>   Or Folly should partake his bed.
>
> What does he then?—Upon my life,
>   'Twas bad example for a deity—
> He takes me Reason for his wife,
>   And Folly for his hours of gaiety.
>
> Though thus he dealt in petty treason,
>   He loved them both in equal measure;
> Fidelity was born of Reason,
>   And Folly brought to bed of Pleasure.

There is another verse of this last song, but so much defaced by stains, and disfigured by indifferent orthography, as to be unintelligible. The little collection contains several other ditties, but rather partaking too much of the freedom of the corps de garde, to be worthy the trouble of transcription or translation.

I have taken more pains respecting these poems than their intrinsic poetical merit can be supposed to deserve, either in the original or the English version; but I cannot divide them from the interest which they have acquired by the place and manner in which they were obtained, and therefore account them more precious than any of the other remains of Waterloo which have fallen into my possession.

Had these reliques of minstrelsy, or any thing corresponding to them in tone and spirit, been preserved as actual trophies of the fields of Cressy and Agincourt, how many gay visions of knights and squires and troubadours, and *sirventes* and *lais*[15], and courts of Love and usages of antique chivalry, would the perusal have excited! Now, and brought close to our own times, they can only be considered as the stock in trade of the master of a regimental band; or at best, we may suppose the compilation to have been the pastime of some young and gay French officer, who, little caring about the real merits of the quarrel in which he was engaged, considered the war by which the fate of Europe was to be decided only as a natural and animating exchange for the pleasures of Paris. Still the gallantry and levity of the poetry compels us to contrast its destined purpose, to cheer hours of mirth or of leisure, with the place in which the manuscript was found, trampled down in the blood of the writer, and flung away by the hands of the spoilers, who had stripped him on the field of battle. I will not, however, trouble you with any further translations at present; only to do justice to my gallant Troubadour, I will subjoin the original French in the postscript to this letter. It is a task of some difficulty; for accurate orthography was not a quality of the original writer, and I am myself far from possessing a critical knowledge of the French language, though I have endeavoured to correct his most obvious errors. I am, dear sister, affectionately yours,

PAUL.

POSTSCRIPT.

CHANSON.

Partant pour la Syrie le jeune et beau Dunois,
Alla prier Marie de bénir ses exploits,
'Faites, O Reine immortelle,' lui dit-il en partant,
'Que j'aime la plus belle, et sois le plus vaillant.'

Il grave sur la pierre le serment de l'honneur,
Et va suivre en guerre le Comte et son seigneur;
Au noble voeu fidèle il crie en combattant,
'Amour à la plus belle, gloire au plus vaillant.'

On lui doit la victoire—'Dunois' dit son Seigneur,
'Puisque tu fais ma gloire je ferai ton bonheur,
De ma fille Isabelle, sois l'epoux a l'instant,
Car elle est la plus belle, et toi le plus vaillant.'

A l'autel de Marie ils contractent tous les deux,
Cette union chérie qui seule les rend heureux;
Chacune Dame à la Chapelle s'écrie en les voyant,
'Amour à la plus belle, honneur au plus vaillant!'

ROMANCE DE TROUBADOUR.

Brûlant d'amour, en partant pour la guerre,
Le Troubadour, ennemi de chagrin,
Pensoit ainsi à sa jeune bergère,
Tous les matins en chantant ce refrain;
　　'Mon bras à ma patrie,
　　Mon coeur pour mon amie,
　　Mourir gaîment pour la Gloire et l'Amour,

C'est le devoir d'un vaillant Troubadour.'

Dans le bivouac le Troubadour fidèle,
La casque au front, la guittarre à la main,
Dans sa delire, à sa jeune bergère,
Chantoit ainsi le joyeux refrain;
  'Mon bras à ma patrie,
  Mon coeur pour mon amie,
  Mourir gaîment pour la Gloire et l'Amour,
  C'est le devoir d'un vaillant Troubadour.'

Dans les combats deployant son courage,
La courage au coeur, la glaive à la main,
Etoit le même au milieu de carnage,
Chaque matin, en chantant le refrain;
  'Mon bras à ma patrie,
  Mon coeur à mon amie,
  Mourir gaîment, pour l'honneur et l'amour,
  C'est le devoir d'un vrai Troubadour.'

Cet brave, helas! deployant son courage,
Aux ennemis en bravant le destin,
Il respiroit sur la fin son ame,
Nommant sa belle, et chantant le refrain;
  'Mon bras à ma patrie,
  Mon coeur à mon amie,
  Mourir gaîment pour l'honneur et l'amour,
  C'est le devoir d'un vrai Troubadour.'

CHANSON DE LA FOLIE.

De prendre femme un jour, dit-on,
L'Amour conduit la Fantasie,

On lui proposa la Raison,
On lui proposa la Folie.—
Quel choix feroit le Dieu fripon,
Chacune d'eux est fort jolie—
Il prit pour femme la Raison,
Et pour maîtresse la Folie.

Il les aimoit toutes les deux,
Avec une constance égale,
Mais l'époux vivant au mieux,
Avec la charmante rivale,
Naquit un double rejeton,
De la double galanterie,
L'amant* naquit de la Raison,
Et le Plaisir de la Folie.

* *Ita* in MS.

LETTER X.

PAUL TO ——, ESQ. OF ——.

The obligation which I contracted to write to you, my dear friend, upon subjects in some degree connected with your statistical pursuits, hangs round the neck of my conscience, and encumbers me more than any of the others which I have rashly entered into. But you will forgive the deficiencies of one who, though for fifteen years doomed to be a farmer, has hitherto looked upon his sheep and cows rather as picturesque objects in the pasture, than subjects of profit in the market, and who, by some unaccountable obtuseness of intellect, never could interest himself about his turnips or potatoes, unless they were placed upon the dinner-table. Could I have got an intelligent Flemish farmer to assist me, I have little doubt that I might have sent you some interesting information from that land of Goshen[1], where the hand of the labourer is never for an instant folded in inactivity upon his bosom, and where the rich soil repays with ready gratitude the pains bestowed in cultivation. Promptitude and regularity, the soul of all agricultural operations, are here in such active exertion, that before the corn is driven out of the field in which it has been reaped, the plough is at work upon the stubble, leaving only the ridges occupied by the shocks. The fertility of the soil is something unequalled, even in our best carse lands, being generally a deep and inexhaustible mould, as favourable for forest-trees as for cultivation. Cheapness is the natural companion of plenty; and I should suppose that

Brussels, considered as a capital, where every luxury can be commanded, is at present one of the economical places of residence in Europe. I began a brief computation, from which it appeared, that I might support myself with those comforts or luxuries which habit has rendered necessary to me, maintaining at the same time decent hospitality, and a respectable appearance, for about the sum of direct taxes which I pay to the public in Scotland. But ere I had time to grumble at my lot, came the comfortable recollection; that my humble home in the north is belted in by the broad sea, and divided from all the convulsions that have threatened the continent, that no contending armies have decided the fate of the world within ten miles of my dwelling, and that the sound of cannon never broke my rest, unless as an early *feu-de-joie*. These, with the various circumstances of safety and freedom connected with them, and arising out of them, are reasons more than sufficient for determining my preference in favour of my own homely home.

But for such as have better reasons than mere economy for chusing a short residence abroad, Brussels possesses great attractions. The English society there, so far as I saw it, is of the very first order, and I understand that of the principal families of the Netherlands is accessible and pleasant. This, however, is wandering from the promised topics—*revenons à nos moutons.*[2]

The farm-houses and cottages in the Netherlands have an air of ease and comfort corresponding with the healthy and contented air of their inhabitants. That active industry, which eradicates every weed, prevents the appearance of waste and disorder, and turns every little patch of garden or orchard-ground to active profit, is no where seen to more advantage than in the Netherlands; and the Flemish painters copied from nature when they represented the groups of trees and thickets in which their cottages are usually embosomed. These thickets, and the woods of a larger scale, which are numerous and extensive, supply the inhabitants with fuel, though there are also coal-mines wrought to considerable extent near Charleroi. The woods are chiefly of beech, but varied with birches, oaks, and other trees. The oaks, in particular, seem to find this a favourite soil, and are to be seen sprouting freely in situations where the surface appears a light and loose sand. In the lower strata, no doubt, they find a clay soil better adapted to their nourishment.

The forests of Flanders were formerly of a more valuable description than at present, for the trees fit for ship-timber have been in a great measure cut down by Buonaparte's orders, in his eager desire to create a navy at Antwerp[3]. Nothing could better mark the immensity of his projects, and the extensive means which he had combined for their execution, than the magnificent dock-yards which he created in that city. The huge blocks of hewn stone, of the most beautiful grey colour and closest grain, each weighing from two to four tons, which were employed in facing the large and deep basins which he constructed, were brought by water from the quarries of Charleroi, at the distance of sixty miles and upwards. The fortifications also, which Buonaparte added to those of the city, were of the most formidable description. Nevertheless the British thunders reached his vessels even in their well-defended dock-yards, as was testified by several of them having been sunk during the bombardment by Sir Thomas Graham[4], of which the masts yet remain visible above water. The people of Antwerp did not speak with much respect of the talents of Carnot, (their governor during the siege,) considered as an engineer, although we have often heard them mentioned with applause in England. They pointed out the remains of a small fascine-battery[5], which was said to be misplaced, and never to have done any execution, as the only offensive preparation made by order of this celebrated mathematician. In other respects the citizens were agreeably deceived in Carnot, whose appointment to the government of the city was regarded with the greatest apprehensions by the inhabitants, who remembered that he had been the minister and instrument of Robespierre. He gave them, however, no reason to complain of him, and the necessary measures which he adopted of destroying such parts of the suburbs as interfered with the fire of the batteries, and the defence of the place, were carried into execution with as much gentleness and moderation as the inhabitants could have expected. The town itself, being studiously spared by the clemency of the besieging general, suffered but little from the British fire, though some houses were ruined by the bombs, and particularly the *Douane*, or French custom-house, whose occupants had so long vexed the Flemings by their extortion, that its destruction was regarded by them with great joy.

Belgium, or Flanders, has of late acquired a new political existence, as a principal part of the kingdom of the Netherlands. I am no friend, in general, to the modern political legerdemain, which transfers cities and districts from one state to another, substituting the 'natural boundaries' (a phrase invented by the French to justify their own usurpations,) by assuming a river, or a chain of mountains, or some other geographical line of demarcation, instead of the moral limits which have been drawn, by habits of faith and loyalty to a particular sovereign or form of government, by agreement in political and religious opinions, and by resemblance of language and manners; limits traced at first perhaps by the influence of chance, but which have been rendered sacred and indelible by long course of time and the habits which it has gradually fostered. *Arrondissements*, therefore, Indemnities, and all the other terms of modern date, under sanction of which cities and districts, and even kingdoms, have been passed from one government to another, as the property of lands and stock is transferred by a bargain between private parties, have been generally found to fail in their principal object. Either a general indifference to the form of government and its purposes, have been engendered in those whom superior force has thus rendered the sport of circumstances; or where the minds of the population are of a higher and more vigorous order, the forced transference has only served to increase their affection to the country from which they have been torn, and their hatred against that to which they are subjected. The alienation of the Tyrol from Austria[6] may be quoted as an example of the latter effect; and it is certain, that this iniquitous habit of transferring allegiance in the gross from one state to another, without consulting either the wishes or the prejudices of those from whom it is claimed, has had the former consequences of promoting a declension of public spirit among the smaller districts of Germany. Upon the map, indeed, the new acquisitions are traced with the same colour which distinguishes the original dominions of the state to which they are attached, and in the accompanying gazetteer, we read that such a city, with its liberties, containing so many thousand souls, forms now a part of the population of such a kingdom: But can this be seriously supposed (at least until the lapse of centuries) to convey to the subjects, thus transferred, that love and affection to their new dynasty of rulers, that reverence for the institutions in church and state, those wholesome and honest prejudices in favour of the political society to which we belong, which go so far in forming the love of our native country? 'Care I for the limbs, the thewes, the sinews of a man—Give me the spirit!'[7]—and when the stipulations of a treaty, or the decrees of a conqueror, can transfer with the lands and houses the love, faith, and attachment of the inhabitants, I will believe that such *arrondissements* make a wholesome and useful part of the state to which they are assigned. Until then the attempt seems much like that of a charlatan who should essay to ingraft, as an useful and serviceable limb, upon the person of one patient, the arm or leg which he has just amputated from another.

But though it seems in general sound and good doctrine, to beware of removing ancient land-marks, and although the great misfortunes of Europe may be perhaps traced to the partition of Poland[8], in which this attempt was first made upon the footing of open violence, yet the union between the Low Countries and the States of Holland must be admitted to form a grand exception to the general rule. It is, indeed, rather a restoration of the natural union which subsisted before the time of Philip the Second[9], than a new-modelled arrangement of territory; the unsettled situation of Flanders, in particular, having long been such as to make it the common and ordinary stage, upon which all the prize-fighters of Europe decided their quarrels. To a people too often abandoned to the subaltern oppression of governors sent from their foreign masters, it is no small boon to be placed under a mild and mitigated monarchy, and united with a nation whose customs, habits, and language, are so similar to their own. Still, however, such is the influence of the separate feelings and opinions acquired during the lapse of two centuries, that many prejudices remain to be smoothed away, and much jealousy to be allayed, and soothed, before the good influence of the union can be completely felt.

The first and most irritating cause of apprehension is the difference of religion. The Flemings are very zealous, and very ignorant catholics, over whom their clergy have a proportional power. The king's declared purpose of toleration has greatly alarmed this powerful body, and the nerve which has thus been touched has not failed to vibrate through the whole body politic. The Archbishop of Liege[10], formerly a great adherent and ally of Buonaparte, has found his conscience alarmingly twinged by so ominous a declaration on the part of a Calvinistic monarch, and has already made his remonstrance against this part of the proposed constitution in a pastoral letter, which is couched in very determined language. But the present royal family are too surely seated, and the times, it may be hoped, too liberal, for such fulminations to interfere with the progress of toleration. Meanwhile the king neglects nothing that fairly can be done to conciliate his new catholic subjects. He has recently pledged himself to use his utmost exertions to recover from the possession of the French the pictures which they carried off from various churches in the Netherlands, and particularly from Brussels and Antwerp. Among the last, was the chef-d'oeuvre of Rubens, the Descent from the Cross[11], which, with two corresponding pictures relative to the same subject, once hung above the high altar in the magnificent cathedral at Antwerp, where the compartments, which they once filled, remain still vacant to remind the citizens of their loss. All the other ornaments of that superb

cathedral shared the fate of this masterpiece, excepting only
a painting which Rubens executed to decorate the chapel in
which he himself lies buried; and which an unusual feeling
of respect and propriety prevented the spoilers from tearing
away from his tomb. The composition of the picture has
something curious; for under the representation of a Holy
Family, and various characters of the New Testament, the
artist has painted his grandfather, his father, his three wives,
and his mistress, the *last* in the character of the Virgin
Mary, to whom the others are rendering homage. He has
also introduced his own portrait, a noble martial figure,
dressed in armour, and in the act of unfurling a banner.
Whatever may be thought of the decorum of such a picture
painted for such a place, the beauty of the execution cannot
be sufficiently admired. While the English traveller is
called upon for once to acknowledge the moderation of the
French, who have left at least one monument of art in the
place to which it was most appropriate, he will probably
wish they had carried off with them the trash of wax
figures, which, to the disgrace of good taste and common
sense, are still the objects of popular adoration. Abstracted
from all polemics, one can easily conceive that the sight of
an interesting painting, representing to our material organs
the portrait of a saint, or an affecting scene of Scripture,
may not only be an appropriate ornament in the temple of
worship, but, like church-music, may have its effect in fixing
the attention, and aiding the devotion of the congregation.
It may be also easily understood, and readily forgiven, that
when kneeling before the very altar to which our ancestors
in trouble resorted for comfort, we may be gradually led
to annex a superstitious reverence to the place itself: But
when, in the midst of such a cathedral as that of Antwerp,

one of the grandest pieces of Gothic architecture which Europe can show,—when among the long-drawn aisles and lofty arches, which seem almost the work of demi-gods, so much does the art and toil bestowed surpass what modern times can present,—when, in the midst of such a scene, we find a wax figure of the Virgin, painted, patched, frizzled, and powdered; with a tarnished satin gown (the skirt held up by two cherubs,) paste ear-rings and necklace, differing in no respect, but in size, from the most paltry doll that ever was sold in a toy-shop; and observe this incongruous and ridiculous *swamy*[12] the object of fervid and zealous adoration from the votaries who are kneeling before it, we see the idolatry of the Romish church in a point of view disgusting and humiliating as that of ancient Egypt, and cease to wonder at the obstinacy of the prelate of Liege and his brethren, who fear the light which universal toleration would doubtless throw upon the benighted worship of their great Diana. In the meanwhile the promise of the king to procure restoration of the pictures, is received by most of the Flemings as a pledge that the religion, which he himself professes, will not prevent his interesting himself in that of the catholics; and I think there can be little doubt that, under the gradual influence of time and example, the grosser points of superstition will be tacitly abandoned here, as in other catholic countries.

The Dutch have a more worldly subject of jealousy in the state of their commerce, which cannot but be materially affected by the opening of the Scheldt, whenever that desirable event shall have taken place, and also by the principal residence of the government being changed from the Hague to Brussels. But they are a reflecting people, and are already aware that the operation of both these changes will be slow and gradual; for commerce is not at once transferred from the channels in which it has long flowed; and for some time, at least, family recollections and attachments will make the royal family frequent residents in Holland, notwithstanding the charms of the palace of Lacken[13]. In the meanwhile the Dutch gain the inestimable advantage of having the battle turned from their gates, and of enjoying the protection of a strong barrier placed at a distance from their own frontier,—blessings of themselves sufficient to compensate the inconvenience which they may for a time sustain, until they transfer their capital and industry to the new channels offered for them by the union.

Nothing could have happened so fortunate for the popularity of the house of Orange as the active and energetic character of the hereditary prince. His whole behaviour during the actions of Quatre Bras and Waterloo, and the wound which (it may almost be said fortunately) he received upon the latter occasion, have already formed the strongest bond of union between his family and their new subjects, long unaccustomed to have sovereigns who could lead them to battle, and shed their blood in the national defence. The military force, which he is at this moment perpetually increasing, is of a respectable description; for, though some of the Belgian troops behaved ill during the late brief campaign, there were other corps, and particularly infantry and artillery, both Dutch and Flemings, whose firmness and discipline equalled those of any regiments in the field. The *brave Belges* are naturally proud of the military glory they have acquired, as well as of the prince who led them on. In every corner of Brussels there were ballad-singers bellowing out songs in praise of the prince and his followers. I, who am a collector of popular effusions, did not fail to purchase specimens of the Flemish minstrelsy, in which, by the way, there is no more mention of the Duke of Wellington, or of John Bull, than if John Bull and his illustrious general had had nothing to do with the battle of Waterloo.

This little omission of the Flemish bards proceeds, however, from no disinclination to the Duke or to England. On the contrary, our wounded received during their illness, and are yet experiencing, during their convalescence, the most affecting marks of kindness and attention from the inhabitants of Brussels. These acts of friendship towards their allies were not suspended (as will sometimes happen in this world) until the chance of war had decided in favour of the English. Even on the 17th, when the defeat of Blucher, and the retreat of the Duke of Wellington, authorised them to entertain the most gloomy apprehensions for their own safety, as well as to fear the vengeance of the French for any partiality they might show towards their enemies, the kind citizens of Brussels were not deterred from the exercise of kindness and hospitality. They were seen meeting the wounded with refreshments; some seeking for those soldiers who had been quartered in their houses, others bestowing their care on the first disabled sufferer they met with, carrying him to their home, and nursing him like a child of the family, at all the cost, trouble, and risk, with which their hospitality might be attended. The people of Antwerp, to which city were transferred upon the 17th and 18th most of those who had been wounded at Quatre Bras, were equally zealous in the task of the good Samaritan, Many of our poor fellows told me, that they must have perished but for the attention of these kind Flemings, whose

'Entire affection scorned nicer hands,'[14]

since many of the highest and most respectable classes threw pride and delicacy aside to minister to the wants of the sufferers. On their part, the Flemings were often compelled to admire the endurance and hardihood of their patients. 'Your countrymen,' said a lady to me, who spoke our language well, 'are made of iron, and not of flesh and blood. I saw a wounded Highlander stagger along the street, supporting himself by the rails, and said to him, I am afraid you are severely hurt. "I was born in Lochaber," answered the poor fellow, "and I do not care for a wound;" but ere I could complete my offer of shelter and assistance, he sunk down at my feet a dying man.' In one house in Brussels, occupied by a respectable manufacturer and his two sisters, thirty wounded soldiers were received, nursed, fed, and watched, the only labour of the medical attendants being to prevent their hosts from giving the patients more wine and nourishing food than suited their situation. We may hope the reciprocal benefits of defence and of hospitality will be long remembered, forming a kindly connection between England and a country which, of all others, may be most properly termed her natural ally.

I have again wandered from agriculture into politics and military affairs, but I have little to add which properly belongs to your department, since I have no doubt that you have already sate in judgment upon the Flemish plough, rake, and hay-fork, presented to the Highland Society by one of its most active members. The most remarkable implement of agriculture which fell under my observation was a sort of hooked stick, which the reaper holds in his left hand, and uses to collect and lay the corn as he cuts it with a short scythe. The operation is very speedy, for one person engaged in it can keep two or three constantly employed in binding the sheafs. But I suppose it would only answer where the ground is level and free from stones.

The furniture of the Flemings, and, generally speaking, their implements of labour, &c. have a curious correspondence with what we have been accustomed to consider as their national character; being strong and solid, but clumsy and inelegant, and having a great deal more substance employed in constructing them than seems at all necessary. Thus the lever of an ordinary draw-well is generally one long tree; and their waggons and barges are as huge and heavy as the horses which draw them. The same cumbrous solidity which distinguishes the female figures of Rubens, may be traced in the domestic implements and contrivances of his countrymen. None would have entertained you more than the apparatus provided for securing a horse while in the act of being shod, a case in which our Vulcans trust to an ordinary halter and their own address. But a Flemish horse is immured within a wooden erection of about his own size, having a solid roof, supported by four massive posts, such as a British carpenter would use to erect a harbour-crane. The animal's head is fastened between two of these huge columns with as many chains and cords as might have served to bind Baron Trenck[15]; and the foot which is to be shod is secured in a pair of stocks, which extend between two of the upright beams. This is hardly worth writing, though ridiculous to look at; but there is something, as Anstey says, 'so clumsy and clunch'[16] in the massive strength of the apparatus, in the very unnecessary extent of the precaution, and in the waste of time, labour, and materials, that it may be selected as an indication of a national character, displaying itself in the most ordinary and trifling particulars.

Adieu, my dear friend; I am sorry I can send you no more curious information upon your favourite subject. But it would be unnecessary to one who is skilled in all the modern arts of burning without fire, and feeding without pasture; and who requires no receipts from Holland to teach him how to lay on so much fat upon a bullock or a pig as will make the flesh totally unfit for eating. Yours affectionately,

PAUL.

LETTER XI.

TO THE SAME.

I have now, my dear friend, reached Paris, after traversing the road from Brussels to this conquered capital through sights and sounds of war, and yet more terrible marks of its recent ravages. The time was interesting, for although our route presented no real danger, yet it was not, upon some occasions, without such an appearance of it as naturally to impress a civilian with a corresponding degree of alarm. All was indeed new to me, and the scenes which I beheld were such as press most deeply on the feelings.

We were following the route of the victorious English army, to which succours of every sort, and reinforcements of troops recently landed in Flanders, were pressing eagerly forward, so that the towns and roads were filled with British and foreign troops. For the war, although ended to all useful and essential purposes, could not in some places be said to be actually finished. Condé had surrendered but a few days before, and Valenciennes still held out, and, as report informed us, was to undergo a renewal of the bombardment. Another and contrary rumour assured us that an armistice had taken place, and that, as *non-combatants*, the garrison would permit a party even as alarming as our own to pass through the town without interruption. I felt certainly a degree of curiosity to see the most formidable operation of modern war, but as I was far from wishing the city of Valenciennes to have been burned for my amusement, we were happy to find that the latter report was accurate. Accordingly we passed the works and batteries of the besiegers unquestioned by the Dutch and Prussian videttes, who were stalking to and fro upon their posts, and proceeded to the gate of the place, where we underwent a brief examination from the non-commissioned officer on duty, who looked at our passports, requested to know if we were military men, and being answered in the negative, permitted us to enter a dark, ill-built, and dirty town. 'And these are the men,' I thought, as I eyed the ill-dressed and ragged soldiers upon duty at the gates of Valenciennes, 'these are the men who have turned the world upside down, and whose name has been the night-mare of Europe, since most of this generation have written man!' They looked ugly and dirty and savage enough certainly, but seemed to have little superiority in strength or appearance to the Dutch or Belgians. There was, however, in the air and eye of the soldiers of Buonaparte, (for such these military men still called themselves,) something of pride and self-elation, that indicated undaunted confidence in their own skill and valour. They appeared, however, disunited and disorganized. Some wore the white cockade, others still displayed the tri-colour, and one prudent fellow had, for his own amusement and that of his comrades, stuck both in his hat at once, so as to make a *cocarde de convenance*, which might suit either party that should get uppermost. We were not permitted to go upon the ramparts, and I did not think it necessary to walk about a town in possession of a hostile soldiery left to the freedom of their own will. The inhabitants looked dejected and unhappy, and our landlady, far from displaying the liveliness of a French-woman, was weeping-ripe, and seemed ready to burst into tears at every question which we put to her. Their apprehensions had been considerably relieved by General Rey[1] having himself assumed the white cockade; but as he still refused to admit any of the allied troops within the city, there remained a great doubt whether the allies would content themselves with the blockade, to which they had hitherto restricted their operations against Valenciennes. The inhabitants were partial, the landlady said, to the English, with whom they were well acquainted, as Valenciennes had been a principal depot for the prisoners of war; but they deprecated their town being occupied by the Prussians or Belgians, in whose lenity they seemed to place but little reliance.

On the road next day we met with very undesirable company, being the disbanded garrison of Condé, whom the allies had dismissed after occupying that town. There is, you may have remarked, something sinister in the appearance of a common soldier of any country when he is divested of his uniform. The martial gait, look, and manner, and the remaining articles of military dress which he has retained, being no longer combined with that neatness which argues that the individual makes part of a civilized army, seem menacing and ominous when that assurance is wanting. If this is the case even with the familiar faces of our own soldiery, the wild and swarthy features, moustaches, and singular dresses of foreigners, added much, as may well be supposed, of the look of banditti to the garrison of Condé. They were indeed a true sample of the desperate school to which they belonged, for it was not many days since they had arrested and put to death a French loyalist officer named Gordon[2], solely for summoning them to surrender the town to the king. For this crime the brother of the murdered individual is now invoking vengeance, but as yet fruitlessly, at the court of the Thuilleries. These desperadoes, strolling in bands of eight or ten or twenty, as happened, occupied the road for two or three miles, and sullen resentment and discontent might easily be traced in their looks. They offered us no rudeness, however, but contented themselves with staring hard at us, as a truculent-looking fellow would now and then call out *Vive le Roi!* and subjoin an epithet or two to show that it was uttered in no mood of loyal respect. At every cross-road two or three dropped off from the main body, after going, with becoming grace, through the ceremony of embracing and kissing their greasy companions. The thought involuntarily pressed itself upon our mind, what will become of these men, and what of the thousands who, in similar circumstances, are now restored to civil life, with all the wild habits and ungoverned passions which war and license have so long fostered? Will the lion lie down with the kid, or the trained free-booter return to the peaceable and laborious pursuits of civil industry? Or are they not more likely to beg, borrow, starve, and steal, until some unhappy opportunity shall again give them a standard and a chieftain?

We were glad when we got free of our military fellow-travellers, with whom I should not have chosen to meet by night, or in solitude, being exactly of their appearance who would willingly say 'Stand' to a true man. But we had no depredations to complain of, excepting the licensed extortions of the innkeepers, a matter of which you are the less entitled to complain, because every prudent traveller makes his bargain for his refreshments and lodging before he suffers the baggage to be taken from his carriage. Each reckoning is therefore a formal treaty between you and mine host or hostess, in which you have your own negligence or indifference to blame, if you are very much over-reached. It is scarce necessary to add, that the worst and poorest inns are the most expensive in proportion. But I ought not to omit informing you, that notwithstanding a mode of conducting their ordinary business, so much savouring of imposition, there is no just room to charge the French with more direct habits of dishonesty. Your baggage and money is always safe from theft or depredation, and when I happened to forget a small writing-box, in which there was actually some money, and which had the appearance of being intended for securing valuable articles, an ostler upon horseback overtook our carriage with it before I had discovered my mistake. Yet it would have cost these people only a lie to say they knew nothing of it, especially as their house was full of soldiers of different nations, whose presence certainly afforded a sufficient apology for the disappearance of such an article. This incident gave me a favourable opinion of this class of society in France, as possessed at least of that sort of limited honesty which admits of no peculation excepting in the regular way of business.

The road from Brussels to Paris is, in its ordinary state, destitute of objects to interest the traveller. The highways, planned by Sully[3], and completed by his followers in office, have a magnificence elsewhere unknown. Their great breadth argues the little value of ground at the time they were laid out, but the perfect state in which the central causeway is maintained, renders the passage excellent even in the worst weather, while the large track of ground on each side gives an ample facility to use a softer road during the more favourable season. They are usually shadowed by triple rows of elms, and frequently of fruit-trees, which have a rich and pleasant effect. But much of the picturesque delights of travelling are lost in France, owing to the very circumstances which have rendered the roads so excellent. For as they were all made by the authority of a government, which possessed and exercised the power of going as directly from one point to another as the face of the country admitted, they preserve commonly that long and inflexible straight line, of all others least promising to the traveller, who longs for the gradual openings of landscape afforded by a road which, in sweet and varied modulation, 'winds round the corn-field and the hill of vines,'[4] being turned as it were from its forward and straight direction by respect for ancient property and possession, some feeling for the domestic privacy and convenience, some sympathy even for the prejudices and partialities of a proprietor. I love not the stoical virtue of a Brutus[5], even in laying out a turnpike-road, and should augur more happily of a country (were there nothing else to judge by) where the public appears to have given occasionally a little way to spare private property and domestic seclusion, than of one where the high road goes right to its mark without respect to either. In the latter case it only proves the authority of those who administer the government, in the former it indicates respect for private rights, for the protection of which government itself is instituted.

But the traveller in France, upon my late route, has less occasion than elsewhere to regret the rectilinear direction of the road on which he journeys, for the country offers no picturesque beauty. The rivers are sluggish, and have flat uninteresting banks. In the towns there sometimes occurs a church worthy of visiting, but no other remarkable building of any kind, and the sameness of the architecture of the 15th century, to which period most of them may be referred, is apt to weary the attention when you have visited four or five churches in the course of two days. The fortifications of the towns are of the modern kind, and consequently more formidable than picturesque. Of those feudal castles which add such a venerable grace to the landscape in many places of England and Scotland, I have not seen one either ruinous or entire. It would seem that the policy of Louis XI.,[6] to call up his nobility from their estates to the court, and to render them as far as possible dependent upon the crown,—a policy indirectly seconded by the destruction of the noble families which took place in the civil wars of the League[7], and more systematically by the arts observed during the reign of Louis XIV.,—had succeeded so entirely as to root out almost all traces of the country having ever been possessed by a *noblesse campagnarde*[8], who found their importance, their power, and their respectability, dependent on the attachment of the peasants among whom they lived, and over whom their interest extended. There are no ruins of their ancient and defensible habitations, and the few, the very few country houses which the traveller sees, resemble those built in our own country about the reign of Queen Anne, while the grounds about them seem in general neglected, the fences broken, and the whole displaying that appearance of waste which deforms a property after the absence of a proprietor for some years.

The furious patriots of the Revolution denounced war against castles, and proclaimed peace to the cottage. Of the former they found comparatively few to destroy, and of the latter, in the English sense of the word, there were as few to be protected. The cultivator of the fields in France, whether farmer or peasant, does not usually live in a detached farm-house or cottage, but in one of the villages with which the country abounds. This circumstance, which is not altogether indifferent, so far as it concerns rural economics, blemishes greatly the beauty of the landscape. The solitary farm-house, with its little dependencies of cottages, is in itself a beautiful object, while it seldom fails to excite in the mind, the idea of the natural and systematic dependence of a few virtuous cottagers upon an opulent and industrious farmer, who exercises over them a sort of natural and patriarchal authority, which has not the less influence because the subjection of the hinds, and their submission to their superior, is in some degree voluntary. A large village, composed of many farmers and small proprietors, and who hire their labourers at large, and without distinction, from amongst the poorer class of the same town, is more open to the feuds and disputes which disturb human society, always least virtuous and orderly when banded in crowds together, and when uninfluenced by the restraints of example, and of authority approaching, as closely as may be, to their own station in society.

Another uncomfortable appearance in French landscape, is the total want of inclosure. The ground is sedulously and industriously cultivated, and apparently no portion of it is left without a crop. But the want of hedges and hedge-row trees gives to an eye accustomed to the richness of England, a strange appearance of waste and neglect, even where you are convinced, on a closer examination, that there exists in reality neither the one nor the other. Besides there is necessarily an absence of all those domestic animals which add so much in reality, as well as in painting and descriptive poetry, to the beauty of a country. Where there are no inclosures, and where at the same time the land is under crop, it is plain that the painter must look in vain for his groups of cattle, sheep, and horses, as the poet must miss his lowing herd and bleating flock. The cattle of France are accordingly fed in the large straw-yards which belong to each *Metairic*, or large farm-house, and the sheep are chiefly grazed in distant tracts of open pasture. The former practice, as a mode of keeping not only the stall-fed bullock, but the cows destined for the dairy, has been hailed with acclamation in our own country by many great agriculturists, and you among others. But until I shall be quite assured that the rustic economics profit by this edict of perpetual imprisonment against the milky mothers of the herd, in proportion to the discomfort of the peaceful and useful animal thus sequestered from its natural habits, and to the loss of natural beauty in the rural landscape, thus deprived of its most pleasing objects, I would willingly move for a writ of Habeas Corpus in favour of poor Crummie[9], made a bond-slave in a free country. At any rate, the total absence of cattle from the fields, gives a dull and unanimated air to a French landscape.

In travelling also through such parts of France as I have seen, the eye more particularly longs for that succession of country-seats, with their accompaniments of parks, gardens, and paddocks, which not only furnish the highest ornaments of an English landscape, but afford the best and most pleasing signs of the existence of a mild and beneficent aristocracy of land-holders, giving a tone to the opinions of those around them, not by the despotism of feudal authority and direct power, but, as we have already said of the farmer, by the gradual and imperceptible influence which property, joined with education, naturally acquires over the more humble cultivator of the soil. It is the least evil consequence of the absence of the proprietor, that with him vanishes those improvements upon the soil, and upon the face of nature, which are produced by opulence under the guidance of taste. The eye in this country seldom dwells with delight upon trees growing, single or in groupes, at large and unconfined, for the sole purpose of ornament, and contrasting their unrestrained vegetation and profusion of shade with such as, being trained solely for the axe, have experienced constant restraint from the closeness of the masses in which they are planted, and from the knife of the pruner. The French forests themselves, when considered in their general effect, though necessarily both numerous and extensive, as furnishing the principal fuel used by the inhabitants, are not generally so disposed as to make an interesting part of the scenery. The trees are seldom scattered into broken groupes, and never arranged in hedge-rows, unless by the sides of the highways. Large woods, or rather masses of plantations, cannot and do not supply the variety of landscape afforded by detached groves, or the rich and clothed appearance formed by a variety of intersecting lines composed of single trees.

The absence of inclosures gives also, at least to our eyes, an unimproved and neglected air to this country. But upon close inspection the traveller is satisfied that the impression is inaccurate. The soil is rich, generally speaking, and every part of the land is carefully cropped and cultivated. Although, therefore, the ground being undivided, except by the colour of the various crops by which it is occupied, has, at first sight, that waste and impoverished appearance to which the inhabitant of an inclosed country is particularly sensible, yet the returns which it makes to the cultivator amply contradict the false impression. It is truly a rich and fertile land, affording in profusion all that can render subsistence easy, and abounding with corn, wine, and oil. When we consider France in this light, it is impossible to suppress our feelings of resentment at the irregular ambition, which carried the inhabitants of so rich a country to lay yet more waste the barren sands of Prussia, and encumber with their corpses the pathless wildernesses of Moscow and Kalouga.

But the hour of retaliation is now come, and with whatever feelings of resentment we regard the provocation, it is impossible to view the distress of the country without deep emotions of compassion. From one hill to another our eye descried the road before us occupied by armed bands of every description, horse, foot, artillery, and baggage, with their guards and attendants. Here was seen a long file of cavalry moving on at a slow pace, and collecting their forage as they advanced. There a park of artillery was formed in a corn-field, of which the crop was trampled down and destroyed. In one place we passed a regiment of soldiers, pressing forwards to occupy some village for their night-quarters, where the peasant must lay his account with finding his military guests whatever accommodation they are pleased to demand from him; in another we might see, what was still more ominous to the country through which the march was made, small parties of infantry or of cavalry, detached upon duty, or straggling for the purpose of plunder. The harvest stood ripened upon the fields, but it was only in a few places that the farmer, amid the confusion of the country, had ventured upon the operation of reaping it, unless where he was compelled by the constraint of a military requisition, or the commands of a commissary. It would have been a new sort of harvest-home for you, and your faithful *Grieve*[10], to have seen the labour of leading in the crop performed by an armed force, and your sheaves moving to head-quarters instead of the farm-yard, under the escort of an armed and whiskered Prussian, smoking his pipe with great composure on the top of each cart. Sometimes odd enough rencounters took place during this operation. A Prussian commissary, with his waggons, met some French peasants driving their carts, which occasioned a temporary stop to both parties. While some of the Frenchmen seemed zealously engaged in clearing way for the military men, others approached the waggons, and having previously contrived to ascertain that none of the Prussians understood French, they loaded them with all the abusive epithets which that language affords; taking care, however, amid the vivacity of their vituperation, to preserve such an exterior of respect in their manner and gestures, as induced the honest Prussians to suppose the Frenchmen were making apologies for the temporary obstruction which they had given to their betters. Thus the one party were showering *coquin*, and *voleurs*, and *brigand* upon the other, who ever and anon with great gravity withdrew their pipes from their mouths to answer these douceurs with *Das ist gut—sehr wohl*[11], and similar expressions of acquiescence. It would have been cruel to have deprived the poor Frenchmen of this ingenious mode of expectorating their resentment, but I could not help giving them a hint, that the commissary who was coming up understood their language, which had the instant effect of sending the whole party to their horses' heads.

The inhabitants hastened to propitiate the invaders, as far as possible, by assuming the badges of loyalty to the house of Bourbon. Nothing marked to my mind more strongly the distracted state of the country, than the apparent necessity which every, even the humblest individual, thought himself under of wearing a white cockade, and displaying from the thatch of his cottage a white rag, to represent the *pavilon blanc*. There was a degree of suspicion, arising from this very unanimity, concerning the motives for which these emblems were assumed; and I dare say the poor inhabitants might many of them have expressed their feelings in the words of Fletcher,—

> 'Who is he here that did not wish thee chosen,
> Now thou *art* chosen? Ask them—all will say so,
> Nay swear't—'tis for the king; but let that pass.'[12]

With equal zeal the inhabitants of the towns were laying aside each symbol that had reference to Buonaparte, and emulously substituting a loyal equivalent. The sign-painter was cleverest at his profession who could best convert the word *Imperiale* into *Royale*; but there were many bunglers, whose attempts produced only a complicated union of the two contradictory adjectives. Some prudent housekeepers, tired apparently of the late repeated changes, left a blank for the epithet, to be inserted when the government should show some permanency.

These numerous testimonies of acquiescence in the purpose of their march, were in some measure lost upon the allied troops. The British indeed preserved the strictest good order and discipline, in obedience to the orders issued and enforced by the commander in chief. But as the army was necessarily to be maintained at the expence of the country through which they passed, heavy requisitions were issued by the commissaries, which the French authorities themselves were under the necessity of enforcing. Still as pillage and free-booting, under pretext of free quarters and maintenance, was strictly prohibited and punished, the presence of the English troops was ardently desired, as a protection against those of other nations.

Our allies the Prussians, as they had greater wrongs to revenge, were far less scrupulous in their treatment of the invaded country. When our road lay along their line of march we found as many deserted villages as would have jointured all Sultan Mahmoud's owls[13]. In some places the inhabitants had fled to the woods, and only a few miserable old creatures, rendered fearless by age and poverty, came around us, begging, or offering fruit for sale. As the peasants had left their cottages locked up, the soldiers as regularly broke them open, by discharging a musket through the key-hole and shattering all the wards at once by the explosion. He who obtains admission by such violent preliminaries is not likely to be a peaceful or orderly guest; and accordingly furniture broken and destroyed, windows dashed in, doors torn down, and now and then a burned cottage, joined with the state of the hamlets, deserted by such of the terrified inhabitants as were able to fly, and tenanted only by the aged and disabled, reminded me of the beautiful lines describing the march of a conqueror,—

> 'Amazement in his van with Flight combined,
> And Sorrow's faded form and Solitude behind.'[14]

A friend of mine met with an interesting adventure at one of these deserted villages. He had entered the garden of a cottage of somewhat a superior appearance, but which had shared the fate of the rest of the hamlet. As he looked around him he perceived that he was watched from behind the bushes by two or three children, who ran away as soon as they perceived themselves observed. He called after them, but to no purpose. The sound of the English accent, however, emboldened the mother of the family to show herself from a neighbouring thicket, and at length she took courage to approach him. My friend found to his surprise that she understood English well, owing to some accident of her life or education, which I have forgotten. She told him her family were just venturing back from their refuge in the woods, where they had remained two days without shelter, and almost without food, to see what havock the spoilers had made in their cottage, when they were again alarmed by the appearance of troops. Being assured that they were English soldiers, she readily agreed to remain, under the confidence which the national character inspired; and having accepted what assistance her visitor had to offer her, as the only acknowledgment in her power, she sent one of the children to pull and present to her guest the only rose which her now ruined garden afforded. 'It was the last,' she said, 'she had, and she was happy to bestow it on an Englishman.' It is upon occasions such as these that the French women, even of the lowest class, display a sort of sentimental delicacy unknown to those of other countries.

Equal distress, but of a very different kind, I witnessed in the perturbation of a Flemish peasant, whose team of horses had been put in requisition to transport the baggage of an English officer of distinction. As they had not been returned to the owner, whose livelihood and that of his family depended on their safety, he had set out in quest of them, in an agony of doubt and apprehension that actually had the appearance of insanity. Our attention was called to him from his having seated himself behind our carriage, and an expostulation on our part produced his explanation. I never saw such a sudden transition from despair to hope, as in the poor fellow's rugged features when he saw, in the descent between two hills, a party of English dragoons with led horses. He made no doubt they could only be his own, and I hoped to see such a meeting as that of Sancho with Dapple, after their doleful separation. But we were both disappointed; the led horses proved to be those of my friend General A ——[15], who probably would not have been much flattered by their being mistaken, at whatever distance, for Flemish beasts of burthen. I believe, however, my ruined peasant obtained some clew for recovering his lost property, for he suddenly went off in a direction different from that which we had hitherto afforded him the means of pursuing. It is only by selecting such individual instances that I can make you comprehend the state of the country between Mons and Paris.

The Prussians having used this military license, the march of such of our troops as pursued the same route became proportionally uncomfortable. A good bluff quarter-master of dragoons complained to me of the discomforts which they experienced from the condition to which the country had been reduced, but in a tone and manner which led me to conjecture, that my honest friend did not sympathize with the peasant, who had been plundered of his wine and brandy, so much as he censured the Prussians for leaving none for their faithful allies;

'O noble thirst!—yet greedy to drink all.'[16]

In the meanwhile it is no great derogation from the discipline of the English army to remark, that some old school-boy practices were not forgotten; and that, where there occurred a halt, and fruit-trees chanced to be in the vicinity, they instantly were loaded like the emblematic tree in the frontispiece of Lily's grammar[17], only with soldiers instead of scholars; and surrounded by their wives, who held their aprons to receive the fruit, instead of satchels, as in the emblem chosen by that learned grammarian. There were no signs of license of a graver character.

In the midst of these scenes of war and invasion, the regulations of the post establishment, which, as is well known, is in France entirely in the charge of the government and their commissaries or lessees, were supported and respected. A proclamation in four different languages, French, German, English, and Prussian, and signed by four generals of the different countries, was stuck up in every post-house. This polyglot forbade all officers and soldiers, whether belonging to the King of France, or to the allies, from pressing the horses, or otherwise interfering with the usual communication of Paris with the provinces. The post-houses were accordingly inhabited and protected amid the general desolation of the country, and we experienced no interruption on our journey.

While the villages and hamlets exhibited such scenes as I have described, the towns appeared to have suffered less upon this awful crisis, because the soldiers were there under the eye of their officers, and in each garrison-town a military commandant had been named for the maintenance of discipline. Some were indeed reeking from recent storm, or showed half-burnt ruins, which had been made by bombardment within a week or two preceding our arrival. Cambray had been carried by escalade by a bold coup-de-main, of which we saw the vestiges. The citizens, who were chiefly royalists, favoured the attack; and a part of the storming party entered by means of a stair-case contained in an old turret, which terminated in a sally-port opening to the ditch, and above in a wicket communicating with the rampart. This pass was pointed out to them by the towns-people. The defenders were a part of the National Guard, whom Buonaparte had removed from the district to which they belonged and stationed as a garrison in Cambray. The garrison of Peronne, formerly called *Peronne la Pucelle*, or the Virgin Fortress, because it had never been taken, were military of the same amphibious description with those of Cambray. The town is strongly situated in the Somme, surrounded by flat ground and marshes, and presents a formidable exterior. But this, as well as the other fortresses on the iron-bound frontier of Flanders, was indifferently provided with means of resistance. Buonaparte in this particular, as in others, had shown a determination to venture his fortunes upon a single chance of war, since he had made no adequate provision for a protracted defence of the country when invaded. It was one instance of the inexperience of the garrison of Peronne, that they omitted to blindfold the British officer who came to summon them to surrender. An officer of engineers, of high rank and experience, had been employed in this mission, and doubtless did not leave unemployed the eyes which the besieged, contrary to custom in such cases, left at liberty. Upon his return he reported the possibility of carrying a horn-work which covers a suburb on the left side of the river. The attempt was instantly made, and being in all respects successful, was followed by the surrender of the garrison, upon the easy conditions of laying down their arms, and returning to the ordinary civil occupations from which Buonaparte's mandate had withdrawn them. So easy had been these achievements that the officers concerned in them would hardly be prevailed upon to condescend to explain such trifling particulars. Yet to me, who looked upon ramparts a little injured indeed by time, but still strong, upon ditches containing twelve feet deep of water and a high glacis surmounting them, upon palisades constructed out of the trees which had been felled to clear the esplanade around the fortifications, the task of storming such works, even though not defended at all, seemed a grave and serious undertaking. In all these towns, so far as I could discover, the feeling of the people was decidedly in favour of the legitimate monarch; and I cannot doubt that this impression is correct, because elsewhere, and in similar circumstances, those who favoured Buonaparte were at no pains to suppress their inclinations. In one or two towns they were preparing little fetes to celebrate the king's restoration. The accompaniments did not appear to us very splendid; but when a town has been so lately taken by storm, and is still garrisoned by foreign troops and subjected to military requisitions, we could not expect that the rejoicings of its inhabitants should be attended with any superfluity of splendour.

Meanwhile we advanced through this new and bewildering scene of war and waste, with the comfortable consciousness that we belonged to the stronger party. The British drums and bugle-horns sung us to bed every night, and played our reveillée in the morning; for in all the fortified towns which we passed there were British troops and a British commandant, from more than one of whom we experienced attention and civility.

When we reached Pont de St Maxence, which had been

recently the scene of an engagement between the Prussians and French, we found more marked signs of hostile devastation than in any place through which we had yet travelled. It is a good large market-town, with a very fine bridge over the Oise, an arch of which had been recently destroyed, and repaired in a temporary manner. The purpose had probably been to defend the passage; and as the river is deep, and the opposite bank is high and covered with wood, besides having several buildings approaching to the bridge, I presume it might have been made a very strong position. It had been forced, however, by the Prussians, in what manner we found no one to tell us. Several houses in this town had been burnt, and most of them seemed to have been pillaged. The cause was evident from the number of embrasures and loop-holes for musketry which were struck out in the houses and garden walls. The attempt to make a village into a place of defence is almost always fatal to the household gods, since it is likely to be burnt by one or other of the parties, and certain to be plundered by both. Military gentlemen look upon this with a very different eye; for I have been diverted to hear some of them, who have given me the honour of their company in my little excursions from Paris, censure a gentleman or farmer with great gravity for having built his house and stationed his court of offices in a hollow, where they were overlooked and commanded; whereas, by placing the buildings a little higher on the ridge, or more towards right or left, they might, in case of need, have acquired the dignity of being the *key* of a strong position, and, in all probability, have paid for their importance by sharing the fate of Hougoumont.

We were informed at St Maxence that the hand of war had been laid yet more heavily upon the neighbouring town of Sénlis, through which lay our direct route to Paris, and near which an action had taken place betwixt a part of Blucher's army and that of Grouchy and Vandamme, which, falling back to cover the French capital after the battle of Waterloo, had accomplished a retreat that placed those who commanded it very high in public estimation. We felt no curiosity to see any more of the woes of war, and readily complied with a proposal of our postillions to exchange the route of Sénlis for that of Chantilly, to which they undertook to carry us by a cross road through the forest. *Le beau chemin par terre*, or fine green-sward road, which they had urged as so superior to the public causeway, had unfortunately not possessed the same power of resisting the tear and wear of cavalry, artillery, and baggage-waggons. It was reduced to a sort of continued wet ditch, varying in depth in a most irregular manner, and through which the four stallions that drew us kicked, plunged, snorted, and screamed, in full concert with the eternal smack of the whips, as well as shrieks, whoops, and oaths of the jack-booted postillions, lugging about our little barouche in a manner that threatened its demolition at every instant. The French postillions, however, who, with the most miserable appliances and means, usually drive very well, contrived, by dint of quartering and tugging, to drag us safe through roads where a Yorkshire post-boy would have been reduced to despair, even though his horses had not been harnessed with ropes, fastened together by running nooses.

The forest of Chantilly was probably magnificent when it was the chase of the princely family of Condé;[18]. but all the valuable timber trees have been felled, and those which now remain appear, generally speaking, to be about twenty years old only, and consist chiefly of birch, and other inferior timber used for fire-wood. Those who acquired the domains of the emigrants after the Revolution were generally speculating adventurers, who were eager to secure what they could make of the subject in the way of ready money, by cutting timber and selling materials of houses, partly in order to secure the means of paying the price, and partly because prudence exacted that they should lose no time in drawing profit from a bargain, of which the security seemed rather precarious.

The town and palace of Chantilly, rendered classical by the name of the great Prince of Condé, afforded us ample room for interesting reflection. The town itself is pleasant, and has some good houses agreeably situated. But in the present state of internal convulsion, almost all the windows of the houses of the better class were closed, and secured by outer shutters. We were told this was to protect them against the Prussians, with whom the town was crowded. These soldiers were very young lads, chiefly *landwehr*, or militia, and seemed all frolicksome, and no doubt mischievous youths. But, so far as I could see, there was no ill nature, much less atrocity, in their behaviour, which was rather that of riotous school-boys of the higher form. They possessed themselves of the jack-boots of our postillions, and seemed to find great entertainment in stumping up and down the inn-yard in these formidable accoutrements, the size and solidity of which have been in no degree diminished since the days of Yorick and La Fleur[19]. But our Prussian hussars were seen to still greater advantage in the superb stables of Chantilly, which have escaped the fury that levelled its palace. The huge and stately vault, which pride, rather than an attention to utility, had constructed for the stud of the Prince of Condé, is forty feet high, two hundred yards in length, and upwards of thirty-six feet in width. This magnificent apartment, the enormity of whose proportions seemed better calculated for the steeds of the King of Brobdignag than for Houyhnhnms[20] of the ordinary size, had once been divided into suitable ranges of stalls, but these have been long demolished. In the centre arises a magnificent dome, sixty feet in diameter and ninety feet in height; and in a sort of recess beneath the dome, and fronting the principal entrance, is a superb fountain, falling into a huge shell, and dashing over its sides into a large reservoir, highly ornamented with architectural decorations. This fountain, which might grace the court of a palace, was designed for the ordinary supply of the stable. The scale of imposing magnificence upon which this building was calculated, although at war with common sense and the fitness of things, must, in its original state of exact order and repair, have impressed the mind with high ideas of the power and consequence of the prince by whom it was planned and executed, and whose name (Louis Henry de Bourbon, seventh Prince of Condé)[21] stands yet recorded in an inscription, which, supported by two mutilated genii, is displayed above the fountain. But what would have been the mortification of that founder could he have witnessed, as we did, the spacious range with all its ornaments broken down and defaced, as if in studied insult; while its high and echoing vault rung to the shouts, screams, and gambols of a hundred or two of the dirtiest hussars and lancers that ever came off a march, while the shrill cries of their half-starved and miserable horses added a wild but appropriate accompaniment. Yet whatever his feelings might have been to witness such pollution, they would have been inferior to those with which his ancestor, the Great Condé, would have heard that the Sarmatian partizans[22] who occupied Chantilly formed part of an invading army, which had marched, almost without opposition, from the frontiers to the capital, and now held in their disposal the fates of the house of Bourbon and of the kingdom of France.

The old domestic of the family who guided me through these remains of decayed magnificence, cast many a grieved and mortified glance upon the irreverent and mischievous soldiers as they aimed the buts of their lances at the remaining pieces of sculpture, or amused themselves by mimicking his own formal address and manner. *'Ah les barbares! les barbares!'*—I could not refuse assent to this epithet, which he confided to my ear in a cautious whisper, accompanied with a suitable shrug of the shoulders; but I endeavoured to qualify it with another train of reflections:—*'Et pourtant, mon ami, si ce n'étoit pas ces gens la!'*—*'Ah oui, Monsieur, sans eux nous n'aurions peut être jamais revu notre bon Duc—Assurément c'est un revenant bon—mais aussi, il faut avouer qu'il est revenu en assez mauvaise compagnie.'*[23]

At some distance from these magnificent stables, of which (as frequently happens) the exterior does more honour to the architect's taste than the inside to his judgment, are the melancholy remains of the palace of the Prince of Condé, where the spectator can no longer obey the exhortation of the poet,—

> *'Dans sa pompe élégante, admirez Chantilly,*
> *De héros en héros, d'âge en âge embelli.'*[24]

The splendid chateau once corresponded in magnificence with the superb offices which we had visited, but now its vestiges alone remain, a mass of neglected ruins amid the broad lake and canals which had been constructed for its ornament and defence. This beautiful palace was destroyed by the revolutionary mob of Paris early in the civil commotions. The materials, with the lead, iron, carpenter work, &c. were piled up, by those who appropriated them, in what was called Le petit Chateau, a smaller edifice annexed to the principal palace, and communicating with it by a causeway, Thus the small chateau was saved from demolition, though not from pillage. Chantilly and its demesnes were sold as national property, but the purchasers having failed to pay the price, it reverted to the public, so that the king, upon his restoration, had no difficulty in reinstating the Duke of Bourbon. The lesser chateau has been lately refitted in a hasty and simple style, for the reception of the legitimate proprietor; but the style of the repairs makes an unavoidable and mortifying contrast with the splendour of the original decorations. Rich embossed ceilings and carved wainscot are coarsely daubed over with whitewash and size-paint, with which the remains of the original gilding and sculpture form a melancholy association. The frames alone remained of those numerous and huge mirrors,

—— 'in which he of Gath,
Goliah, might have seen his giant bulk
Whole without stooping, towering crest and all.'[25]

But the French artizans, with that lack of all feeling of *convenance*, or propriety, which has well been described as a principal deficiency in their national character, have endeavoured to make fine things out of the frames themselves, by occupying the room of the superb plates of glass with paltry sheets of blue paper, patched over with gilded *fleurs-de-lis,* an expedient the pitiful effect of which may be easily conceived. If I understood my guide rightly, however, this work ought not to be severely criticised, being the free-will offering of the inhabitants of Chantilly, who had struggled, in the best manner their funds and taste would admit, to restore the chateau to something like an habitable condition when it was again to be possessed by its legitimate owner. This is the more likely, as the furniture of the duke's own apartment is plain, simple, and in good taste. He seems popular among the inhabitants, who, the day preceding our arrival, had, under all the unfavourable circumstances of their situation, made a little fete to congratulate him upon his restoration, and to hail the white flag, which now once more floated from the dome of the offices, announcing the second restoration of the Bourbons.

Beside the little chateau are the vestiges of what was once the principal palace, and which, as such, might well have accommodated the proudest monarch in the world. It was situated on a rock, and surrounded by profound and broad ditches of the purest water, built in a style of the richest Gothic architecture, and containing within its precincts every accommodation which pomp or luxury could desire. The demolition has been so complete that little remains excepting the vaults from which the castle arose, and a ruinous flight of double steps, by which visitors formerly gained the principal entrance. The extent, number, and intricacy of the subterranean vaults were such as to afford a retreat for robbers and banditti, for which reason the entrances have been built up by order of the police. The chateau, when in its splendour, communicated with a magnificent theatre, with an orangery and greenhouse of the first order, and was surrounded by a number of separate parterres, or islands, decorated with statuary, with *jets d'eau*, with columns, and with vases, forming a perspective of the richest architectural magnificence. All is now destroyed, and the stranger only learns, from the sorrowful tale of his guide, that the wasted and desolate patches of ground intersected by the canals, once bore, and deserved, the names of the Gallery of Vases, the Parterre of the Orangerie, and the Island of Love. Such and so sudden is the downfall of the proudest efforts of human magnificence. Let us console ourselves, my dear friend, while we look from the bartizan of the old mansion upon the lake, and its corresponding barrier of mountains, that the beauties with which Nature herself has graced our country are more imperishable than those with which the wealth and power of the house of Bourbon once decorated the abode of Chantilly.

I may add, that the neighbourhood of Chantilly exhibits more picturesque beauty than I had yet remarked in France.

PAUL.

LETTER XII.

PAUL TO HIS SISTER.

Your question, my dear sister, What do I think of Paris?
corresponds in comprehensive extent with your desire
that I would send you a full and perfect description of that
celebrated capital; but were I to reside here all my life,
instead of a few weeks, I am uncertain whether I could
distinctly comply with either request. There is so much in
Paris to admire, and so much to dislike, such a mixture of
real taste and genius, with so much frippery and affectation,
the sublime is so oddly mingled with the ridiculous, and
the pleasing with the fantastic and whimsical, that I shall
probably leave the capital of France without being able
to determine which train of ideas it has most frequently
excited in my mind. One point is, however, certain;—that,
of all capitals, that of France affords most numerous objects
of curiosity, accessible in the easiest manner; and it may be
therefore safely pronounced one of the most entertaining
places of residence which can be chosen by an idle man.
As for attempting a description of it, that, you know, is far
beyond the limits of our compact, which you must have
quite forgotten when you hinted at such a proposal. The
following sketch may not, however, be uninteresting.

If we confine our observation to one quarter of Paris
only, that, namely, which is adjacent to the Royal Palace, I
presume there is no capital which can show so many and such
magnificent public edifices within the same space of ground.
The Tuilleries, whose immense extent makes amends for

the deficiencies of the architecture, communicate with the royal gardens, which are used as public walks, and these again open into the Place de Louis Quinze[1], a large octagon, guarded by a handsome balustrade, richly ornamented at the angles, having, on the one hand, the royal gardens with the range of the palace, on the other the Champs Elysees, a large space of ground, planted and laid out in regular walks like those of Hyde-Park. Behind is the extensive colonnade of a palace, called by Buonaparte the Temple of Victory, and since the Restoration the Temple of Concord.[2] Another large and half-finished temple was rising in the front by the command of Buonaparte, which was dedicated to the honour of soldiers who had died in battle. The building was to have been consolidated solely by the weight of the massive stones made use of, and neither wood, iron, or lime, was to be employed in its construction; but schemes of ambition as ill-cemented interrupted its progress. A line of buildings extend on either hand, forming a magnificent street, called La Rue Rivoli, which runs parallel with the iron palisade of the garden of the Tuilleries.

It was on the second night after my arrival in Paris, that, finding myself rather too early for an evening party to which I was invited, I strolled out, enjoying the pure and delicious air of a summer night in France, until I found myself in the centre of the Place de Louis Quinze, surrounded, as I have described it, by objects so noble in themselves, and so powerfully associated with deep historic and moral interest. 'And here I am at length in Paris,' was the natural reflection, 'and under circumstances how different from what I dared to have anticipated! That is the palace of Louis le Grand, but how long have his descendants been banished from its halls, and under what auspices do they now again possess them!

This superb esplanade takes its name from his luxurious and feeble descendant; and here, upon the very spot where I now stand, the most virtuous of the Bourbon race expiated, by a violent death inflicted by his own subjects, and in view of his own palace, the ambition and follies of his predecessors. There is an awful solemnity in the reflection, how few of those who contributed to this deed of injustice and atrocity now look upon the light, and behold the progress of retribution. The glimmering lights that shine among the alleys and parterres of the Champs Elysees, indicate none of the usual vigils common in a metropolis. They are the watch-fires of a camp, of an English camp, and in the capital of France, where an English drum has not been heard since 1436, when the troops of Henry the Sixth were expelled from Paris. During that space, of nearly four centuries, there has scarce occurred a single crisis which rendered it probable for a moment that Paris should be again entered by the English as conquerors; but least of all could such a consummation have been expected at the conclusion of a war, in which France so long predominated as arbitress of the continent, and which had periods when Britain seemed to continue the conflict only in honourable despair.'

There were other subjects of deep interest around me. The lights which proceeded from the windows and from the gardens of the large hotel occupied by the Duke of Wellington,[3] at the corner of the Rue des Champs Elysees, and which chanced that evening to be illuminated in honour of a visit from the allied sovereigns, mingled with the twinkle of the camp-fires, and the glimmer of the tents; and the music, which played a variety of English and Scottish airs, harmonized with the distant roll of the drums, and the notes of that beautiful point of war which is performed by our bugles at the setting of the watch. In these sounds there was pride and victory and honour, some portion of which descended (in imagination at least) to each, the most retired and humblest fellow-subject of the hero who led, and the soldiers who obeyed, in the achievements which had borne the colours of Britain into the capital of France. But there was enough around me to temper the natural feelings of elation, which, as a Briton, I could not but experience. Monuments rose on every side, designed to commemorate mighty actions, which may well claim the highest praise that military achievement alone, abstracted from the cause in which it was accomplished, could be entitled to. From the centre of the Place Vendome, and above the houses of the Rue Rivoli, arose the summit of the celebrated column which Buonaparte had constructed upon the plan of that of Trajan; the cannon taken at Ulm and Austerlitz affording the materials of its exterior, and which is embossed with a detailed representation of the calamities and subjection of Austria. At no great distance lay the Bridge of Jena[4], an epithet which recalls the almost total annihilation of the kingdom of Prussia. In the front of the Tuilleries are placed, on a triumphal arch, the Venetian Horses[5], the trophies of the subjugation of Italy, and in the neighbouring Louvre are deposited the precious spoils of victories gained and abused in every country of Europe; forming the most resistless evidence, that the hand which placed them there had once at its arbitrary disposal the fortunes of the civilized world. No building among the splendid monuments of Paris, but is marked with the name, or device, or insignia of an emperor, whose power seemed as deeply founded as it was widely extended. Yet the gourd of the prophet[6], which came up in a night and perished in a night, has proved the type of authority so absolute, and of fame so diffused; and the possessor of this mighty power is now the inhabitant of a distant and sequestered islet, with hardly so much freewill as entitles him to claim from his warders an hour of solitude, even in the most solitary spot in the civilized world. The moral question presses on every bosom, Was it worth while for him to have climbed so high to render his fall the deeper, or would the meanest of us purchase the feverish feelings of gratified ambition, at the expence of his reflections, who appeared to hold Fortune chained to his footstool? Could the fable of the Seven Sleepers[7] have been realized in Paris, what a scene of astonishment would have been prepared for those who, falling asleep in 1813, awakened from their torpor at the present moment! He who had seen the pope place the crown upon the head of Napoleon, and the proud house of Austria compelled to embrace his alliance, Prussia bent to the dust beneath his footstool, England excluded from each continental connection of commerce or alliance, Russia overawed and submissive, while Italy, Germany, and the greater part of Spain, were divided as appanages among his brothers and allies,—what would have been the surprise of the waking moment which should have shown him the Prussian cannon turned upon the bridges of Paris, and the sovereigns of Austria, Russia, and Prussia, with the representatives of almost all the other nations of Europe, feasting in the capital of France with the general and minister of England, supported by a force which made resistance equally frantic and hopeless! The revolution of ages must have appeared to him to have been accomplished within the space of little more than twenty-four months.

From this slight sketch, you may have some general idea of the magnificence of that quarter of Paris which adjoins to the Tuilleries, crowded as it is with palaces, public monuments, and public buildings, and comprehending in its circuit ornamented gardens and extended walks, open to the inhabitants for exercise or pleasure. I ought also to describe to you the front of the palace itself, a magnificent range of buildings, corresponding with the Louvre, another immense royal mansion, from which the Tuilleries is only divided by the superb square, called La Place du Carousel. The only screen betwixt this square and the court of the Tuilleries, is a magnificent railing of wrought iron, which gives freedom to the eye, not only to survey the extended front of the chateau, but to penetrate through the central vestibule of the palace into the gardens beyond, and as far as the Champs Elysees. In the centre of this screen the public have admittance to the court-yard of the palace, beneath a triumphal arch, which Buonaparte erected in imitation of that of Septimius Severus. The effect of this monument seems diminutive when compared to the buildings around; the columns, made of a mixed red and white marble, are rather gaudy, and the four celebrated Venetian horses, formed of Corinthian brass, which occupy the top of the arch, have been injudiciously harnessed with gilded trappings to a gilded car, driven by a gilded Victory. It is said Buonaparte intended to have placed his own figure in the car; but it came to his ears (for he was self-tormentor enough to enquire after such matters) that the disaffected had hailed it, as likely to afford a good opportunity for calling him mountebank with impunity, since, while they should point to the chariot, the epithet *Le Charlatan* might easily be substituted for *Le Char le tient*[8]. Thus a threatened pun saved Napoleon's image one descent at least by preventing its temporary elevation; and it also saved the

French taste the disgrace of adding another incongruity to the gilded car, harness, and driver. This monument is now undergoing considerable alterations. The Austrians are busy in exchanging for plain slabs of marble, the tablatures placed around the arch: The sculptures almost all relate to the humiliation of the Emperor of Austria, there represented cap in hand before Buonaparte, who appears covered and in an authoritative posture. The French rebelled against the mutilation of this monument at its commencement, and attempted something like a riot, but were instantly called to order by a strong Prussian guard. The work now goes on quietly, and not without some respect to the feelings of the Parisians; for there are blinds of wood put up before the scaffolding, to save their eyes the mortification of seeing its progress. It is not doubted that the horses themselves will be removed in due time.*

In the meanwhile the statue of Buonaparte[9], which was last year taken down from the pillar in the Place Vendome, is said to have experienced an odd transition. It had been exchanged for a certain number of busts and small figures of Louis XVIII., just as a large piece of coin of one reign is given for an equivalent in the small money of another. The figure of the abdicated emperor for some time found refuge in the yard of an artist, by whom it has since been sold to an Englishman. The purchase is believed to be made in behalf of the Duke of Wellington, in which case the statue will be a striking ornament to the palace destined by national gratitude as an acknowledgment at least of the debt, which even the wealth and generosity of Britain cannot pay in full.

To return to the works of Buonaparte. It cannot be

---

* This removal has since taken place.

denied that he showed great ability and dexterity in availing himself of that taste for national display, which is a leading feature of the French character. Yet this was, at least, as much evinced in the address with which he adopted and carried through the half-accomplished plans of Louis XIV. and his successors, as in any work of original genius which can be decidedly traced to his own design. The triumphal arch, and the pillar in the Place Vendome, are literal, almost servile, imitations of the column of Trajan and the arch of Severus. But the splendid extension of the Louvre, by the combination of that striking pile with the Tuilleries, upon the side which had been left unfinished, although the work of Buonaparte, and bearing his name, is, in fact, only a completion of the original design of Louis XIV. One original plan Napoleon may indeed claim as his own—the project, namely, of erecting a stupendous bronze figure of an elephant[10] upon the site of the Bastile. The sort of castle, or Howdar, with which this monstrous statue was to have been accoutred, was designed for a reservoir, the water of which, being discharged through the trunk into a large cistern, or fountain, surrounding the pedestal on which the animal was placed, was to supply with water all that quarter of Paris. The model of this gigantic grotesque is exhibited in stucco near the place which it was designed to have occupied, and such is the deference of the present government for the feelings of *la gloire nationale*, that they have not yet ventured to avow, that, in a time of national poverty and distress, they mean to dispense with erecting a monument, which, after being accomplished at immense expence, must appear *bizarre* and fanciful, rather than grand and impressive. In the meanwhile they are, in justice to the ancestors of the present king, reclaiming for the Bourbons those public buildings, which, by inscriptions and emblems, Napoleon had consecrated to his own dynasty. N.'s are every where disappearing, or undergoing a conversion into H.'s and B.'s,[11] an operation in which the royal stone-cutters are as much called upon to exert their dexterity as the poor sign painters in Roye, Peronne, and Cambray, They have, indeed, the same benefit of experience, having, not very long ago, accomplished the counterpart of the metamorphosis. Such are the minute and ridiculous consequences which indicate a change of government, as much as the motion of straws, twigs, and withered leaves upon the surface, indicates the progress and subsiding of a torrent.

On the whole, it must be acknowledged, that Buonaparte, though unscrupulous in appropriating the merit of his predecessors, bent an earnest and active attention to perfecting whatever grand or magnificent plans they had left uncompleted, thus establishing his own reputation as heir of the monarchy, as well as of the revolution. His ambition to distinguish himself sometimes soared beyond popular prejudice, and hurried him into extravagancies of expence, which the Parisians seem in general to deem unnecessary. Such is the plan of his *Rue de l'Empereur*, now *Rue de la Paix*, a fine street, running from the Place Vendome to the Boulevard des Capucines, which not only boasts a breadth corresponding to the magnificence of the buildings, but is actually accommodated with *two gutters*, one on each side, instead of that single kennel in the centre, where the filth floats or stagnates in all the other streets of Paris. But even the Emperor Napoleon, in the height of his dignity, dared not introduce the farther novelty of a pavement on each side. This would be, indeed, to have destroyed that equality between horse and foot, walkers, drivers, and driven, which appears to give such delight to a Parisian, that, if you extol to him the safe pavements and foot-paths of an English street, or road, he will answer with polite composure—'*C'est tres bien pour Messieurs les Anglois—pour moi, J'aime la totalité de la rue.*' Good phrases, saith Justice Shallow, are and ever must be commended; and this, of *la totalité de la rue*, reconciles a Parisian walker to all the inconveniences of being ridden down or driven over. But the privilege of *totality* by no means reconciles the aged, the timid, the infirm, not to mention females and children, to the accidents to which they are exposed. At present these are multiplied by the numerous accession of strangers, all of whom drive in their own way, and give their own mode of warning, which the pedestrian must construe rightly upon his own peril. Here he hears the *Hey! hey!* of a member of the English Four-in-hand Club; there he is called to attention by the *Gare! Gare!* of a Parisian petit maitre, or a German Freyherr; and having escaped all these hair-breadth risks, he may be ridden down at the next turning by a *drosky*, the driver of which, a venerable Russian charioteer, with a long beard flowing down to his girdle, pushes right on to his destined course with the most unperturbed apathy, without giving passengers warning of any kind to shift for themselves.

The risk, however, to pedestrians, does not form my only objection to the French metropolis, abstracted always from those splendid streets which belong to the quarter of the Tuilleries. The rest of Paris, excepting the *Boulevards*, a peculiar sort of open suburb by which it is surrounded, is traversed by narrow streets, which divide buildings dark, high, and gloomy, the lower windows grated with projecting iron rails of the most massive description, and the houses belonging to persons of importance opening by what is called a *porte cochere*, or carriage-entrance, into courts, which intervene between them and the street. By thus sequestering their mansions, the great do indeed deprive the shop-keeper, or roturier, who lives opposite, of the powers of looking upon the windows of his neighbour the duke, count, or marquis. Nevertheless, mansions constructed upon this unsocial and aristocratic plan, by which the splendour of the habitations of the noble and wealthy is reserved and veiled, as too dazzling and precious to form a part of the public street, cannot contribute to the general beauty of the city in which they are placed. I do not, however, mean to say that the other quarters of Paris, though gloomy, dark, and traversed chiefly by these narrow and perilous passes, are devoid of a strong and peculiar interest. On the contrary, the constant appearance of public edifices, distinguished in history, of Gothic churches and halls, of squares and *places*, surrounded by stately buildings perpetually, even in the most disagreeable quarters of Paris, reminds us that we are in a capital early distinguished for arts and arms, and where even the rudeness and inconvenience of many streets, joined to the solid, massive, and antique structures to which they give access, argue at once early importance and ancient dignity.

It appears a remarkable peculiarity to a British eye, when Paris is viewed from a distance, that over buildings so closely piled together, there arises not that thick and dense cloud of smoke which sometimes graces and dignifies, but more frequently deforms, a view of London, or any other large town in our island. This is owing to the Parisians using wood for fuel, and that frequently in the shape of charcoal, but always sparingly, and in stoves, instead of our sea-coal burnt in open chimneys. Seen from the heights of Montmartre, or the dome of St Genevieve, Paris exhibits a distinct mass of houses, steeples, and towers, unclouded, but also unsoftened, by the dusky canopy which hangs over a British city. My Parisian friends laughed heartily, and, on the whole, deservedly, at my regretting the absence of this dusky accompaniment, which, laying aside associations, does nevertheless add a shadowy importance, and even a softness, to the landscape; or, admitting associations, and pleading on those to which we are accustomed, gives an assurance of business and life to what, without such an indication of living bustle, seems not unlike the appearance of the town in the Arabian tale, whose inhabitants had been all petrified, I own this is a prejudiced feeling, and do not contest the right which a Frenchman has to associate with the cloud which overhangs our metropolis, all that is disgusting, and perhaps unhealthy, in the gross evaporation of our coarser fuel.

The Seine is usually appealed to by the Parisians as the principal beauty of their city, and it is at least one of its greatest conveniences. But Lord Chesterfield furnished an answer to the proud question, whether England could show the like—'Yes—and we call it Fleet-ditch.'[12] This gasconade is like that of the French veteran lecturing upon invasion, who spits upon the ground, and says to his audience, '*Voila la Tamise*,'—a hyperbole which may be excused from ignorance, as no French soldier has happened to see the Thames for many a century, excepting as a guest or a prisoner in England. But, laying jests aside, the Seine is far from having the majestic appearance of the Thames, being diminutive both in depth and breadth, and strait-waist-coated by a range of ungraceful quays, a greater deformity than those of London, because rendered conspicuous by the narrowness of the stream. The river being divided also at two intervals by small islands, completely occupied by buildings, we are induced to entertain a contemptuous opinion of the Seine, as completely subjugated and tyrannized over by the despotic authority of human art. Several of the walks along its side are nevertheless most interesting, particularly the Quai de Voltaire, from which the passenger views the superb and long extent of colonnade belonging to the Louvre, while farther down the river are seen the gardens of the Tuilleries and the trees of Les Champs Elysees.

The finest views of Paris are to be seen from the heights of Montmartre, which rise as close behind the city as the Calton-hill in respect to Edinburgh, and from some of the steeples, particularly that of St Genevieve, a magnificent new church of Grecian architecture, originally dedicated to the titular saint of Paris; next polluted by the appellation of the Temple of Reason; then solemnly entitled the Pantheon, because it was to be the place for depositing the bodies of departed sages and patriots; and lastly restored by Buonaparte to the character of a Christian church, without taking away its destination as a general mausoleum for departed worth. The honours, however, of those who received this distinction were not always permanent. There was 'no snug lying in the abbey.'[13] Several of those revolutionary chiefs whose remains the faction of the day had installed in this sanctuary, were torn from thence shortly afterwards, and thrown, like the corpse of Sejanus, into the common-sewer of the city. The bodies of other heroes of the day have been withdrawn in secret, lest they should suffer the same fate. In some instances the temporary tenant of the tomb was dispossessed, and made to give way to a popular character of more recent celebrity. Thus the corpse of Mirabeau was removed from the Pantheon to make room for that of Marat;[14] on which occasion one of the family of the former returned thanks to heaven for an expulsion, which, as he expressed himself, 're-established the honour of his house.' The corpse of the villain Marat, after having had at least the honour of one bloody sacrifice, in the trial and execution of a man who had offered an insult to his temporary monument, was soon after, 28th July, 1793, dragged from the church, and thrown into the common-sewer of the Rue de Montmartre. At length, weary or ashamed of their own versatility, the National Convention, in the year 1795, decreed that no citizen should receive the honours of the Pantheon until ten years after his death; a decree which amounted almost to an universal sentence of exclusion in a country where the present occupies solely the attention of the public. Of all those to whom the various legislative bodies of France decreed this posthumous distinction, there have only remained in the Pantheon the tombs of two authors, Voltaire and Rousseau. The remains of these distinguished literary characters were deposited here, during the early fervour of the Revolution, with shouts, and with hymns, and with tears, and with transports of that universal philanthropy, which shortly afterwards made its real character evident to the world. A painted wooden sarcophagus, much like a deal packing-box in form and materials, is laid above the grave of each, with a mouldering inscription expressive of what the Legislative Assembly intended to do for the honour of the philosophers whose talents illumined the 18th century. But the rotten board on which their decrees are registered, frail as it is, has proved a record more permanent than the power that placed it there.

The monuments of despotism are more durable than those of anarchy; and accordingly some of Buonaparte's generals and senators are buried in the Pantheon, and, though men of inferior note, have been suffered to enjoy in quiet that repose which even the tomb could not secure for the republican demagogues.

In visiting this church, or temple, I was entertained by the dry answer of an Englishman, who had followed us up to the dome without the observation of the sexton. Our guide seemed a little hurt at the stranger's presumption, and from time to time addressed to him a few words of reprehension, stating the risk he run of being bewildered in the vaults, and perhaps shut up there. As I perceived my countryman did not understand in what he had given offence, I explained to him the sexton's remonstrance. 'Tell him,' answered the stranger, with great gravity, 'that if the misfortune he threatens had really befallen me, I would have had only to call out *Sixpence*, and all Paris would have come to my rescue.' With deference, however, to this honest specimen of John Bull, the access of the public to what is worthy of notice in Paris is much less impeded by a functionary stretching forth his hand for a fee than is the case in London; and when we recollect the mode in which the various departments of St Paul's and Westminster Abbey are secured by a dozen of petty turnpikes and tax-gatherers, we may judge more fairly of the sexton of St Genevieve.

The liberality of the French nation, in affording every possible means to the public of enjoying the collections of curiosities, or of scientific objects, made for their behalf, instead of rendering them sources of profit to some obscure pensioner, pervades all their establishments; and strangers, for whose ease and convenience even greater facilities are afforded than are given to the natives, are called upon to acknowledge it with gratitude. If there be in this open display of the treasures which they possess some traces of national pride, it is in this case an honest and fair pride, and those who derive so much benefit from its effects ought to be the last to question its motive. One or two of these objects of curiosity I shall briefly notice in my next letter, not with the purpose of giving a regular description of them, but to mark, if I can, by a few characteristic strokes, the peculiarities which attracted my own attention.

Adieu; I rest ever your affectionate

PAUL.

LETTER XIII.

THE SAME TO THE SAME.

I have already said, my dear sister, that of all capitals in the world, Paris must afford the most delightful residence to a mere literary lounger; and if we add, that his fortune is limited (as is usually the case with such a character,) it will suit him, after a little experience, as well in point of economy as of taste. The *Jardin des Plantes*, the National Library, the Collection of French Monuments, the National Institute, above all the Grand Museum in the Louvre, are gratuitously opened to his inspection and use, while theatres, and public amusements of various kinds, in the evening, may be frequented for little expence.

I know that nothing in Paris would delight you more than the *Jardin des Plantes*. This grand botanical garden, of several acres extent, richly stocked with the most varied and curious productions of the vegetable world, is equally interesting to the scientific student, and to the idler, who seeks only for shaded walks and interesting and beautiful points of view. The variety of the ground, the disposition of the trees, and the neighbourhood of the Seine, afford the last in considerable variety; while the shade, so grateful in this warm climate, is secured by many a long alley and avenue. The establishment is maintained entirely at the expence of the public. The learned in physics may there have the advantage of a chemical laboratory, of lectures upon botany and natural history by men of approved science, of an anatomical collection, and a valuable library, composed of works relative to natural history. There is also a menagerie upon a great scale of splendour, as well as of comfort to the animals with which it is tenanted. Those which are of a dangerous description are properly secured, but still with due attention to their habits and convenience. The bears, for example, inhabit subterranean residences, each of which opens into a sunk area, of depth enough to prevent escape, but where Bruin may repose himself, or take exercise, at his pleasure. I seldom pass this place without seeing some of the Prussian or Russian soldiers engaged in talking to and feeding the bears, whom, in this southern clime, they probably regard as a kind of countrymen. The elephant, a most magnificent animal of the kind, has, as befits his good sense and civilized behaviour, a small paddock around his cabin, secured from the public by a strong palisade. He had a mate some years ago, but is now a widower; very good humoured, however, and familiar with the passengers. Gentler animals, such as the varieties of the deer species, are allowed space in proportion to their size; and it is only the fiercer tribes of Africa and Asia, lions, tigers, and leopards, which are committed to strict confinement. These also are kept clean, and made as comfortable as circumstances will permit; and on the whole, it is impossible to conceive an institution of the kind managed with more respect to the feelings and convenience of the creatures contained in it. If a stranger is curious to know the names of the various animals, there is always some Frenchman near, who, either merely to do the honours to Monsieur l'Etranger, or at most for *quelque chose pour boire*, walks with you through the collection, and displays at once his eloquence, and that sort of information which is frequently found among the Parisians, even of the lower orders. To me, who am no naturalist, such a guide seems often as interesting a specimen as any in the collection. The contrast of his meagre looks and tattered dress, with the air of patronage which he assumes towards the stranger under his charge; his pompous encomiums on the objects he exhibits; his grave injunctions not to approach too near the grates of the more dangerous quadrupeds; the importance with which he gives the scientific appellation of each animal, condescendingly adding that which is in more vulgar use; and the polite gratitude of his '*Monsieur est tres honnete*,' when he pockets his little gratuity, and puts on the *schako*[1], which he has hitherto held in his hand for the sake of aiding his eloquence,—all these points brought together give a character of the lower rank not to be met with out of France, and rarely out of Paris.

The antiquary who visits Paris must be deeply interested by a visit to the Museum des Monumens Français, assembled by Mons. Le Noir[2] in the church, convent, and gardens of Les petits Augustins. This collection proved a sort of asylum for such monuments of art as could be saved from popular fury during the first revolutionary fever, comprehending the tombs of princes, legislators, and heroes. When the churches were sacked and pillaged, and the property of the clergy was confiscated to the use of the nation, Mons Le Noir had the courage to attempt to save from impending ruin objects invaluable for the history of the arts and for that of the nation, and he had the address to devise a probable mode of succeeding in a plan, which, in these furious days, might have been represented as savouring of aristocracy and *incivisme*[3]. He obtained from the National Assembly a recommendation to their Committee of Alienation, to watch over and protect the monuments of art in the churches and domains which they had confiscated to national use.

This was followed by a warrant, authorising a committee of Sçavans[4], of whom Le Noir was most active, to select and transport to Paris these reliques of antiquity, and there to arrange them in one general collection, so as to afford a view of the progress of the arts during the several periods of French history. Much exertion accordingly has been made, and upon the whole with considerable success, to dispose this various and miscellaneous collection according to centuries, and at the same time to place the productions of each aera in the best and fittest order. You accompany therefore at once the progress of the arts and that of history, as you wander from hall to hall, and compare the rude images of Clovis and Pharamond[5] with what the Italian chisel produced to commemorate departed greatness, in that happy epoch which the French artists call *Le Siecle de la Renaissance*. Several monuments, the size of which rendered them unfit for a cloister, are erected in the gardens; and particularly the tomb of Abelard and Heloïse, with those of Des Cartes, Moliere, La Fontaine, Boileau,[6] and others dear to French literature.

Yet such is the caprice of the human mind, that even from this rich mental feast we return with some degree of dissatisfaction. The inspection of the Museum inspired me at least with a feeling greater in degree, but similar in origin, to that with which I have regarded a collection of English portraits—

'Torn from their destined page—unworthy meed
Of knightly counsel or heroic deed,'—[7]

and compiled to illustrate a Grainger[8], at the expence of many a volume defaced and rendered imperfect. Far deeper is that sensation rooted, when we consider that the stones accumulated around us have been torn from the graves which they were designed to mark out and to protect, and divided from all those associations arising from the neighbourhood of the mighty dead. It is also impossible, with the utmost care and ingenuity, that the monuments should be all displayed to advantage; and even the number of striking objects, huddled together, diminishes the effect which each, separately, is calculated to produce upon the mind. These wayward reflections will arise, and can only be checked by the recollection, that without prosecution of the plan wisely adopted and boldly prosecuted, the reliques around us would have ceased to exist, and that the ingenious collector, far from being the plunderer of a wreck, has saved and protected its scattered fragments, which must have otherwise perished for ever.

If, in the Museum of Monumens Français, we contrast with advantage the principle and mode by which the collection is formed, with the effect produced by the present arrangement, and pardon, for the sake of the former, the necessary imperfections attached to the latter, no such favourable result can be drawn by the reflecting traveller who visits the inimitable collection of paintings and statues in the Louvre, called the Central Museum of the Arts. It is indeed, abstractedly, a subject of just pride to a nation, that she can exhibit to strangers this surpassingly magnificent display of the works of human genius when in its most powerful and active mood, awakened as it were from the sleep of ages, and at once bringing to the service of art such varied talent as never was nor will be equalled. But if, with these exulting considerations, it were possible for the French to weigh the sum of evil which they have suffered and inflicted to obtain this grand object of national vanity, they might well view the most magnificent saloon in Europe as a charnel-vault, and the works of Raphael, Titian, and Salvator, as no better than the sable and tattered scutcheons which cover its mouldering walls. Each picture, indeed, has its own separate history of murder, rapine, and sacrilege. It was perhaps the worst point in Buonaparte's character, that, with a firm and unremitting attention to his own plans and his own interest, he proceeded from battle to plunder, less like a soldier than a brigand or common highwayman, whose immediate object is to rifle the passenger whom he has subdued by violence or intimidation. But Napoleon knew well the people over whom he was called to rule, and was aware that his power was secure, despite of annihilated commerce and exhausted finances, despite of his waste of the lives of Frenchmen and treasure of France, despite of the general execration of the human race, echoed from the Baltic to the Mediterranean, providing he could prove to the Parisians that he was still the Emperor of the World, and Paris its capital. *Savans*, therefore, *amateurs*, and artists, whose skill and taste might supply the deficiency of his own, regularly attended upon his military expeditions; and when a city had surrendered, or had otherwise fallen into his power, whatever it possessed in public or private property evincing excellence in the arts, was destined to augment the Central Museum, and furnish a topic of consolation to those Parisians whose sons perhaps had fallen in battle under its walls. For this purpose every town in Italy was ransacked, and compelled by open violence, or a still more odious influence exercised under pretext of treaties, to surrender those specimens of sculpture and painting whose very names had become associated with the classical situations, from which a true admirer of the arts would have deemed it sacrilege to have torn them. The Low Countries were compelled to yield up those masterpieces of the Flemish school, which are prized by amateurs as almost equal to those of Italy. Dresden, long famous for its collection of paintings, which Frederick the Great contented himself with admiring, was plundered to the bare walls. Berlin and Potzdam underwent a similar fate; and while Buonaparte affected to restore to the subdued monarch of Prussia his crown and kingdom, he actually pillaged his palaces of their most precious and domestic ornaments. Vienna was severely ransacked, with every inferior town in the emperor's dominions, and that even at the period of an alliance cemented by Buonaparte's union with a daughter of the house of Austria. The ancient capital of the czars was destined to consign its old magnificence to the same accumulated heap of spoil. But there the robber's arm was shortened, and the plunder of the Kremlin was retaken ere it had crossed the Beresina. The very ornaments of the apartments were acquired by the same iniquitous means which had filled them with paintings and statues. The twelve granite pillars which supported the Hall of Sculpture were plundered from Aix la Chapelle, and the beautifully-wrought bronze folding doors at the upper end of the Grand Saloon were the spoils of a church at Rome. *Omnis Thais Thaida olet.*[9] The collection in all its parts, magnificent and unmatched as it is, savours of the cruelty, perfidy, and rapine by which it was accumulated.

Many have therefore been tempted to think that there was less wisdom or justice than magnanimity in the conduct of the allies during the preceding year, who, to save the feelings of the French, which in this case had no title to a moment's consideration, sacrificed the justice due to their own despoiled countries, and let pass the opportunity of giving a great moral lesson, without inflicting on France a single hardship excepting what might flow from her wounded vanity. But Prussia, it seems, was satisfied with a promise (ill kept by the restored family) that her property should be redelivered when affairs were settled in France; and for the other nations no stipulation seems to have been made. If the allies on this occasion neglected to reclaim by force their own property when in their power, it would nevertheless have been just, and perhaps prudent, in the Bourbon family, to have of their own accord relinquished spoils which could only remind them of their own misfortunes. But they were too anxious to establish themselves in the opinion of their new subjects as good Frenchmen, to recollect that justice, open and even-handed, is the first duty of a monarch. They were afraid to face the clamour which would have stigmatized an act of honest restitution as the concession of cowardice. As Buonaparte had been the heir of the Revolution, they were willing to be the heirs of Buonaparte, and appear to have been as little disposed to the doctrine of restitution as the worthy corregidor of Leon, who succeeded to the treasures of Captain Rolando's subterranean mansion.[10] At least they were not unwilling, like the sons of a usurer, to possess treasures of such value, without sharing the guilt of the original acquisition. They did not reflect that every token which carried back the Frenchman's recollection to the emperor, must excite comparisons, among the thoughtless and unprincipled, highly unfavourable to the legitimate possessor of the crown.

The day of reckoning is at length arrived. The Museum,

when I first arrived in Paris, was still entire. But Blucher, who was not, it seems, to be foiled a second time, has since made several visits, attended by a German artist, for the purpose of ascertaining and removing the pictures which belong to Prussia, or to the German states now united with her. The French guardians of the Museum also attended, no longer to decide upon the point of view in which the spoils of nations should be disposed, but to plead, occasionally and timidly, that such a picture formed no part of the cabinet of Potzdam, but had been stolen from some other collection. These demurrers were generally silenced by a *'Tais toi,'* or *'Halt maul,'** from the veteran of Laon and Waterloo, who is no friend to prolonged discussions. If you ask, whether Prussia has recovered all the pictures which had been carried off at different times, I fancy I may return the same emphatic answer given by an old Scotch serving-man, when his master asked him if he had been careful to pack up all his wardrobe at leaving a friend's house,—*'At least*, your honour.' Not that I suppose the Prince-Marshal has got a single article to which the French had any just title, but the late enlargement of the dominions of Prussia has greatly extended her claims of restitution in right of states and cities newly annexed to her dominions. Still, however, though nearly a hundred pictures have in this manner gradually disappeared, I have not missed one of those masterpieces to which the attention of the visitor is earliest directed and longest riveted. It is when the claims of Italy and the Netherlands shall be enforced that the principal disgorging of spoil will take place; and when that day comes, I believe it will drive some of the French

---

* 'Hold your tongue.'

amateurs to actual distraction. Their attachment to these paintings and statues, or rather to the national glory which they conceive them to illustrate, is as excessive as if the Apollo and Venus were still objects of actual adoration; and on the day of their departure I anticipate them exclaiming with Micah, 'Ye have taken away my gods and go your ways, and what have I more?—How then say ye unto me, what aileth me?'[11]

It is, however, understood to be definitively settled by the allied sovereigns, that the French must undergo this mortification; as is evident by the generals, at the capitulation of Paris, having refused to sanction an article of the treaty proposed by the French, for securing the possession of these monuments. It is a severe mortification doubtless; but, independent of the undeniable justice of the measure, it is wholesome that the French should have in future no trophies to appeal to as memorials, that they had exercised a power over other states, which their victors never had courage to retaliate; as ensigns of past conquest, and as the incentive to new wars. The contents of the Museum have been found by bitter experience to perpetuate recollections, which, for the peace of France and of Europe, ought to be effaced as speedily and absolutely as possible. Such associations render the removal of the objects which excite them as necessary a precaution, as the burning of Don Quixote's library[12] to prevent the recurrence of his phrenzy.

With respect to the arts, you know I pretend to no skill in the province of the amateur; but the best judges seem to allow that the dispersion of this immense collection is by no means unfavourable to their progress and improvement. We readily admit, and each spectator has felt, that nothing can be more magnificent, more august, more deeply impressive, taken as a whole, than that noble gallery, prolonged to an extent which the eye can hardly distinctly trace, and crowded on every side with the noblest productions of the most inspired artists. Fourteen hundred paintings, each claiming rank as a masterpiece, disposed upon walls which extend for more than twelve hundred feet in length, form, united, a collection unparalleled in extent and splendour. But a part of this charm vanishes when we have become familiar with the *coup d'oeuil*; and the emotions of surprise and pleasure which the transient visitor receives, are gained in some degree at the expence of the student, or studious amateur. In a saloon of such length and height, lighted too from both sides, it is impossible that all the pictures can be seen to advantage; and, in truth, many cannot be seen at all. In a selection where all is excellent, and worthy of studious and heedful attention, this is a disadvantage of no common kind. But it is not the only one. Each of these paintings, almost without exception, have in them something excellent; but, independent of the loss which they sustain in common, by being so much crowded together, and by making part rather of one grand and brilliant whole, than subjects important enough for detached and separate consideration, the merit of some of these *chefs d'oeuvre* so far exceeds that of others, as altogether to divert the attention from objects of inferior, though still of exquisite merit. Few, possessing even the most eager love for the art, though they have consumed hours, days, weeks, and months, in the Museum, have been able to escape that fascination which draws them to the Transformation of Raphael, the Communion by Domenichino, the Martyrdom of the Inquisitor, and some other masterpieces. About fifty pictures at most therefore are copied, studied, examined, and worshipped, while more than twenty times that number are neglected and unseen, and, with all their admitted excellence, draw as little attention as the Nymphs and Graces in the suite of Venus. This shews that the appetite of taste, as well as of epicurism, may be satiated and rendered capricious by the exhibition of too rich and sumptuous a banquet, and that, our capacity of enjoyment being limited, there is no wisdom in an injudicious accumulation of means for its gratification. To the young student in particular, the feelings of satiety are peculiarly hazardous; for either he becomes accustomed to indulge a capricious and presumptuous contempt of works which he has slightly studied, or he is deterred from boldly and vigorously venturing upon a laborious and difficult art, when he sees that excellence of a pitch to which he dare not aspire, may, in company with the ultimate efforts of genius, be insufficient to secure respect and attention.

It might be added, that there are particular points, in which even those distinguished and selected patterns of supereminence which throw every inferior degree of merit into shadow, lose, in some degree, the full impression of their own merit, by being disjoined from the local associations with a view to which they were painted. This is especially the case with the religious subjects executed for altar-pieces, and for the ornaments of chapels, where the artist had laboured to suit not only his size of figures and disposition of light to the place which the painting was to occupy, but had also given them a tone of colouring and a general character, harmonizing with the solemnity, not only of the subject, but of the scene around. To many a thorough-paced and hackneyed connoisseur, who considers the finest painting merely as a subject for his technical criticism, the divesting it of these exterior accompaniments will seem of little consequence. But those who love the art for the noble and enthusiastic feelings by the excitement of which it is best applauded, will feel some difference in considering a scripture-piece over the altar of a Gothic church, and in viewing the same painting where it forms part of an incongruous assemblage of landscapes and flower-pieces, with a group of drinking boors[13] placed on the one side, and an amour of Jupiter upon the other.

These observations apply only to the ostentatious assemblage of so many and such various specimens of the art in one extensive gallery. But had this objection not existed—had these paintings been so disposed in various apartments as to give each its appropriate situation, and secure for each that portion of attention which it merits, still objections would remain to the whole system. There is no wisdom in venturing as it were the fortunes of the world of art in one single collection, exposed to total and irredeemable loss either from accidental fire, or the havoc of war, or popular phrenzy. Had the Museum existed during the first years of the Revolution, its danger must have been most imminent, and twice during the space of a very few months has it narrowly escaped the risks which must have attended it had Paris been stormed.

Independent even of these considerations, and admitting this general accumulation of the treasures of art to be as desirable as it is certainly august and impressive, I should still hesitate to say that Paris is the city where they ought to be reposited. The French school, though it has produced many good artists, has been as remarkable for wanting, as the Italians for possessing, that dignity and simplicity of feeling which leads to the sublime. Poussin alone excepted, there is a flutter and affectation, a constraint of attitude to create point, and a studied contrast of colour and light to bring out effect, which marks the national taste; and from the charms of such Dalilahs, as Dryden calls similar flourishes in poetry,[14] they never have weaned themselves, nor ever will. Their want of real taste and feeling may be estimated by the unawed audacity with which they have in several notorious instances undertaken to repair, and even to alter, the master-pieces which conquest and rapine had put within their power. The same deficiency of real taste is evinced by the rash comparisons which they make between their schools of music and painting and those of Italy, in which Gay's lines still describe the present Parisian as well as him of his own day:

> Mention the force of learned Corelli's notes,
> Some squeaking fiddler of their ball he quotes;
> Talk of the spirit Raphael's pencil gives,
> Yet warm with life, whose speaking picture lives,
> 'Yes, sir,' says he, 'in colour and design,
> Rigaut and Raphael are extremely fine.'[15]

Where the taste of those with whom he must naturally associate is systematically deficient, the young artist may lose as much through the influence of a French preceptor, as he could gain by studying in the Museum. I might also hint how little a capital like Paris, containing so many temptations to idleness and dissipation, is a safe abode for the young artist. But enough has been said to justify the sacrifice now exacted from France, however it may lower her pride and mortify her vanity. First, it is a demand of justice, and therefore must be enforced; and next, the artist, though he must in future extend his travels, and visit various cities in search of those excellencies which are now to be seen collected in the Louvre, will have greater benefit from the experience which has cost him some toil; and if he must traverse Switzerland and Italy, to view the sculptures of ancient Greece, and the paintings of modern Rome, he will have the double advantage of taking lessons on his route from Nature herself, in the solitary grandeur of the one and the profuse luxuriance of the other.

The taste of the French seems to be turned more towards the Hall of Sculptures than the Gallery of Paintings, and I think I can trace something of a corresponding partiality in the works of David[16], their greatest living artist, whose figures, though often nobly conceived and disposed, have a hardness of outline resembling statuary. My own taste (formed probably on habit, for we see few good statues in Britain,) would have inclined otherwise, and I grieve to say I was rather disappointed with some of those statues of antiquity from which I expected most pleasure. One monument can disappoint no one—I mean the Apollo Belvidere[17], the sublime simplicity of whose attitude, and the celestial expression of his countenance, seem really more than mortal. It is said there is a chance of his visiting England: while I looked upon so exquisite a specimen of ancient art, I could not muster virtue enough to wish the report false; but writing in my solitary closet, and in mature consideration, I do hope sincerely that neither by purchase, nor gift, or otherwise, however fairly, will Britain possess herself of that or any other the least part of those spoils, since the French would eagerly grasp at such a pretext for alleging that we sought the gratification of our own selfish ends, while we affected to render justice to others. Indeed, unless I am much mistaken, the personage whose taste might be most gratified by such an acquisition would not enter into a transaction calculated to throw the slightest shade of suspicion on the pure faith of Britain, to acquire all that Phidias ever carved, or Raphael painted. This fine statue, and the other specimens of art, seem to rise in value with the French as the hour of parting with them approaches. They talk to them, weep to them, kneel to them, and bid adieu to them, as if they were indeed restored to the rank of idols. But Baal boweth down, Nebo stoopeth—the hammer and wedge have given awful note of preparation; the Venus, the Dying Gladiator, and many other statues, have been loosened from their pedestals, and stand prompt for returning to their native and appropriate places of abode. Many a lowering eye and frowning brow marks the progress of these preparations; and such is the grotesque distress in the countenance of others, that, as Poins says of Falstaff, if it were not for laughing I could pity them.[18]

After all, however, they are not objects of compassion, even in the despoiled state, as they express themselves, to which they are likely to be reduced. France possesses, as public property, besides the paintings of her own school, a noble collection formed by the Bourbon race, and the Borghesé pictures, honestly bought and paid for by Buonaparte. She has also to boast the gallery of the Luxembourg palace, containing that splendid series of historical pictures by Rubens, commemorating the principal actions in the life of Mary de Medicis,[19] to the brilliancy of which there can only be objected the incongruous mixture of mythological and allegorical personages, with characters of historical reality. But this mixture of truth and fiction, and men and genii, and heathen gods and Christian emblems, seems to me so inconsistent, that, could I entertain the ambitious hope of possessing a picture of Rubens, I would prefer one of his boar-hunts, or groupes of peasants going to market, to the most splendid picture in the Luxembourg gallery.

At Malmaison[20] there are also some fine paintings, besides a number of good copies from the pictures of the Museum. This was the abode of Josephine, of whom all speak with regret and affection. I was particularly struck with the figure of a dancing Nymph, in marble, which, to my poor judgment, might have been placed beside any of the Grecian monuments in the Halls of Sculpture, without suffering much disparagement. It was cut by Canova[21], that eminent artist, who, as he remonstrated formerly against the transference of the works of art from Italy, has now the satisfaction of superintending their restoration to that classical land.

This ample subject has exhausted my paper. I remain, dear sister, affectionately yours,

PAUL.

LETTER XIV.

PAUL TO THE MAJOR.

Your appetite for military details, my dear Major, is worthy of one who assisted at the defence of Bergen-op-Zoom in the year 1747, since it cannot be sated with the ample feast which I sent you from Waterloo. Here indeed I see little around me but military of all nations; but how to describe the gay, glittering, and at the same time formidable scene, a scene too so new to all my habits, is a point of no little difficulty. Paris is one great camp, consisting of soldiers of almost all nations, and is under the military authority of the Prussian Baron Muffling[1], as commandant for the allies. You are not ignorant of the proceedings which led to this extraordinary crisis, but I shall briefly recall them to your memory.

The only division of the French army which remained entire after the rout of Waterloo, was that of Grouchy and Vandamme, which, by a retreat that did these generals the highest honour, was not only conducted unbroken under the walls of Paris, but gained some accession of strength from the wrecks of the main army. Upon their arrival they found matters in a most singular state of crisis. Buonaparte had anticipated the tidings of the field of Waterloo, and brought, like a certain general renowned in song[2], the news of his own defeat to the good city of Paris. It would seem that he expected the Liberalists would now, in this last and critical danger, have made common cause with him, strengthened his hands with all the power that unanimity could bestow upon a dictator, called upon the nation to rally around his standard, and tried yet one desperate chance for conquest. But he had measured his importance according to former, not according to existing circumstances. The rump of the old Conventionalists saw no more to overawe them in Buonaparte defeated, than their predecessors of the Long Parliament[3] had seen in Richard Cromwell. They instantly made known to him, and with no friendly voice, that the times demanded his resignation; they called his ministers before them authoritatively, and intimated by every movement their intention to take the reins of government into their own hands. Napoleon had no alternative left him but that of defiance or of abdication. In the former case, he might indeed have dissolved the refractory chambers, for the troops, and the lower class of the Parisian populace, who were armed under the name of Federés[4], were resolute in his behalf. But he was not resolute in his own determination. It was in vain that his brother Lucien[5], who, having resumed the thorny path of politics, was disposed to tread it with his former audacity, urged him to march a body of troops to the chambers, dissolve them at once, and take the full power into his own hands. Success over the chambers was indeed certain, but its consequences would have called upon Napoleon to live or die with the troops who should achieve it: of the first he had little hope, and for the last slender inclination. He therefore attempted by a compromise to transfer his crown, now entwined with thorns, to the head of his infant son[6]. The proposition was for some time evaded by the Assembly, and Buonaparte's adherents could only procure an indirect and dubious assent to this condition. Lucien pleaded and Labedoyere bullied in vain[7]; and the chambers having possessed themselves of this brief and precarious authority, began such a course of debate as Swift ascribes to his Legion Club,—

> 'While they sit and pick their straws,
> Let them dream of making laws.'[8]

Instead of active preparations to oppose or avert the progress of foreign invaders, the Parisians saw with astonishment their senators engaged in discussions of abstract theory, or frivolous points of form. A matter-of-fact man, who wished to know the distance betwixt Saint Quentin (then Lord Wellington's head-quarters) and Paris, was called to order, as going into matter irrelevant to the subject of debate. The question, however, was not mal-apropos. Grouchy's army arrived, and the allies were not long behind him. The chambers, who had by this time assumed all the old-fashioned mummery and jargon of the Convention, sent forth a deputation of its members, decorated with three-coloured scarfs, to harangue the soldiers and the federés; and they were conjured by the member who proposed the deputation to apprise the soldiers, that the representatives were ready to mix with them in their ranks, since, to those who fell, the day of their death would be that of their *resurrection*. It was supposed that Mons. Garnier[9], not much accustomed to such terms, had meant to say *immortality*, but this impropriety of expression greatly maimed the energy of his eloquence.

The representatives went forth with their fine scarfs. They harangued the soldiers and the armed banditti called federés upon the original principles of liberty and the unprescriptible rights of man, and recommended to them, as a rallying word, *Vive la Nation, Vive la Liberté!* But the charm was as ineffectual as that used by the Abbess of Andouillets[10]. The soldiers and federés only answered with shouts *of Vive l'Empereur*. The representatives affected to consider these acclamations as referring to Napoleon II., and having, like the Duke of Buckingham[11], thanked their loving friends and countrymen for sentiments which they had never expressed, they returned to make their report to the chambers. There was, in truth, only one point of union between these assemblies of *soi-disant* legislators and the French troops, which was an obstinate determination, founded upon a combined sense of crime and fear of punishment, to resist to the uttermost the restoration of the legitimate sovereign, although every wise man in France had long seen it was the sole measure which promised to avert the impending ruin of the country. Upon this topic the most furious speeches were made, the most violent resolutions entered into; and the Lower Chamber, in particular, showed that it wanted only time and power to renew the anarchy, as it had adopted the language, of the early Revolution. But there were cold fits to allay this fever, and the perturbation of mind by which individuals began to find themselves agitated broke out amid their bullying ridiculously enough. Merlin of Douai[12] (an old hack'd engine of Philip Egalité, and Robespierre, under the last of whom he promulgated the bloody edict against suspected persons,) announced to the Chamber of Representatives his having received an untimely visit of two persons in a fiacre, demanding to speak to him on the part of the president of the provisional government; that the hour being one in the morning, he had refused them admittance—happily so refused them—since, in the unanimous opinion of Merlin himself, of his wife, and honest Regnault de St Jean d'Angely[13], these untimely visitors could mean nothing good to his person. On this annunciation, vigorous measures were proposed for the protection of Monsieur Merlin, when Boulay de la Meurthe[14] stopped further proceeding, by informing the assembly that the supposed emissaries of royalty were in fact what they called themselves, messengers from the president upon a matter of emergency, which they had communicated to himself upon being refused access to Merlin. One member's terrors were excited by seeing in the street a wounded officer, those of another broke out upon spying—not a peer, as used to be the cause of alarm in St Stephen's[15]—but sight more appalling, a royal Garde de Corps in full uniform under the gallery. These alarms were faithfully reported to the chambers, and though the wiser representatives suppressed their own fears, there were many indications that they did not less deeply entertain them.

The anxiety of the government and of the chambers was singularly contrasted by the extreme indifference of him who had been the origin of all the turmoil and bloodshed, and who continued for some time to travel from the palace of Bourbon Elyseés to Malmaison and back again, to give fetes there, and to prepare for a journey no one could say whither, with as much composure as if the general distraction concerned him as little, or less, than any other temporary sojourner in France. To complete this scene of characteristic affectation, he sent a message to the chambers to request copies of two books which he desired might be placed at his disposal. But the near approach of the allies at length accelerated his departure, and on the 29th June, when they were within three leagues of the city, he finally left the capital, which he had lately called his own, to make the best defence or capitulation they could. At first the chambers resolved upon defence. But the means were very imperfect.

When Buonaparte, before leaving Paris for Avesnes, consulted Carnot on the means necessary for the defence of the metropolis, the latter is said to have estimated them at two hundred millions, and the labour of three years. 'And when that sum of treasure and, labour has been expended, sixty thousand good troops,' continued the ex-director, 'and a sustained assault of twenty-four hours, may render it all in vain.' Nevertheless Buonaparte undertook preparations for this gigantic and hopeless task. The heights of Montmartre were fortified with extreme care, and amply supplied with artillery. The village of Saint Denis was also strongly garrisoned, and a partial inundation being accomplished by means of stopping two brooks, the water was introduced into the half-completed canal De l'Ourcq, the bank of which being formed into a parapet, completed a formidable line of defence on the northern side of the city, resting both flanks upon the Seine. The populace of Paris had laboured at these lines with an enthusiasm not surpassed in the most exalted phrensy of the Revolution; nor were their spirits or courage at all lowered by the approach of the conquering armies of England and Prussia, in the act of being supported, if need were, by the whole force of Russia and Austria. They confided in what had repeatedly and carefully been impressed upon their minds,—that Paris could only fall by treachery; and boasted that they had now Massena, and Soult, and Davoust, (as much celebrated for military talent as for the atrocity which he displayed in the defence of Hamburgh,)[16] to direct the defence of the capital, instead of Marmont, by whom, in the preceding year, they were taught to believe it had been basely betrayed.

PAUL'S LETTERS TO HIS KINSFOLK

But although the line of defence to the north was such as to justify temporary confidence, the city on the opposite side was entirely open, excepting the occupation of the villages of Issy, and the heights of St Cloud and Meudon. These two points, if they could have been maintained, would have protected for a time that large and level plain which extends on the south side of Paris, and which now presented no advantages for defence, excepting an imperfect attempt at a trench, and a few houses and garden-walls accommodated with loop-holes for the use of musquetry. On this defenceless side, therefore, the allied generals resolved to make the attack, and the Prince-Marshal[17] on the 30th June crossed the Seine at St Germains, and, occupying Versailles, threatened the French position at Meudon, Issy, and the heights of St Cloud, while the Duke of Wellington, holding Gonesse, opened a communication with the Prussians by a bridge at Argenteuil. The French, though their situation was desperate, did not lose courage, and one gleam of success shone on their arms. General Excelmans, by a well-conducted assault, surprised the Prussians who occupied Versailles, and made prisoners some cavalry. But the French were assaulted in their turn, driven from the heights of St Cloud, from Issy, and from Meudon, and forced close under the city itself. This happened on the 2d July, and Blucher had already sent to the British general to request the assistance of a battery of Congreve's rockets[18],—a most ominous preparation for the assault which he meditated. Meanwhile the wealthy and respectable Parisians were equally apprehensive of danger from their defenders and from the assailants. The temper of the French soldiers had risen to phrenzy, and the mob of the Fauxbourgs, animated by the same feelings of rage, vomited threats and execrations both against the allies and against the citizens of Paris who favoured the cause of peace and legitimacy. Such was the temper of this motley garrison, as formidable to the capital as the presence of an incensed enemy, when upon the 3d July the terms of capitulation between the allies and Massena[19], who acted as commander in chief of the French, were arranged and signed, Paris once more subjected to the mercy of Europe, and the Queen of Provinces a second time made a bondswoman.

A brief but fearful period of anarchy passed ere the French army, now men without a cause and without a leader, evacuated Paris and its vicinity, and ere their yet more savage associates, the federés, could be prevailed upon to lay down the arms with which they still threatened death and devastation to each royalist, or rather to property and all its possessors. The firmness of the National Guards is universally acknowledged to have saved Paris in that awful moment, when, in all human probability, the first example of plunder would have been followed both by the populace and by the foreigners, and a scene of universal blood, rapine, and conflagration, must have become the necessary consequence.

There are indeed fervent politicians, whom now and then of an evening we have heard breathe an ardent wish that Paris had been burnt to the ground. These are words soon spoken in the energy of patriotic hatred, or a desire of vengeance for outraged morality; but if we can picture to ourselves without shrinking those horrid scenes which ensue,

'Where the flesh'd soldier, rough and hard of heart,
In liberty of bloody hand shall range,
With conscience wide as hell,'[20]

we ought yet to remember upon how many thousands such dreadful vengeance must have fallen, who can only be justly considered as common sufferers by the very acts of aggression of which Europe has such just reason to complain, and how many thousands more age and incapacity exempted even from the possibility of having been sharers in the offence. It is impossible to look around upon this splendid capital without remembering the affecting plea which the Deity himself condescended to use with his vindictive prophet: 'Should not I spare Nineveh, that great city, wherein are six score thousand persons that cannot discern between their right hand and their left, and also much cattle?'[21] Least of all ought we to wish that any part of the British forces had been partakers in the horrid license that must have followed on such a catastrophe, during which the restraints of discipline and the precepts of religion are alike forgotten in the headlong course of privileged fury. It was observed of the veteran army of Tilly, that the sack of Magdeburg[22] gave a death-blow to their discipline, and we know how the troops of France herself were ruined by that of Moscow. In every point of view, therefore, as well with regard to the agents as the sufferers, the averting the destruction of Paris, when it appeared almost inevitable, has added to the glories which the Duke of Wellington has acquired in this immortal campaign. For it is not to be denied, that to his wise and powerful interference was chiefly owing the timely arrangement of the articles of capitulation, in consequence of which the King of France again obtained possession of his capital, and the allied armies became the peaceful garrison of Paris.

By the time I reached the capital the political convulsions had entirely subsided, and the royal government, to all external appearance, was in as quiet an exercise of authority as if Louis XVIII. had never been dispossessed of the throne. But the public mind was not as yet accustomed to consider the change as permanent, being influenced and agitated by a thousand gloomy reports of plots and conspiracies, as the sea after the storm has subsided continues still to heave and swell with the impulse it has received. It was said, in particular, that Labedoyere, who had been found concealed in Paris, and there arrested, was agent of a conspiracy, in which the federés of the fauxbourgs, with the disbanded soldiers of the army of the north, were to be enlisted. One party of the conspirators was to wear the dress and arms of the Parisian National Guard, and so accoutered were to assault simultaneously the hotels of the Emperors of Austria and of Russia, of the King of Prussia, of Lord Castlereagh, of the Duke of Wellington, and of Blucher; while other bands, disguised in the uniforms of the allied troops, should storm the posts of the National Guard, and particularly those maintained at the palace of the Tuilleries. That a project so wild and impracticable should have been seriously attempted, I can hardly credit; but that so many reckless and desperate men as were now in Paris were meditating something of peril and violence, is extremely probable, for at this very time all the guards maintained on the illustrious personages I have mentioned were on a sudden strongly reinforced, and unusual strictness was exercised by the centinels in challenging those who approached their posts. Indeed, the great and combined military force would have rendered any such conspiracy an effort of fruitless, though perhaps not bloodless, phrenzy.

The internal duty of Paris is chiefly performed by the National Guard, who, in dress and appearance, remind me very much of the original or blue regiment of Edinburgh Volunteers[23]. They furnish picquets for the various guards upon public places, and around the Tuilleries; a severe duty for the respectable class of citizens of whom these regiments are composed, since I suppose at least five hundred men are required for the daily discharge of it. But the corps is very numerous, and a consciousness that the peace of the city and security of property depend upon its being regularly and punctually performed, reconciles these citizen-soldiers to their task.

The guards upon the king's person and palace are entrusted to the Gardes de Corps, or household troops, fine-looking men, very handsomely, though not gaudily, dressed. They are said, with few exceptions, to have behaved with great loyalty in the late trying crisis; but as they are an expensive corps, holding the rank of gentlemen, and being paid accordingly, it is supposed their numbers will be much limited in future. They are very civil in their deportment, and in the discharge of their duty, particularly to English strangers. My infirmities perhaps claimed a little compassion, and it is no discredit to them that I have seen Messrs. les Gardes de Corps feel the claim, and make a little way, by the influence of voice and authority, for one who was not so able to make it for himself. And indeed there was a kind of chivalrous feeling in most of these gentlemen, a modesty of demeanour, a gentleness of conduct towards the crowd, and a deference to the claims of hospitality, a sense, in short, that he who has the momentary power should use it with tenderness and forbearance, which might be mere urbanity, but which a professed aristocrat is apt to consider as mixed with a higher feeling. This corps, I have been informed, suffered much in attending the king to the frontiers; a few, who had been selected from Buonaparte's followers in a spirit of conciliation, returned to their first vocation; but the rest followed their master as far as they were permitted, and experienced much hardship and distress in consequence, besides the actual slaughter of many of their companions. A stranger is an indifferent judge of such matters, but I am so old-fashioned as to think that a body of real men-at-arms, chosen from the younger sons of the nobility and gentry, is not only a graceful institution as a defence and ornament to the throne, but may in France be the means of retrieving the real military character, so dishonoured and disgraced of late years.

There is another armed force, of a very different description, frequently seen in Paris,—the patroles of the modern gens d'armes, or military police; men picked out for the office, and who, in files of two or four, upon foot or horseback, constantly parade every part not only of Paris, but of France. Their dress and arms are those of heavy dragoons, and therefore they may be at first thought less adapted for discharging their peculiar duty, which is that of police-officers. But there is a very perfect system, of which these are the agents, and when, as in the case of the late effort of Buonaparte, the police seems to have proved ineffectual, it is not the fault of the inferior and operative agents, but of those superintendants from whom they receive their signals. These gens d'armes were the agents so dreaded under the imperial government, whose appearance made every knee tremble, and every cheek grow pale. If they are less formidable under a legitimate government, it is because even the enemies of the constitution may shelter their crimes beneath the laws instituted for the protection of innocence. Through all France, however, the ubiquity of the police is something striking and singular. In the most retired scene which you can choose, if you see a solitary horseman, or still more, if you see two riding together, it is five to one that they belong to the gens d'armerie. At this moment they have full employment for their address and omnipresence; and I believe it is exercised in no common degree, unless we should believe the scandal of the *royalistes purs*, who pretend that Fouché under the Bourbons is a much more tractable person than Fouché under the Republic and under Buonaparte.

The National Guards, Gardes de Corps, or household troops, and the Gens d'Armes, compose the only French military force to be at present seen in Paris. Mareschal M'Donald, Duke of Tarentum,[24] is intrusted with the difficult task of disbanding and reorganizing the army beyond the Loire, the remnants, namely, of the old imperial army. M'Donald is equally remarkable for military skill and loyalty; his march from the extremity of Italy to unite himself with Moreau[25], previous to the battle of Novi[26], and the successful retreat which he made even after losing that dreadful and well-fought action, against the redoubted Suwarrow, prove his military talent, as his behaviour during Buonaparte's last invasion has established his military faith. Your question is ready, I know, my dear Major, *Which* of the M'Donalds is he? for of true blood you unquestionably have already deemed him. To satisfy a wish so laudable, I can inform you, from the best authority, that the Mareschal is descended of that tribe or family of the M'Donalds of Clanronald who are called MacEachan, or Sons of Hector, as claiming their descent from a cadet of the house of Clanronald, so named. The father of the Duke of Tarentum was engaged in our affair (I love a delicate expression) of 1745,[27] and was very useful to Prince Charles Edward during his rash enterprize. He was a Highlander, bred to the church, and educated in France. He spoke, therefore, Gaelic, English, French, and Latin, and was, besides, intelligent, bold, and faithful. He was one of the seven who embarked with the unfortunate Chevalier when his expedition of knight-errantry had utterly failed. On his return to France, MacEachan took the more general name of his tribe, and appears to have preferred the military service to resuming his studies for the church. His son is now one of the most respectable characters whom the French army list presents to us. I had letters to him from his friends in Sky, but had not the good fortune to meet him at Paris. He was more usefully engaged; and, by all accounts, the king could not have reposed confidence in a more loyal and gallant character. How should it be otherwise? Is he not a Scotchman, and a M'Donald?—eh, Major?

Of foreign troops, all included, there are generally said to be in France to the number of a million; but I am informed, from the best authority, that they do certainly amount to EIGHT HUNDRED THOUSAND MEN, an assembly of troops scarce paralleled save in the annals of romance. Of these the British, Prussians, and Russians, are nearest to Paris, so stationed as to have an army of one hundred and fifty thousand men within a day's march of the city.

The Austrians are chiefly in the South of France. The French complain more of the severity of the usage which the inhabitants receive from them, than of the rest of the allies. Those whom we see here are part of the Emperor's Hungarian guards, selected men, of fine and tall figure, which is set off by their white dress. They are unquestionably, in point of exterior appearance, the handsomest of the allied

troops; but such bulky men want the hardy and athletic look
of the British, Russians, or Prussians. Tell the ladies also that
this same white uniform looks better upon a line of troops in
the field, than on an individual officer in a ball-room, whose
appearance involuntarily, and rather unfairly, reminds me
of the master of a regimental band. The hussar uniforms
of Austria are very handsome, particularly those of the
Hungarians, to whose country the dress properly belongs.

The Russians are in the neighbourhood in very considerable force. I was present at a splendid review[28] which was
made of these northern warriors by the Allied Sovereigns,
the Duke of Wellington, &c. The principal avenue of the
Champs Elysees was crowded with troops of all sorts; and
the reflection of the sun upon their arms appeared almost
intolerably bright. The monarchs, generals, and their suite,
occupied the centre of the Place Louis Quinze, almost the
very spot in which Louis XVI. was beheaded, and for more
than two hours the troops defiled before them without a
pause, in a close column, whose front occupied the whole
space afforded by the breadth of the avenue. The infantry
were fine, firm, steady-looking men, clean, handsome,
but by no means remarkable for stature. From the green
uniform, and the short and sturdy make of the Russians,
the French nicknamed them *Cornichons*, as if they resembled
the green cucumbers, so called when pickled. They had a
formidable train of artillery, in the highest possible order,
and were attended by several regiments both of dragoons
and cuirassiers. The cuirassiers of the guard had burnished
steel breastplates, which glanced to the sun, and made a
noble display. The cuirasses of the other regiments seemed
to be of hammered iron. The cavaliers were remarkably fine
men; the horses, excepting those of the officers, seemed to

be of an inferior description, and rather weak for that sort of service; but the general effect was indescribably grand. The troops swept on, wave rolling as it were after wave, to the number of at least twenty thousand men, the sound of one band of martial music advancing as the other died away, and the column moving on as if the procession would stretch out to the crack of doom. During this grand display of the powers of the North, the ground was kept by the regular Cossacks of the Russian guard, very fine men, and under good discipline. The irregular Cossacks, and light troops of a similar description, are only occasionally seen in Paris; but their Hettman, Prince Platow, is a constant resident in the capital, and to him these children of the desert are occasionally summoned. The appearance of the proper Cossack is prepossessing. He has high features, keeps his long blue coat strictly clean, and displays some taste for splendour in his arms and accoutrements, which are often richly decorated with silver. But the Tartar tribes, whom the French unite under the same appellation, have frequently a most uncouth and savage appearance. Cloaks of sheep-skin, bows, arrows, shields made of dried hides, and other appointments savouring of the earliest state of society, were seen among them; from which the French, whom even invasion, with all its ills, cannot deprive of their jest, call them *Les Cupidons de Nord*. I saw one man who had come with his tribe from near to the Great Wall of China, to fight against the French under the walls of Paris! The poor fellow was in the hospital from a very natural cause, the injury which his feet had sustained in so long a march. But these wilder light troops were judiciously kept at a distance from Paris, where the splendour and wealth of the shops formed rather too strong temptations for Tartar morality.

The Prussian troops have gradually assumed a more respectable exterior, as the new clothing, at the expence of France, has been completed and delivered. They are a handsome fair-haired race of men; their uniforms almost exclusively blue and red. Both they and the Russians seem to think, that the beauty of the male form consists in resembling as much as possible a triangle, or rather a lady in an old-fashioned pair of high stays. So they draw their waists tight by means of a broad belt, or some similar contrivance, and stuff out and pad the breast and shoulders till the desired figure is attained. Almost all of them are young men summoned to arms by the situation of Europe, and their own country in particular,—a call which was obeyed with such ardent enthusiasm, that I suppose no civilized kingdom ever had under arms, as a disposable force, so large a proportion of its population. Many regiments are composed of *landwehr*, or militia, and some of volunteers. It necessarily follows, from this intermixture of various descriptions of force, that they cannot be all under the same degree of strict military discipline; and to this must be attributed the irregularities they committed upon their march, and which were sometimes imputed to them in their quarters. They have never been accused, however, of gross violence, of assailing life or honour, or of wantonly injuring the churches or public buildings, crimes which were objected to the French armies in Prussia. Their resentment, indeed, was stirred at the name of the bridge of Jena, and they had made preparations for the destruction of that useful and beautiful edifice. But the intercession of the Duke of Wellington procured a delay, until the King of Prussia upon his arrival repealed this hasty and vindictive order.

I saw a large body of these troops quartered in the

celebrated Chateau de Montmorency. The owner of this fine seat, and the beautiful domain annexed, was attached to Buonaparte, had fled upon Napoleon's first exile, and had returned to share his triumph. The brief interval before the battle of Waterloo, which compelled him to a second retreat, had been employed in refitting the chateau with painting, pannelling, and sculpture, in the most expensive style. The Prussians were now busily undoing all that he had commenced, and the contrast between recent repair and the work of instant destruction was very striking. The rich furniture was stripped by the female followers of the camp, and the soldiers were boiling their camp-kettles with the gilded frames of pictures, the plate-glass windows were smashed to pieces, and the breaches repaired by old jackets and pantaloons. One of my friends, who had been long in the Spanish war, observed with composure, that the chateau was in a way of being handsomely *rumped*, a technical word for what was going on, which you may insert at my peril in your collection of military phrases. When quartered upon inhabited houses, the French chiefly complained of the extent of the Prussians' appetite, as a craving gulf, which they found it very difficult to satisfy. They were not otherwise cruel or ill-natured; but, like the devouring cannibal in the voyages of Aboulfouaris,[29] their hunger could not be lulled to sleep longer than three hours at a time. Much of this was undoubtedly greatly exaggerated.

It is certain, however, that means have been put into the power of the Prussian officers to indulge themselves in the pleasures of Paris to an extent which their pay and allowances, if limited to those drawn in their own country, could not possibly have afforded. They are the principal customers to the expensive *restaurateurs*, the principal frequenters of coffee-houses, of theatres, and of the Palais Royale, at regular and irregular hours,—all indications of an expence not within the ordinary reach of subaltern officers. It is said, that some of our German subsidiary troops made application to the Duke of Wellington to be put upon the same footing with the Prussians in these extra advantages. His Grace, we are assured, expressed to them (with the fullest acknowledgment of their meriting every indulgence which could be wisely bestowed) his decided opinion, that all expedients which tended to place the soldier upon a different footing of expence and luxury in France, than he held in his native country, were injurious to discipline, detrimental to the character of the army, and to the interest of the sovereign. His practice expresses the same doctrine. The British troops receive regularly the allowances and rations to which they would be entitled in England, and which are here raised at the expence of France; but neither directly nor indirectly do they obtain further indulgence. The strong sense and firmness for which the Duke is as much distinguished as for skill in arms and bravery in the field of battle, easily saw that the high and paramount part which Britain now holds in Europe, that pre-eminence, which, in so many instances, has made her and her delegates the chosen mediators when disputes occurred amongst the allied powers, depends entirely on our maintaining pure and sacred the national character for good faith and disinterested honour. The slightest complaint, therefore, of want of discipline or oppression, perpetrated by a British officer or soldier, has instantly met with reprehension and punishment, and the result has been the reducing the French to the cruel situation of hating us without having any complaint to justify themselves for doing so, even in their own eyes. Our officers of rank have, in many instances, declined the quarters appointed them in private houses; and, where they were accepted, have arranged themselves in the mode least likely to derange the family, and declined uniformly the offers to accommodate them with wine, or provisions, which were made as a matter of course. They receive the reward of this moderation in the public respect, which, however the French may dislike us as a nation, they are compelled to pay to individual merit and courtesy.

On the other hand, strange and alarming whispers are thrown abroad respecting the situation of the Prussian army. It is hinted, that they are somewhat out of controul, and look up less to the king than to their generals as their paramount superiors. Blucher holds the first rank ostensibly; but it is pretended, that General Gneisenau, so celebrated for his talents as a quarter-master-general, possesses most real influence. Much of this is supposed to be exerted by means of secret societies, particularly that called The Order of Faith and Honour[30]. This association, which derived its first institution from the laudable and patriotic desire of associating against French tyranny, has retained the secret character with which it was necessarily invested, when the foreign enemy possessed the fortresses of Prussia, but which now seems useless at least, if not capable of being rendered hazardous. Almost all the officers of this army belong to this order, which is a sort of institution that has peculiar charms for Germans; and it is said to be an object of jealousy to the government, though it cannot be supposed dangerous while headed by the loyal Blucher.

Our forces, in general, are admired for their appearance under arms, although, like their countrymen under Henry V.,

They are but warriors for the working day,
Their gayness and their gilt is all besmirch'd
With rainy marching on the painful field.[31]

The serviceable state of the men, horses, and equipments, fully compensates, to the experienced eye, every deficiency in mere show.

The singular dress of our Highlanders makes them particular objects of attention to the French. In what class of society they rank them, may be judged from part of a speech which I heard a French lady make to her companion, after she had passed two of these mountaineers: '*Aussi j'ai vu les sauvages Americains.*' It was very entertaining to see our Highlanders making their bargains upon the Boulevards, the soldier holding his piece of *six sols* between his finger and thumb, with the gripe of a smith's vice, and pointing out the quantity of the commodity which he expected for it, while the Frenchman, with many shrugs and much chattering, diminished the equivalent as more than he could afford. Then Donald began to shrug and jabber in his turn, and to scrape back again what the other had subtracted; and so they would stand for half an hour discussing the point, though neither understood a word which the other said, until they could agree upon *le prix juste.*

The soldiers, without exception, both British and foreigners, conduct themselves in public with civility, are very rarely to be seen intoxicated, though the means are so much within reach; and, considering all the irritating circumstances that exist, few quarrels occur betwixt them and the populace. Very strong precautions are, however, taken in case of any accidental or premeditated commotion. A powerful guard of Prussians always attends at the Pont

Neuf and Pont Royale, with two pieces of artillery turned upon each bridge, loaded with cannister-shot, horses saddled, matches burning, and all ready to act on the shortest warning. The other day an unpleasant accident took place. Some of the Parisian populace, while the Prussian officer of the day was visiting a post, quarrelled with the orderly soldier who held his horse; the animal took fright, and escaped the man's hold; the officer came out, and was hustled and insulted by the mob. In the meanwhile, the orderly-man galloped off, and returned with about thirty of his companions, who charged with their lances couched, as if they threatened death and destruction; but, with much dexterity, tilted up the point of the spear when near a Frenchman's body, and reversing the weapon, only struck with the butt. They made five or six of the most tumultuous prisoners, who were carried before Baron Muffling, reclaiming loudly the safeguard of the police, and demanding to be carried before a French judge. But, in the present situation of this capital, the commandant preferred subjecting them to military chastisement; and a truss of straw being laid down for each culprit, they were stretched out, and received a drubbing *a la militaire* with the reins and girths of the hussars' horses. The appearance of the sufferers acted as a sedative upon the temper of the mob, none of whom chose to seek further personal specimens of the Prussian discipline. It seemed a strong measure to the English spectators; but the question is, Whether a good many lives were not saved at the expence of the shoulders of those sufferers; for where combustibles are so plenty, the least spark of fire must be trodden out with as much haste as may be. In other frays, it has happened that Prussian soldiers have been killed; in which case, the district where the accident happened is subjected to severe contributions, unless they can arrest the perpetrator. The Palais Royale, where such scenes are chiefly to be apprehended, is trebly guarded every night by a company of the National Guard, one of British, and one of Prussians.

As a matter of courtesy between the allied powers, the duty of mounting guard upon the person of the monarchs is performed by the troops of each nation in succession: So that our guardsmen mount guard on the Emperor of Russia, the Russians on the Emperor of Austria, and the Highlanders, perhaps, on the King of Prussia, in rotation; —a judicious arrangement, which tends to show both the French and the allied troops the close and intimate union of the sovereigns in the common cause of Europe. The important post of Montmartre, which, in its present state of strong fortification, may be called the citadel of Paris, is confided to the care of the British, who keep guard with great and unusual strictness. Even foreign officers are not admitted within these works, unless accompanied by an Englishman. The hill is bristled with two hundred pieces of cannon; and they make frequent discovery of military stores and ammunition buried or concealed. All these will fall to our share; and, I trust, the two hundred guns will be sent to keep company with the hundred and fifty taken at the battle of Waterloo.

In the meanwhile, it is a strange and most inconsistent circumstance, that the Castle of Vincennes[32], within three miles of Paris, lying in the midst of these armies, and of no more strength than the White Tower of London, or any other Gothic keep, affects to hold out against the allied army. The commandant, although he has hoisted the white flag, will neither receive a Royalist nor an allied soldier within the castle, and gives himself great airs of defiance, as encouraged by an impunity which he only owes to contempt, and to the reluctance of the allied sovereigns to increase the King of France's difficulties and unpopularity by punishing the gasconade as it deserves.

I do not observe that the soldiers of the allied nations intermix much in company with each other, although they seem on kind and civil terms when occasionally thrown together. The Museum, which is open to all ranks and conditions, frequently, besides its other striking beauties, exhibits a moving picture of all the nations of Europe in their military dresses. You see the tall Hungarian, the swarthy Italian, the fair-haired Prussian, the flat-faced Tartar, English, Irish, Guardsmen, and Highlanders, in little bands of two or three, strolling up and down a hall as immense as that of the Caliph Vathek[33], and indulging their curiosity with its wonders. The wildest of them appeared softened and respectful, while forming a part of this singular assemblage, which looks as if all the nations had formed a rendezvous at Paris by military representation. Some of their remarks must of course be very entertaining. One or two I caught. 'By—, Jack,' said an English dragoon to his comrade, pointing to a battlepiece by Salvator[34], 'look at the cuirasses—they have got the battle of Waterloo here already.'—'Pooh, you blockhead,' said the other, 'that an't the battle of Waterloo; don't you see all the horses have got long tails?' I asked a Highland serjeant, who was gazing earnestly on the Venus de Medicis, 'How do you like her, countryman?'—'God bless us—is your honour from Inverness?' was the first exclamation, and then, 'I am told she is very much admired—but I'll show your honour a much better proportioned woman,'—and the ambitious serjeant, himself a remarkably little man, conducted me to a colossal female figure, eight feet high. There is no disputing with the judgment of artists, but I am afraid the beauties of this statue are not of a kind most obvious to the uninitiated.

Where there are monarchs at the head of conquering armies, the pomp of war must of course be displayed in its full glories. We have reviews of many thousands every morning, from seven o'clock until ten or eleven. That of the British cavalry was very much admired, notwithstanding the dust which enveloped their movements. The Russians and Prussians exhibited upon another occasion the manoeuvres of a mock engagement, the Emperor commanding the Prussian army, and the King of Prussia, in the dress of a colonel of the Russian guards, enacting the general of the Muscovites. After the battle, the two potentates met and greeted each other very handsomely. On another occasion, the Prussians entertained us with a rehearsal of the battle of Issy, or the movements of the French army and their own in the attack and defence of that village, upon the 2nd of June.[35] At one of these reviews the Russians were commanded by the emperor to charge in line, expressly for the gratification of the English general. You know it is surmised, that the British claim pre-eminence over all other nations, because the steadiness and bottom of the individual soldiers permit them to hazard a general charge in line, whereas the column is adopted for the purpose of attack by the French and all other foreigners. Perhaps this was designed as a rebuke to our national vanity. However, the Russians went through the manoeuvre admirably well, dressing a line of very great length with the utmost accuracy, during an advance of half a mile.

It must be owned, that a politician more gloomy than

myself, might draw evil augury from the habits, which the reigning sovereigns of Europe may possibly acquire by being for years the inmates of camps, and compelled by the pressure of the imminent crisis to postpone the duties of the sovereign to those of the general. War has been described as 'the game of princes;' and we know how easily the habit of gambling is acquired, and how irresistible it soon becomes. If it should happen that these powerful monarchs, influenced by the military ideas and habits which have been so long uppermost, should find a state of peace a tedious and dull exchange for the animating perils of war, it will be one instance, among many, of the lasting evils which French aggression, and the necessary means of counteracting it, have entailed on the kingdoms of Europe. I confide, however, something in the wisdom of these princes, and a great deal in the pacific influence of a deity whose presence we all deprecate, notwithstanding the lessons of wisdom which she is supposed to teach—I mean the Goddess of Poverty.

Two circumstances struck me in the grand military spectacle which I have mentioned,—the great number of actors, and, comparatively speaking, the total absence of spectators. The scale of the exhibition cannot indeed be wondered at, considering the importance of the actors:

> Ha! Majesty, how high thy glory towers,
> When the rich blood of kings is set on fire![36]

But, in the neighbourhood of so populous a city as Paris, the inhabitants of which have been so long famous for their attachment to public spectacles, one might have thought spectators enough would have been found besides the military amateurs not immediately engaged, and a few strangers. But I never saw above a hundred Frenchmen, and those of the very lowest order, looking on at these exhibitions, not even at that made in the Place Louis Quinze, under their very eyes. This is the strongest sign of their deeply feeling their present state of humiliation, and proves, more than a thousand others, that they taste the gall in all its bitterness, and that the iron has entered into their soul. In my next letter to my friend Peter, I will communicate what else I have observed on the state of the public mind in France. But I must first acquit myself of my promise to our ghostly father, the parson.

Your's entirely,

Paul.

Postscript. By the bye, you must allow me to add to my Waterloo anecdotes, one which relates to a gallant countryman of ours, in whose family you well know that we feel the interest of old and sincere friendships: I mean Colonel Francis Hepburn, of the 3d regiment of Guards, who had the distinguished honour of commanding the detachment sent to the relief of Hougoumont, when it was attacked by the whole French division of Jerome Buonaparte. He had the charge of maintaining, with his own single battalion, this important post, when the communication was entirely cut off by the French cavalry, and it was not until they were repulsed, that he was reinforced by two battalions of Hanoverians and one of Brunswickers. Colonel Woodforde of the Coldstream Guards, who in the morning reinforced Lieutenant-Colonel Macdonell, commanded in the house and garden, and Colonel Hepburn in the orchard and wood. I am particular in mentioning this, because the name of Lieutenant-Colonel Home,[37] who acted under

Colonel Hepburn, appeared in the Gazette instead of his, by a mistake incidental to the confusion of the day, which rendered it impossible accurately to distinguish individual merit. The error has been admitted, but there is a difficulty in correcting it publicly, though there can be none in making our friends in Scotland acquainted with the real share which the relative of our deceased friend, the best and kindliest of veterans, had, in the most memorable battle that ever was fought, and which in no degree takes away from the admitted gallantry of his countryman, Lieutenant-Colonel Home. Colonel Hepburn, as you will remember, was engaged in the Spanish war, and severely wounded at the battle of Barossa.

LETTER XV.

PAUL TO THE REVEREND MR ——,
MINISTER OF THE GOSPEL AT ——.

Do not blame me, my dear friend, if I have been long in fulfilling my promise to you. Religion, so ample a field in most countries, has for some time been in France an absolute blank. From my former letters you must have learned, that in Flanders the catholic system still maintains itself in great vigour. The churches are full of people, most of them on their knees, and their devotion, if not enlightened, seems fervent and sincere. One instance I saw with peculiar pleasure, at Malines—Two *Religieuses*, sisters of charity, I believe, entered the church at the head of a small school of about twenty poor children, neatly, though coarsely, dressed, and kneeled down with them to their devotions. I was informed, that the poor nuns had dedicated their little income and their whole time, struggling occasionally with all the difficulties incident to a country convulsed by war and political revolutions, to educate these children in the fear of God, and in useful knowledge. Call them nuns, or call them what you will, I think we will neither of us quarrel with an order who thus employ their hours of retirement from the world.

I was less edified by the frequent appearance of a small chapel and an altar, on the side of the road, where the carman will sometimes snatch a flying prayer, while his huge waggon wanders on at the will of the horses. But your own parishioners sometimes leave their horses' heads for less praise-worthy purposes, and therefore much cannot be said on that score. The rites and solemnities of the catholic church made less impression on me than I expected; even the administration of high mass, though performed by a cardinal, fell far short of what I had anticipated. There is a fidgetting about the whole ceremony, a perpetual dressing and undressing, which seems intended to make it more elaborate and complex, but which destroys the grandeur and simplicity so appropriate to an act of solemn devotion. Much of the imposing exterior may now indeed be impaired—the church was the first object of plunder wherever the French came, and they have left traces of their rapacity which will not soon be erased. The vestments look antiquated and tawdry, the music is but indifferent, the plate and jewels have all vanished. The priests themselves are chiefly old men, on whom the gaudy dresses with which they are decorated, sit awkwardly, and who seem in many instances bowed down by painful recollections, as much as by infirmity. In a word, the old Dame of Babylon[1], against whom our fathers testified so loudly, seems now hardly worth a passing attack, even in the *Nineteenthly* of an afternoon's sermon[2], and is in some measure reduced to the *pavé*[3]. Old John Bunyan himself could hardly have wished to see her stand lower in influence and estimation, than she does in the popular mind in France; and yet a few years, and the Giant Pope will be, in all probability, as innoxious as the Giant Pagan.[4] Indeed, since his having shared the fate of other giants, in being transported, like a show, from place to place, by the renowned charlatan Buonaparte, his former subjects have got familiar with his terrors, and excommunication scarcely strikes more horror than the *fee fau fum* of a nursery tale.

It is remarkable, that this indifference seems to have extended to the enemies, as well as the subjects, of the catholic church. When Rome was stormed in 1527, the chief amusement of the reformed German soldiers was insulting the rites of the Roman religion, and ridiculing the persons of their clergy. But in 1815, when the conquering armies of two protestant kingdoms marched from Brussels to Paris, the idea of showing scorn or hatred to the catholic religion never occurred to any individual soldier. I would gladly ascribe this to punctuality of discipline; but enough was done, by the Prussians at least, to show, that that consideration alone would not have held back their hands, had they felt any temptation to insult the French through the medium of their religion. But this does not seem to have appeared to them a vulnerable point, and not a crucifix or image was touched, or a pane of painted glass broken, that we could see or hear of, upon the route.

In the churches which we visited, very few persons seemed to attend the service, and these were aged men and women. In Paris this was still more remarkable; for, notwithstanding the zeal of the court, and the example which they exhibit of strict attention to the forms of the church,—an example even too marked for good policy,—those of the city of Paris are empty and neglected. It is melancholy to think that, with the external forms and observances of religion, its vital principles also have fallen into complete disuse and oblivion. But those under whose auspices the French Revolution commenced, and by whom its terrors were for a time conducted, found their own interest intimately and strictly connected with the dissolution of the powerful checks of religious faith and moral practice. And although the Directory afterwards promulgated, by a formal edict, that France acknowledged the existence of a Supreme Being, and, with impious mockery, appointed a fete in his honour, all opportunity of instruction in religious duties was broken off by the early destination of the youth of France to the trade of arms. A much-esteemed friend at Paris happened to have a domestic of sense, information, and general intelligence above his station. His master upon some occasion used to him the expression, 'It is doing as we would be done by,—the Christian maxim.' The young man looked rather surprised; 'Yes,' repeated my friend, 'I say it is the doctrine of the Christian religion, which teaches us not only to do as we would be done by, but also to return good for evil.'—'It may be so, sir,' answered the valet; 'but I had the misfortune to be born during the heat of the Revolution, when it would have been death to have spoken on the subject of religion, and so soon as I was fifteen years old, I was put into the hands of the drill serjeant, whose first lesson to me was, that, as a French soldier, I was to fear neither God nor devil.' My friend, himself a soldier, and a brave one, but of a very different cast of mind from that which was thought necessary for the service of France, was both shocked and astonished at this strong proof of the manner in which the present generation had been qualified from their childhood to be the plagues of society. The consideration, that they were thus perverted in their early youth, and rendered unfit for all purposes but those of mischief, is the best consolation for such French patriots as mourn over the devastation which has overwhelmed the youth of their country.

Buonaparte, who, when not diverted from his purpose by his unsatiable ambition, had strong views of policy, resolved upon the re-establishment of the church as a sort of outwork to the throne. He created accordingly archbishops, bishops, and all the appendages of a hierarchy. This was not only intended that they might surround the imperial throne, with the solemn splendours of a hierarchy, and occasionally feed their master's ears with flattery in their pastoral charges,—an office which, by most of them, was performed with the most humiliating baseness,—but also in order to form an alliance between the religious creed which they were enjoined to inculcate, and the sentiments of the people towards the imperial dignity. The imperial catechism, promulgated under authority, proclaimed the duties of the catechumen to the emperor, to be love, obedience, fidelity, and military service; the causes assigned were Napoleon's high and miraculous gifts, his immediate mission from the Deity, and the consecration by the pope; and the menace to disloyalty was no less than eternal condemnation—here and hereafter. I am sorry to say, that this summary of *jus divinum* was not entirely of Buonaparte's invention; for, in a Prussian catechism for the use of the soldiers, entitled, '*Pflichten der Unterthanen*,' (the Duties of Subjects,) and printed at Breslau, in 1800, I find the same doctrines expressed, though with less daring extravagance. Buonaparte reaped but little advantage from his system of church government, partly owing to the materials of which his monarchy was constructed, (for the best and most conscientious of the clergy kept aloof from such promotion,) partly from the shortness of his reign, but principally from the stern impatience of his own temper, which could not long persist in apparent veneration for a power of his own creating, but soon led the way in exposing the new prelates to neglect and contempt.

We must learn to look with better hope upon the more

conscientious efforts for re-establishing the altar, which have been made by the king. Yet we cannot but fear, that the order of the necessary reformation has been, to a certain extent at least, the reverse of what would really have attained the important purposes designed by the sovereign. The rites, forms, and ceremonies of a church, all its external observances, derive, from the public sense of religion itself, the respect which is paid to them. It is true, that, as the shell of a nut will subsist long after the kernel is decayed, so regard for ceremonies and forms may often remain when true devotion is no more, and when ignorant zeal has transferred her blind attachment from the essence of religion to its mere forms. But if that zeal is quenched, and that attachment is eradicated, and the whole system is destroyed both in show and in substance, it is not by again enforcing the formal observances which men have learned to contemn and make jest of, that the vivifying principle of religion will be rekindled. Indeed, far from supposing that the foundation of the altar should be laid upon the ritual of the Romish church, with all the revived superstitions of the twelfth century, it would be more prudent to abandon to oblivion, a part at least of what is shocking to common sense and reason; which, although a Most Christian King might have found himself under some difficulty of abrogating when it was yet in formal observance, he certainly cannot be called upon to renew, when it has fallen into desuetude. The catholics of this age are not excluded from the lights which it has afforded; and the attempt to re-establish processions, in which the officiating persons hardly know their places, tales of miraculous images, masses for the souls of state criminals, and all the mummery of barbarous ages, is far from meeting the enlarged ideas which the best and most learned of them have expressed. The peculiar doctrines of their church prohibits, indeed, the formal rejection of any doctrine or observance which she has once received; but I repeat, that the time is favourable in France for rebuilding the Gallican church on a more solid basis than ever, by leaving room for the gradual and slow reformation introduced by the lapse of time, instead of forcing back the nineteenth century into the rude and degrading darkness of the ages of excommunications and crusades. It is with the hearts of the French, and not with the garments of their clergy, that the reformation, or rather the restoration, of religion ought to commence; and I conceive the primary object should be securing the instruction of the rising generation in religious and moral duties, as well as in general education, by carefully filling up the ranks of the parochial clergy, on whose patient and quiet attention to the morals of their flocks the state of the nation must depend, and not upon the colour of a cap, the tinkle of a bell, or the music of high mass.

The truth is, that the king's most natural and justifiable zeal for the establishments of religion, which were his chief consolation in adversity, has already given alarm to several classes of his subjects. Bigotted, or interested priests have been already heard misrepresenting the intentions of their sovereign, so far as to affirm, he means to restore to the church all her rights, and impose anew upon the subject the burdens of tithes, and the confusion which must arise from the reclamation of the church lands. How these reports, malignantly echoed by the enemies of the royal family, sound in the ears of men of property, I leave to your own judgment; and can only regret that it is as difficult as it is desirable, for the king to oppose them by a public contradiction.

It is chiefly in the southern districts, where the French protestants still maintain themselves, that this alarm is excited,
cherished, and fostered, by those who care for neither
one religion nor the other, further than as the jealousies
and contentions of both may be engines of bloodshed,
depression, and revolution. In the province of Languedoc
especially, the angry passions of both parties are understood
to be at full tide; and it unfortunately happens that the
contending parties are there envenomed by political hatred.
Buonaparte, whose system of national religion included
universal toleration, extended his special protection to the
professors of the reformed doctrines, and by an organic law
concerning worship, published in the year X[5], guaranteed to
them the free exercise of their religion, being the first public
indulgence which had been extended to them since the
revocation of the Edict of Nantes[6]. A system of consistories
was established for their internal church government; and
so highly were they favoured, that the public exercise of the
catholic religion, by processions or other ritual observances
performed without the walls of the church, was positively
prohibited in such towns as had consistorial churches
belonging to the protestants. This distinction in favour of
a body of subjects, amounting, it has been computed, to
two millions of souls, attended by the triumph conferred by
the interdiction of the catholic rites where their eyes could
be offended by them, raised the spirits of the protestants as
much as it exasperated and depressed those of the catholics.
They took their ranks in political contest accordingly; and
although interests of various kinds prevented the rule from
being absolute, yet it was observed, during the last convulsions
of state, that the catholics of the South were in general
royalists, whereas many of the protestants, in gratitude for

past favours conferred on their church, in jealousy of the family of Bourbon, by the bigotry of whose ancestors their fathers had suffered, and confiding in the tolerant spirit of Buonaparte, lent too ready and willing aid to his usurpation. During that event, and those which followed, much and mutual subject of exasperation has unfortunately taken place between these contending parties. Ancient enmities have been awakened, and, amid contradictory reports and statements, we can easily discover that both parties, or individuals at least of both, have been loud in their appeal to principles of moderation when undermost, and very ready when they obtained the upper hand to abuse the advantages which the changes of the state had alternately given to them. This is a deep and rankling wound, which will require to be treated with no common skill. The protestants of the South are descendants of the ardent men who used to assemble by thousands in the wilderness—I will not say with the scoffer, to hear the psalms of Clement Marot sung to the tune of *Reveillez vous, belle Endormie*[7]—but rather, as your Calvinistic heroes of moor and moss[8], in the days of the last Stuarts, are described by a far different bard, dear in remembrance to us both, for the affectionate sympathy and purity of his thoughts and feelings; when in the wilderness

—— 'arose the song, the loud
Acclaim of praise: The whirling plover ceased
Her plaint; the solitary place was glad,
And on the distant cairns the watcher's ear
Caught doubtfully at times the breeze-borne note.'[9]

On the other hand, the catholics are numerous, powerful in the hope of protection and preference from the crown, and eager to avenge insults, which, in their apprehension, have been aimed alike at the crown and the altar. If we claim for the protestants, whose nearer approach to our own doctrines recommends them to our hearts as objects of interest, the sympathy which is due to their perilous situation, let us not, in candour, deny at least the credit of mistaken zeal to those whom different rites divide from us. In the name of that Heaven, to whose laws both forms of religion appeal, who has disclaimed enforcing the purest doctrines by compulsion, and who never can be worshipped duly or acceptably by bloody sacrifices, let us deprecate a renewal of those savage and bloody wars, which, founded upon difference of religious opinion, seem to convert even the bread of life itself into the most deadly poison. British interference, not surely so proposed as to affront France's feelings of national independence, a point on which late incidents have made her peculiarly irritable—but with the earnest and anxious assurances of that good-will, for which our exertions in behalf of the royal family, and our interest in the tranquillity of France, may justly claim credit,— might, perhaps, have some influence with the government. But in what degree, or how far it may be prudent to hazard it, can only be known to those upon whom the momentous charge of public affairs has devolved at this trying crisis. We need not now take up the parable of Lord Shaftesbury, when he compared the reformed churches of France and Savoy to the sister of the spouse in the Canticles, and asked the astonished peers of Charles the Second, 'What shall be done for our sister in the day when she shall be spoken for?'[10] But it is certain, that the security of the protestant religion abroad is now, as in the days of that statesman, a wall and defence unto that which we profess at home; and at all times, when England has been well administered, she has claimed and exercised the rights of intercession in behalf of the Reformed Churches. I trust, however, that our mediation will be, in the present case, unnecessary, and that the king himself, with the sound judgment and humane disposition which all parties allow him to possess, will show himself the protector of both parties, by restricting the aggressions of either. In the meanwhile, admire the singularity of human affairs. In Ireland discontents exist, because the catholics are not possessed of all the capacities and privileges of their protestant fellow subjects;—in the Netherlands the catholic clergy murmur at the union, because the king has expressed his determination to permit the free exercise of the protestant religion amid his catholic dominions;—and in the south of France the sword is nearly drawn, upon the footing of doubts, jealousies, and apprehensions of mutual violence, for which neither party can allege any feasible ground, except mutual dislike and hatred. We may without offence wish that all of them would qualify their zeal for the doctrinal part of their religion with some part of that meekness of spirit, which would be the best proof of its purity.

To return to the religious and moral state of France. It is remarkable that the dissolution of religious principle, the confusion of the Sabbath with the ordinary days of the week, the reduction of marriage to a state of decent and legal concubinage, from which parties can free themselves at pleasure, have, while thus sapping the foundations of the social affections, as well as of religious faith, introduced more vices than crimes, much profligacy, but less atrocity than might have been expected. A Frenchman, to whom you talk of the general decay of morality in his country, will readily and with truth reply to you, that if every species of turpitude be more common in France, delicts of that sort against which the law directs its thunders, are much more frequent in Britain. Murders, robberies, daring thefts, such as frequently occur in the English papers, are little known in those of Paris. The amusements and habits of the lower orders are, on all occasions of ordinary occurrence, more quiet, peaceable, and orderly than those of the lower English. There are no quarrels in the street, intoxication is rarely practised even by the lowest of the people, and when assembled for the purpose of public amusement, they observe a good-humoured politeness to each other and to strangers, for which certainly our countrymen are not remarkable. To look at the thousands of rabble whom I have seen streaming through the magnificent apartments at Versailles without laying a finger upon a painting or an article of furniture, and afterwards crowding the gardens without encroaching upon any spot where they could do damage; to observe this, and recollect what would be the conduct of an English mob in similar circumstances, compels one to acknowledge, that the French appear, upon such occasions, beyond comparison the more polished, sensible, and civilized people. But release both parties from the restraints imposed by the usual state of society, and suppose them influenced by some powerful incentive to passion and violence, and remark how much the contrast will be altered. The English populace will huzza, swear, threaten, break windows, and throw stones at the Life Guards engaged in dispersing them; but if a soldier should fall from his horse, the rabble, after enjoying a laugh at his expence, would lend a hand to lift him to his saddle again. A French mob would tear him limb from limb, and parade the fragments in triumph upon their pikes. In the same manner, the Englishman under arms retains the same frank, rough loyalty of character, without the alert intelligence and appearance of polished gallantry which a French soldier often exhibits to strangers. But it would be an outrage to our countrymen to compare the conduct of the two armies when pursuing a defeated enemy, or entering a country as invaders, when every evil passion is awake, and full license is granted to satiate them.

The cause of so extraordinary a contrast may, I think, be expressed in very few words. The French act from feeling, and the British from principle. In moments, therefore, when the passions are at rest, the Frenchman will often appear, and be in reality, the more amiable of the two. He is generally possessed of intelligence and the power of reflection, both of which are great promoters of that limited sort of honesty which keeps the windy side of the law. He piques himself upon some understanding and perception of the fine arts, by which he is told his country is distinguished, and he avoids the rudeness and violence which constitute a barbarian. He is, besides, habitually an observer of the forms and decencies of society, and has ample means of indulging licentious passions without transgressing. The Frenchman is further, by nature and constitution, a happy and contented mortal, content with little, and attached to luxuries of the more simple kind; and a mind so constituted is usually disposed to extend its cheerfulness to others. The Englishman is, in some degree, the reverse of all this. His intelligence seldom goes beyond the art to which he is trained, and which he most frequently practises with mechanical dexterity only; and therefore he is not by habit, unless when nature has been especially bountiful, much of a reasoning animal. As for pretending to admire or understand the fine arts, or their productions, he would consider such an effort of taste as the most ridiculous affectation, and therefore readily treats with contempt and disrespect what he would upon system be ashamed to understand. Vice and crime are equally forbidden by the Englishman's system of religious morals; if he becomes stained with gross immorality, he is generally ready to rush into legal delict, since, being divested of the curb of conscience, and destroyed in his own esteem, he becomes, like a horse without a bridle, ready to run upon any course which chance or the phrenzy of the moment may dictate. And this may show why, though the number of vicious persons be greater in France than in England in an enormous ratio, yet the proportion of legal criminals is certainly smaller. As to general temper and habits, the Englishman, less favoured in climate and less gay by constitution, accustomed to be a grumbler by his birth-right, very often disdains to be pleased himself, and is not very anxious to please others. His freedom, too, gives him a right, when casually mixed with his betters, to push, to crowd, to be a little riotous and very noisy, and to insult his neighbours on slight provocation, merely to keep his privileges in exercise. But then he is also taught to respect the law, which he invokes as his own protection; to weigh and decide upon what is just and unjust, foul and fair; to respect the religion in which he has been trained, and to remember its restraints, even in the moment of general license. It might indeed be wished that some of the lighter and more amiable qualities of the French could be infused into our populace. But what an infinitely greater service would the sovereign render to France, who should give new sensibility to those moral feelings which have too long lain torpid in the breasts of her inhabitants!

This great end can only be reached by prudent and prospective regulations; for neither religion nor morality can be inforced upon a nation by positive law. The influence of parochial clergy, and of parochial schools, committed to persons worthy of the important trust, are, as I before hinted, the most obvious remedies. But there are others of a prohibitory and preventive nature. It is in the power of government to stop some grand sources of corruption of morals, and to withdraw their protection and licence at least, from those assemblies which have for their direct object the practice of immoralities of every sort. The Palais Royale, in whose saloons and porticos Vice has established a public and open school for gambling and licentiousness, far from affording, as at present, an impure and scandalous source of revenue to the state, should be levelled to the ground, with all its accursed brothels and gambling houses,—rendezvouses, the more seductive to youth, as being free from some of those dangers which would alarm timidity in places of avowedly scandalous resort. Gaming is indeed reduced to all the gravity of a science, and, at the same time, is conducted upon the scale of the most extensive manufacture. In the *Sallon des Etrangers*, the most celebrated haunt of this Dom-Daniel[11], which I had the curiosity to visit, the scene was decent and silent to a degree of solemnity. An immense hall was filled with gamesters and spectators; those who kept the bank, and managed the affairs of the establishment, were distinguished by the green shades which they wore to preserve their eyes, by their silent and grave demeanour, and by the paleness of their countenances, exhausted by constant vigils. There was no distinction of persons, nor any passport required for entrance, save that of a decent exterior; and on the long tables, which were covered with gold, an artizan was at liberty to hazard his week's wages, or a noble his whole estate. Youth and age were alike welcome; and any one who chose to play within the limits of a trifling sum, had only to accuse his own weakness if he was drawn in to deeper or more dangerous hazard. Every thing seemed to be conducted with perfect fairness; and indeed the mechanical construction of the E O tables[12], or whatever they are called, appears calculated to prevent the possibility of fraud. The only advantage possessed by the bank (which is, however, enormous) is the extent of its funds, by which it is enabled to sustain any train of reverse of fortune; whereas most of the individuals who play against the bank are in circumstances to be ruined by the first succession of ill luck; so that ultimately the smaller ventures merge in the stock of the principal adventurers, as rivers run into the sea. The profits of the establishment must indeed be very large to support its expences. Besides a variety of attendants who distribute refreshments to the players gratis, there is an elegant entertainment, with expensive wines, regularly prepared about three o'clock in the morning, for those who choose to partake of it. With such temptations around him, and where the hazarding an insignificant sum seems at first venial or innocent, it is no wonder if thousands feel themselves gradually involved in the whirlpool whose verge is so little distinguishable, until they are swallowed up with their time, talent, and fortune, and often also both body and soul. This is Vice with her fairest vizard; but the same unhallowed precincts contain many a secret cell for the most hideous and unheard-of debaucheries, many an open rendezvous of infamy, and many a den of usury and of treason; the whole mixed with a Vanity-fair of shops for jewels, trinkets, and baubles, that bashfulness may not lack a decent pretext for adventuring into the haunts of infamy. It was here where the preachers of the Revolution first found, amidst gamblers, desperadoes, and prostitutes, ready auditors of their doctrines, and active hands to labour in their vineyard. In more recent times, it was here that the plots of the Buonapartists were adjusted, and the number of their partizans recruited and instructed concerning the progress of the conspiracy; and from hence the seduced soldiers, inflamed with many a bumper to the health of the Exile of Elba, under the mystic names of *Jean de l'Epee*, and *Caporal Violet*, were dismissed to spread the news of his approaching return, and prepare their comrades to desert their lawful sovereign. In short, from this central pit of Acheron,—in which are openly assembled and mingled those characters and occupations which, in all other capitals, are driven to shroud themselves in separate and retired recesses—from this focus of vice and treason have flowed forth those waters of bitterness of which France has drunk so deeply. Why, after having occasioned so much individual and public misery, this source of iniquity is not now stopped, the tenants expelled, and the buildings levelled to the ground, is a question which the consciences of the French ministers can best answer. Thus far at least is certain, that, with the richest soil, and the most cultivated understandings, a people brave even to a fault, kind-tempered, gay, and formed for happiness, have been for twenty years the plague of each other and of Europe; and if their disorders can be plainly traced to want of moral character and principle, it cannot be well to maintain amongst them, for the sake of sharing its polluted profits, such a hot-bed of avowed depravity.

If the French have no strong sense of religion or its precepts, they are not without a share of superstition; and an impostor is at present practising among them, who, by all accounts, is as successful as Joanna Southcote[13] herself. This lady, a woman, I am assured, of rank and information, pretends, like Baron Swedenborg[14], to an immediate intercourse with the spiritual world, and takes her ecstatic trances for the astonishment of parties of good fashion, to whom, on her return to her senses, she recounts the particulars of her visit to the spiritual world, and whom she treats with explanations of their past lives, and predictions of the future. It is said her art has attracted the attention of some men of high rank in the armies of our allies.

If you disbelieve the powers of this lady, you may also distrust the apparition of *l'Homme Rouge*, or the red man, said to have haunted Napoleon as the daemon did Ras Michael, and advised him in matters of importance. He was, saith the legend, a little muffled figure, to whom, whenever he appeared, access was instantly given, for the spectre was courteous enough to request to be announced. At Wilna, before advancing into Russia, while Buonaparte was engaged in tracing the plan of his march, he was told this person requested to speak with him. He desired the attendant to inform his summoner that the Emperor was engaged. When this reply was communicated to the unknown, he assumed an authoritative voice and accent; and, throwing open his cloak, discovered his dress under it, which was red, without mixture of any other colour. 'Tell the Emperor,' said he, 'that *l'Homme Rouge* MUST speak with him.' He was then admitted, and they were heard to talk loud together. As he left the apartment, he said publicly, 'You have rejected my advice! you will not again see me till you have bitterly repented your error.' The visits of *l'Homme Rouge* were renewed on Buonaparte's return from

Elba; but before he set out on his last campaign, Napoleon again offended his familiar, who took leave of him for ever, giving him up to the red men of England, who became the real arbiters of his destiny. If you have not faith enough for this marvellous story, pray respect the prophecy which was made to Josephine, by one of the negroe sooth-sayers in the West Indies, that she should rise to the highest pinnacle of modern greatness, but without ever being a *queen*; that she should fall from thence before her death, and die in an hospital. I can myself vouch for the existence of this prophecy before the events which it was supposed to predict, for it was told me many years ago, when Buonaparte was only general of the army of Italy, by a lady of rank who lived in the same convent with Josephine. The coincidence of the fortune-teller's presages with the fact, would have been marred by the circumstances of the ex-empress's death, had not somebody's ingenuity discovered that her house, as the name *Mal-maison* implies, had once been a hospital. Buonaparte, it is well known, had strange and visionary ideas about his own fated destiny, and could think of fortune like the Wallenstein of the stage. The following lines from that drama, more grand in the translation of Coleridge than in the original of Schiller, seem almost to trace the career of Napoleon:—

> 'Even in his youth he had a daring soul:
> His frame of mind was serious and severe
> Beyond his years; his dreams were of great objects.
> He walk'd amid, as if a silent spirit,
> Communing with himself: Yet have I known him
> Transported on a sudden into utterance
> Of strange conceptions; kindling into splendour,

His soul reveal'd itself, and he spoke so
That we look'd round perplex'd upon each other,
Not knowing whether it were craziness,
Or whether 'twere a God that spoke in him.

Thenceforth he held himself for an exempted
And privileged being, and, as if he were
Incapable of dizziness or fall,
He ran along the unsteady rope of life,
And paced with rapid step the way to greatness;
Was Count, and Prince, Duke Regent, and Dictator,
And is all, all this too little for him;
He stretches forth his hands for a King's crown,
And plunges in unfathomable ruin.'[15]

Farewell, my dear friend; light and leisure are exhausted in this long detail, concerning the religion of which the French have so little, and the superstition of which they have a considerable portion.

You will groan over many parts of this epistle, but the picture is not without its lights. France has afforded many examples, in the most trying crisis, of firmness, of piety, of patience under affliction; many, too, of generosity and courtesy and charity. The present Royal Family have been bred in the school of adversity, and it is generally allowed that they have the inclination, though perhaps they may mistake the means, of ameliorating the character of the nation, to the government of which they have been so providentially restored.

LETTER XVI.

PAUL TO HIS COUSIN PETER.

I am in the centre, you say, of political intelligence, upon the very area where the fate of nations is determined, and send you no intelligence. This seems a severe reproach; for in England, with a friend in the foreign-office, or the advantage of mixing in a certain circle of society, one can always fill up a letter with political events and speculations some days sooner, and somewhat more accurately, than they appear in the newspapers. But they manage matters otherwise in France. The conferences between the ministers of the allied powers and those of Louis XVIII., are conducted with great and praise-worthy secrecy. They are said to be nearly concluded; but a final arrangement will probably be postponed by an expected change of ministry in the Tuilleries.

All politicians were surprised (none more than thou, Peter) at the choice which the king made of his first ministry. That Fouché, who voted for the death of his brother, Louis XVI., who had been an agent of Robespierre and a minister of Buonaparte—who, in the late Revolution, was regarded as a chief promoter of the unexpected and unnatural union between the discontented patriots, or Liberalists, and the followers of Buonaparte,—that he should have been named minister of police under the restored heir of the Bourbons, seemed wonderful to the royalists. His companions in the provisional government saw themselves with equal astonishment put under the *surveillance* of their late associate, in his new character; and the letters between him and Carnot, when the latter applied to Fouché, agreeably to the royal proclamation, that a place of residence might be assigned to him, fully, though briefly, express their characteristic feelings. '*Ou veux tu que ge m'en vais, Traitre?*' signed, CARNOT, was a brief question, to which the minister of police as briefly replied, '*Ou tu veux, Imbecille,*'[1] FOUCHÉ.

There are two ways of considering the matter;—with reference to the minister who accepted the office, and with regard to the sovereign who nominated him.

On the former point little need be said. Times of frequent and hasty changes, when a people are hurried from one government to another, necessarily introduce among the leading statesmen a versatility of character, at which, those who are remote from the pressure of temptation, hold up their hands and wonder. In looking over our own history, we discover the names of Shaftesbury and Sunderland[2], and of many other statesmen eminent for talent, who changed their political creed with the change of times, and yet contrived to be employed and trusted by successive governments who confided in their fidelity, at least while they could make that fidelity their interest. Independent and steady as the English boast themselves, there were, during the great civil war, persons who made it an avowed principle to adhere to the faction that was uppermost, and support the administration of the day, enough to form a separate sect, who, in the hypocritical cant of the times, assumed the name of Waiters upon Providence. This prudential line of conduct has been rendered so general in France, during the late frequent changes of government, as to give matter for a catalogue of about four hundred and fifty pages, which has been recently published, under the name of the *Dictionnaire des Girouettes*[3], in which we find the names of almost all the men distinguished for talents, or influence, now alive in France, with a brief account of the changes of their political lives. The list grew so scandalously comprehensive, that the editor announces his intention of suppressing, in a second edition, all those who had changed only *once*, considering them, comparatively, as men of steady political faith and conscience. They must know little of human nature, who can suppose the result would be otherwise with the mass of mankind in times, when universal example sanctioned changes of principle, which were besides pressed upon each individual by ambition, by avarice, by fear, by want, in short, by their interest under the most pressing and seductive forms. The conduct of Fouché, therefore, is by no means singular; although, if it be true, that, in assuming power under Buonaparte, his real wish was to serve the king, his case merits a particular distinction,—whether favourable or no, may be reasonably doubted.

That Fouché should have accepted power was, therefore, in the order of things, as they have lately gone in France. But, that the king should have trusted, or at least employed him, and that his appointment should have given acknowledged satisfaction to the Duke of Wellington and to Lord Castlereagh[4], thou, Peter, wilt think more difficult to account for. Consider, however, that Fouché was at the head of a numerous faction, comprehending the greater part of that third party in the state, which, as uniting all shades of those who use the word Liberty as their war-cry, are generally called Liberalists. If these were divided from the king in the moment of his return, what remained to him save the swords of a few nobles and men of honour, the scattered and subdued bands of La Vendée, and the inert wishes of the mass of the population, who might indeed cry *Vive le Roi*, but had plainly shewed they loved their own barns better than the house of Bourbon. The bayonets of the allies, indeed, surrounded Paris, but Buonaparte was still in France and at large, the army of the Loire continued independent and unbroken, many garrisons held out, many provinces were still agitated; and the services of Fouché, who held in his hand the various threads of correspondence through the distracted kingdom, who knew the character and principles of each agitator, and the nature of the materials he had to work with, who possessed, in short, that extent of local and personal knowledge peculiar to one who had been long the head of the French police, were essentially necessary to the establishment of the royal authority, and to preventing a scene of blood and total confusion. That Fouché served the king with great address, cannot be doubted, and his admission into the high office of trust, which he has for some time enjoyed, was a great means of calming the public mind, and restoring to confidence those, who, feeling themselves involved in the general defection, might otherwise have been rendered desperate by the fear of punishment. Talleyrand[5], also, whose loyalty to the house of Bourbon, during the last usurpation, was never doubted, is understood to have expressed his strong sense of the peremptory necessity of receiving Fouché and his party into power at least, if not into confidence. So much, therefore, for the propriety, or rather necessity, of a measure, which looked strange enough when viewed from a distance, which could not be agreeable to the king personally, and which had its political inconveniences; but, nevertheless, was at the time essential to the royal interest. The first benefit which resulted from this appointment was the close and vigilant pursuit that compelled Napoleon to surrender to the English. The same activity exercised by this experienced politician and his agents, decided and secured a bloodless counter-revolution in most of the towns in France. Upon the general interests of Europe, Fouché is well understood to have entertained such just and moderate views as were acceptable to the ministers of the allied powers, and particularly to those of Britain.

Notwithstanding these advantages, it is not supposed that Fouché will keep his ground in the ministry, and it is supposed the change will occasion the resignation of Talleyrand. As the king's party appears better consolidated, and his power becomes more permanent, the faction of the *Royalistes purs et par excellence*[6] acquires members and courage, and becomes daily more shocked with the incongruity of Fouché's high place in the administration. His influence is supposed to have one effect, which, if true, is a very bad one—that, namely, of delaying the selecting and bringing to punishment the more notorious agents of the last usurpation. All who know this nation must be aware of what importance it is that their ruler should not seem to fear them; and the king must be aware that his authority will seem little more than an idle pageant till he shall show he is possessed of the power of maintaining it. On the other hand, nothing can be more impolitic than to keep up the memory of this brief usurpation, and the insecure and jealous feelings of all connected with it, by long hesitation on the choice of victims to the offended laws. The sooner that two or three principal criminals can be executed, some dangerous agitators banished, and a general amnesty extended to all the rest,[7] without exception, the sooner and the firmer will the royal authority be established. We have as yet had only one example of severity in the fate of Labedoyere, although no good reason can be given why others of superior consequence, such as Ney and Massena, should not share his fate. But the death of this comparatively subordinate agent has acted as a sedative upon the spirit of faction. Last week nothing was heard but threats and defiance, and bold declarations, that the government would not, and dared not, execute the sentence. The rights of the Bourbons seemed to have been so long in *abeyance*, that it was thought scarce possible to be guilty of treason against them, or that they should dare to regard and punish it as such. This is a popular feeling which the king must remove by a display of firmness, or it will most assuredly once more remove his throne. Accordingly the execution of this criminal has had some effect, and the tone of mutiny and defiance is greatly lowered. The handsome sufferer, however, finds the usual degree of favour in the eyes of the fair. One lady talked of his execution as *un horreur*, an atrocity unequalled in the annals of France.—'Did Buonaparte never order such executions?'—'Who? the Emperor?—never.'—'But the Duc d'Enghien[8], madam?' continued the persevering querist.—'*Ah! parlez moi d'Adam et d'Eve*,' was the reply. A retrospective of three or four years was like looking back to the fall of man; and the exclamation affords no bad key to the French character, to whom the past is nothing, and the present every thing.

The attacks upon Fouché in our English newspapers are said to have no small share in unsettling his power, by seeming to express the opinion of our nation against him. I have great reason to doubt whether his successor may not be appointed out of a class to whom we are, as a nation, less acceptable. For, with a few exceptions, I do not think that the English are so much disliked, even by the military men and Imperialists, as they are by the nobility and pure royalists. This class of politicians, whatever may be thought of their bias to despotism, numbers among them so much of high honourable feeling and sincere principle, that I willingly look for some apology for their entertaining sentiments towards England and Englishmen, which, to say the least, are an indifferent requital for our former hospitality and our late effective assistance. I will, therefore, make every allowance for the natural prejudice which they entertain against us for having, as they may conceive, stopped short in the services which it was in our power to have rendered them, and declined to back their pretensions to complete restoration of the rights and property which they had forfeited in the king's cause. I will permit them to feel as Frenchmen as well as royalists, and to view, with a mingled feeling, the victory of Waterloo and the capture of Paris, although their own interest and that of the king was immediately dependent on the success of the allies. I can suppose, that it is painful for them to see foreigners residing at Paris as lords of the ascendant; and it may be a laudable sensibility to the misfortunes of their country, which makes them at this moment retreat from the duties of hospitality, and shun mixing in society with those whose best blood has been so recently shed in the king's service. I can even forgive them, that, being conscious of their weakness in point of numbers and influence (unless through that of the sovereign), they are glad to snatch opportunities of making common cause with the bulk of their countrymen at the expence of foreigners, and are therefore fain to lead the cry against the allies, and especially against our country, in order to show, that whatever may be their interests, their hearts have always been French. But while we pardon the motives, we must be allowed to smile at the effects of this animosity. One would almost suppose while hearing them, that our interference in the affairs of France was altogether gratuitous and unnecessary, and had only prevented a grand *re-action*, by which Napoleon would have been walked out of the kingdom as he had walked into it, and a counter-revolution accomplished, as nearly resembling that which concludes the Rehearsal, as the last revolution seemed in ease and celerity to rival that of King Phys. and King Ush.[9] in the same drama. They even extol the conduct of those commandants upon the frontier, who, in defiance of their sovereign's mandate, and with a brutal indifference to human life, maintain, without motive, or means, or hope, a senseless opposition to the allied troops. Some of them have been honourably acquitted when brought to trial; all are praised and caressed, as having maintained the frontiers of France against foreigners, instead of being shot or degraded for the bloodshed occasioned by their resistance both to their country and to the king's allies. Upon the same principle, I suppose the governor of Vincennes, who still holds out his old Donjon, is to be considered as a true patriot, although he, and those who think like him, have no object in view but to show a reckless and unavailing resistance to their victors. In one of the king's proclamations[10] to his subjects on his restoration, he has been made to take credit, that not one of his own followers had been permitted to draw a sword in defence of his rights, &c. If the state of the royal army was indeed justly rated at twenty-four thousand men and forty pieces of cannon, as given in an order of the day signed by the Duke of Feltre, on 7th April 1815, we may justly complain of the mistaken tenderness which withheld such a force from the conflict, and demand of the King of

France a reckoning for the lives of forty thousand brave men killed in his quarrel, many of whom might have been saved by such a reinforcement. But if the attendants of the king consisted chiefly of a few hundred officers and gardes de corps, to whom the timely arrival of *cinq Cent Suisses* (that is, not five hundred Swiss, as a sanguine Englishman was led to interpret the phrase, from the pleasure with which he heard the incident detailed, but five individuals of the corps called *les Cent Suisses,*) was hailed as a timely reinforcement, it should be considered, that, since the days of chivalry are ended, and since no single knight can now rout a legion of cuirassiers with his own good sword, the king must have owed his restoration to Wellington and Blucher; and those who only walked forward in the path which our swords hewed out for them ought to bear with some patience the measures to which their own proved weakness, and the experienced art and strength of their powerful adversaries, compel us to have recourse. It was, I think, Edward I., who replied with scorn to a competitor for the Scottish crown, in whose cause he had invaded Scotland, when, after the victory at Dunbar,[11] he ventured to remind him of his pretensions, *Ne avons nous autre chose a faire que a vous reaumeys gagner?** Such an answer we might have returned to Louis XVIII., had we inclined to support any other competitor among the ample choice which the provisional government held out to us; and although we claim no merit for following the open path of faith and loyalty to an unfortunate ally, we ought at least to escape the censure of those who have been most benefited by our exertions, and who confessedly were unable or unwilling to assist themselves.

* *i.e.* 'Have we nothing to do but to conquer kingdoms for you?'

In the meanwhile, if it is meant to confine the king's choice of ministers to the faction of *royalistes purs*, we are afraid his choice will be limited; for, excepting a few individuals who have been employed in Russia, where strangers are more readily promoted to offices of confidence than elsewhere, we know few who have had the means of acquiring experience in state business. Brave, loyal, and gallant, the French noblesse are by their charter; but the heat of temper which confounds friends and foes; the presumption which pushes direct to its object without calculation of obstacles; a sense of wrongs received, and a desire of vengeance, make them dangerous counsellors at such a crisis as the present.

From the more violent portion of the opposite faction, (inclusive of the Imperialists, who are now hastily melting into the ranks of the general opposition,) the king can, I fear, look for little cordiality, and only for that degree of support which he can make it their interest to afford him. Still, however, there are many cases where ability without principle may be successfully employed, when it would be unsafe to trust to principle unguided by experience and prudence; just as a proprietor will sometimes find it his interest to employ, in the management of his affairs, a skilful knave rather than an honest fool. This is taking an extreme case: there are many degrees between a *jacobin enragé* and a *royaliste pur*, and some of the wisest and best of each party will perhaps at length see the necessity of joining in an administration exclusive of neither, which should have at once for its object the just rights of the throne, and the constitutional liberties of the subject. To such a coalition, the king's name would be, indeed, a tower of strength; but founded upon a narrower basis, must run the risque of falling itself, and bearing to ground all who adhere to it.

It must be owned, nevertheless, that the general rallying point of the *Liberalists* is an avowed dislike to the present monarch and his immediate connections. They will sacrifice, they pretend, so much to the general inclinations of Europe, as to select a king from the Bourbon race; but he must be one of their own chusing, and the Duke of Orleans is most familiar to their mouths. And thus these politicians, who assume the title of *Constitutional Royalists*, propose to begin their career by destroying hereditary succession, the fundamental principle of a limited monarchy. In Britain, we know that the hereditary right of succession is no longer indeed accounted divine and indefeasible, as was the principle of *our* ancient *royalistes purs et par excellence*. But the most sturdy whig never contended that it could be defeated otherwise than by abdication or forfeiture, or proposed the tremendous measure of changing the succession purely by way of prevention or experiment. In the most violent times, and under the most peculiar circumstances, the Exclusion Bill[12], although founded upon an acknowledged and plausible ground of incapability, and levelled against the person of a successor, not of an existing monarch, was rejected as a dangerous innovation on the constitution. It is in order to prevent, as far as possible, such violent and hazardous experiments, that we impute the faults of monarchs not to themselves, but to their ministers, and view, in a political sense, the well-known maxim, that the king can do no wrong. For the same reason, in the height of popular indignation against James II., the word *abdication* was selected in preference to *desertion* or *forfeiture*, to express the manner in which the throne became vacant at the Revolution. But the doctrine now held in France strikes at the very foundation of hereditary right, being founded on no overt act of the sovereign tending to affect the liberties of his subjects, but upon jealousies and fears that he has, or may call, evil counsellors around him, who, at some time or other, will persuade him to attempt the re-establishment of the feudal rights of the nobility and the domination of the church. In this grand counterpart to our constitutional maxim, it is not even alleged that the king *has* done wrong, but it is assumed that he *will* do wrong, and proceedings are to be grounded on this prediction as if the evil foreseen already existed. The fact seems to be, that the objections of this faction to the present line is much more a matter of taste or caprice than they are willing to acknowledge. The vanity of the nation, and especially of this class of statesmen, who have not the least share of it, is affronted at being compelled to receive back from the conquering hand of the allies the legitimate monarch, in whose causeless expulsion they had assisted. They would willingly have had a bit of sugar with the wholesome physic which was forced upon them by English and Prussian bayonets, and they still long for something which may give them an ostensible pretext to say, that their own conduct had not been entirely inconsistent, nor their rebellion altogether fruitless. Hence the obstinacy of Buonaparte's two chambers to the very last, in rejecting Louis XVIII. Hence the nicknames of *Le Prefet de l'Angleterre*, and Louis *l'Inevitable*, which their wit attached to the restored monarch; and to this feeling of mortified vanity, less than to any real fears of aggression upon their liberties, may be traced their wish to have a king whose title should be connected with the Revolution, and who might owe his crown more to their courtesy than to his own right. But who will warrant those that set such a dangerous stone rolling, where its course will stop? The body now united in one mass of opposition to the *royalistes purs* comprehend among themselves a hundred various shades of difference, from the Constitutionalist of 1814 to the Republican of 1793, or the Imperialists of Buonaparte's time. It happened regularly in the French revolution, that so soon as one point was gained or yielded, which the popular party represented as an ultimatum, new demands were set up by demagogues, who affected to plead still higher doctrines of freedom than those with which their predecessors had remained satisfied; the force of those who had been satisfied with the concessions being uniformly found insufficient to defend the breach they themselves had stormed, until all merged in anarchy, and anarchy itself in military tyranny. We have seen already the progress of an Orleans faction, as well as its fatal termination. We have no desire to give another whirl to the revolutionary E O table, or once more to shuffle the cards for the chance of turning up such trumps as will best suit the political gamblers of the Palais Royale.

Besides these two violent parties, one of which aims to restore the abrogated tyranny of priests and seigneurs, and the other to render a hereditary monarchy an elective one at a sweep, there are two classes of great importance, namely, the army and the mass of the people. Much must undoubtedly depend on the disposition of the former, which has been for some time accustomed to act as a deliberative body, and which, however mutilated and disjoined, will, like the several portions of a snake, continue long to writhe under the same impulses by which it was agitated when entire. Every effort is now making to place this formidable engine in the hands of the crown, by the dissolution and new-formation of the regiments, by recruits, and by the addition of separate corps, levied in the places most attached to the royal interest. But this is, in a great measure, counteracted by the insane policy which, as we have already noticed, applauds in military men the very conduct that indicates, as in the case of Huningen[13], and other places defended after the king's restoration, an opposition to his mandates; and if bravery alone shall be accounted a sufficient apology for rebellion, the French government will certainly have enough of both. Were a breach, therefore, to take place at this moment between the King and the Constitutionalists, I have little doubt that great part of the army would take part with the latter, though perhaps more out of pique than principle. The Royalists, with all their vehemence in words, have already shewn how infinitely inferior they are to the opposite party in intrigue, as well as in audacity; and discontented soldiers may be seduced to declare for a change of dynasty, or for a republic, as readily as for a Buonaparte. Besides, distant and secure as is Napoleon's present place of exile,[14] we have but scotched the snake, not killed him;[15] and while life lasts, especially after his extraordinary return from Elba, there will not be wanting many to rely upon a third *avatar* of this singular emanation of the Evil Principle. This is an additional and powerful reason for the king to avoid, in thought, act, and deed, the slightest innovation on the liberties of his subjects as ascertained by the constitutional charter, as certain to provoke a contest in which he would prove inferior.

If you ask me, then, what are the legitimate resources of this unfortunate monarch, placed between the extremes of two violent factions, I would answer, that, under God, I conceive them to rest upon the good-will of the mass of the people of France. The agitators and intriguers of both parties bear an exceedingly small proportion to the numbers of those who only desire peace, tranquillity, and the enjoyment of the fruits of their industry, under a mild and steady government. With this class of people Louis XVIII. is deservedly popular; their tears attended his expulsion, and their rejoicings his return.[16] It is true that this general feeling of good-will and affection was not strong enough to bring them to the field, though it threw great obstacles in the way of the usurper. But it is also true, that this class of Loyalists were taken totally at unawares, and became only apprized of their danger when it was too late to take measures for encountering a veteran army, masters of all the fortresses in the kingdom. The general class of proprietors are also (for the present) disheartened, drained of the young and active spirits whom Buonaparte sacrificed in his wars, rendered callous by habit to the various changes of government, and more passive under each than it is possible for Englishmen to comprehend. But there is very generally among the middling orders in France, and among all, indeed, who are above the lowest vulgar, a kind and affectionate feeling towards the king, well deserved by his mild and paternal character, and which further experience of the blessings of peace, and of a settled government, will kindle into zealous attachment. The best policy of the monarch is, to repress the ardent tempers of the clergy and nobles; to teach them that their real interest depends upon the crown; and that they will themselves be the first sufferers, if they give pretext for a new attack upon the Bourbons, by setting up pretensions equally antiquated and ill adapted with a free government. At the same time it may be necessary for the king, by exhibiting vigour and decision in his measures, to convince the more violent of the opposite faction that they cannot renew their attempts against the throne with the facility and impunity which heretofore have attended them. The very violence with which these parties oppose each other affords the king the means of mediating betwixt both. Let the people at length see clearly that the king desires no more than his own share in the constitution, but that he stands prepared to defend his own rights, as well as theirs. It may, perhaps, take some time to awaken the indifferent from that palsy of the mind which we have alluded to, and to put to rest the jealous fears of the proprietors of national property. But good faith and persevering steadiness on the part of the crown may accomplish both, and with these fears will subside the hopes entertained by those who delight in change; revolution will become difficult in proportion as its chance of success shall disappear; the ardent spirits who have frequented its dangerous paths will seek more pacific avenues to wealth and distinction; and from being her own plague and the terror of her neighbours, France may again be happy in herself, and the most graceful ornament of the European commonwealth.

Upon the subject of awakening France to her true interests, use might surely be made of the principle uppermost in the heart of every Frenchman, and which is capable of guiding him to much good or evil, the interest, namely, which high and low take in the glory of their country. Through the abuse of this sentiment, (noble in itself, because disinterested,) Napoleon was enabled to consolidate his usurped government in such a manner that it required all his own rashness to undermine it. Did the people ask for bread?—he showed them a temple. Did they require of him the blood of their children?—he detailed to them a victory,—and they retired, satisfied that, if they suffered or wept, France had been rendered illustrious and victorious. It cannot be, that so strong and disinterested a sentiment should be applicable to evil purposes alone; nor do I believe the French so void of reflection or common sense, as not to be made capable, by experience, of valuing themselves as much upon personal freedom, an equal system of laws, a flourishing state of finance, good faith to other nations, and those moral qualities which equally adorn a people and individuals, as they now esteem their country decorated by an unnecessary palace, or by a bloody and fruitless victory. It is true, that the reformation must begin where the corruption was first infused, and that, although converts may be gained gradually to the cause of sound reason, yet we must necessarily be obliged to wait the effects of a better education upon the rising race, before real and genuine patriotism can be generally substituted for what is at present merely national vanity.

This appetite for glory has of late been fed with such unsubstantial food, as has apparently rendered the French indifferent to the distinction betwixt what is unreal and what is solid. Any thing connected with show and splendour,—any thing, as Bayes says, calculated to surprise and elevate, is what they expect from their governors, as regularly as the children of London expect a new pantomime at Christmas. Buonaparte contrived to drown the murmurs which attended his return to Paris, in the universal speculation which he excited by announcing his purpose of holding a *Champ de Mai*, which is much the same as if William III. had paved the way to the throne by summoning a *Wittenagemot*[17]. In England, some would have thought the Prince of Orange had lost his senses, and some, that he was speaking Dutch. But all in England knew the meaning of a National Convention, the denomination by which William distinguished the assembly which he convoked. In Paris, it was exactly the contrary—the people did not want to see a national convention, or a national assembly either—they knew, like Costard, 'whereuntill that did amount;'[18] but the Champ de Mai was something new, something not easily comprehended; and it would have been a motive with many against expelling Buonaparte prematurely, that they would have lost the sight of the Champ de Mai. And thus they sacrificed their good sense to their curiosity, and showed their minds were more bent on the form of the assembly than on its end and purposes. After all, the *fete* was indifferently got up, and gave little satisfaction, notwithstanding the plumes and trains of the principal actors. But still it had its use. The Bourbons have been compelled also to sacrifice to this idol; and the king is himself obliged, contrary to his own good sense and taste, to conform to this passion for theatrical effect. A man was condemned to death, to whom it had been resolved to extend the royal pardon, and the king imagined, *tout bonnement*, that he had nothing to do but issue one from his chancery. But no—that would have been to defraud the public of their share in the scene. So he was advised to go (by pure accident) in the course of his evening drive, into some remote corner of the city, where he was to meet (also accidentally) with the municipality, who were to fall on their knees, and beg mercy for this delinquent, which the king was then to grant with characteristic grace and bounty, and all the by-standers were to shout *Vive le Roi*. It must not be supposed that a nation, so shrewd and ingenious as the French, are really blinded by these exhibitions *got up* for their amusement. But they are entertained for the time, and are no more disgusted with the want of reality in the drama, than with the trees upon the stage for being made of pasteboard. They consider the accompaniments as of more importance than the real object of the representation, and fall under the censure due to Prior's

———— idle dreamer,
Who leaves the pye to gnaw the streamer.[19]

To reclaim hawks which have been accustomed to so wild a flight, requires all the address of a falconer. Yet there is at the bottom a strong fund of disinterested patriotism to work upon; for who will deny its existence to a people, the bulk of whom have, on all occasions, thought always of the nation, and never of themselves individually? Should, therefore, the present king meet with a minister calculated, like Fabius[20], to arrest immediate dangers, and protract or evade angry discussions, until such a long train of quiet shall have elapsed, that men's minds have become estranged from all ideas of force and violence, he may, even in his own time, lay such a foundation of a better system, as will lead future Frenchmen to place their pride less in vain parade or military glory, than in the freedom, arts, and happiness of France.

The approaching meeting of the National Representatives[21], if they meet, as the time so peremptorily demands, in the spirit, not of partizans, but of conciliators, may do much to accelerate so desirable an issue. But it is too much to be feared, that it will be found very difficult to assemble such a body of representatives, as may be justly considered as the organ of the nation. Could such a senate be convoked,

we should hear on every side the language of peace and
moderation, nor would the debates be warmer or more
obstinate, than is necessary for elucidation of the measures
proposed. Such an assembly, in the name of the proprietors
of France, would deprecate the senseless agitation of
theoretical questions, would recommend brief sentence on
a limited and narrow selection of the principal agents of the
last usurpation, whose fate seems essential to the vindication
of justice, and the intimidation of the disaffected; and when
that painful duty was executed, would proceed with joy
to the more agreeable task of promulgating such a general
amnesty as should throw a perpetual veil over the crimes
and errors of that unhappy period. I might add, that such
a senate would proceed by secret committees to tent the
wounds of the country, to turn their attention towards
the state of religion and morals, and to ensure the means
of bringing up the rising generation, at least, free from
the errors of their fathers. In their adjustment of foreign
relations, such a council of state would recollect, that if
the country had suffered reiterated humiliation, it was in
consequence of reiterated aggression; and, avoiding painful
and irritating discussions concerning the past, they would
offer by such moderation the surest guarantee for peace
and amity in future. Such would be the language of the
representatives of the people, did they really speak the sense
of the proprietors of France—not that those proprietors are
sufficiently enlightened to recommend the special measures
for attaining peace and tranquillity, but because they are
sighing for that state of good order to which the measures
of an enlightened representation ought to conduct them.
But I have doubts whether this calm and wise course can be
expected from the senators to be shortly assembled, since we

hear of nothing on all sides but the exertions made by the two political factions of Royalists and Liberalists to procure returns of their own partizans. We must, therefore, prepare to witness a warm, and, perhaps, a deadly war waged between two contending parties, of which one proposes a complete re-action and restoration of things, as they stood in the reign of Louis XV., with the advantages perhaps of new confiscations to avenge those by which they were themselves ruined, and the other proposing a gratuitous and uncalled-for alteration of the laws of succession, while each is content to hazard in the attempt a renewal of the horrors of the Revolution.

You may wonder that a spirit should be expected to prevail among the representatives so different from that of the mass of the people by whom they are chosen. The cause seems to be, that those gradations, not of rank only, but of education, intelligence, and habits of thinking upon political men and measures, which enable Englishmen both to chuse representatives, and to watch their conduct when chosen, cannot at present be said to exist in France. Those who propose themselves as candidates are men altogether distinct in their habits of thinking from the voters whom they are to represent. They are considered as politicians by profession, as men belonging to a class entitled exclusively to be chosen, and who, when chosen, relieve their electors from all further trouble in watching or directing their political conduct. The electors may assemble in their organic colleges, and may give their suffrages to a candidate for the Chamber of Representatives; but it will be in the same manner as they might chuse a person to repair the town-clock, when almost all the voters are ignorant of the means which the artist is to adopt for its regulation, and probably some of them cannot tell the hour by the dial-plate when the machine is put in order. On the contrary, the class in England upon whom the election of parliament devolves, is trained to their task by long habit, by being freeholders, members of common councils, vestries, and other public bodies, or by hearing business of a public nature discussed upon all occasions, whether of business or pleasure, and are thereby habituated to consider themselves as members of the body politic. Though, therefore, many may be seduced by interest, biassed by influence, or deluded by prejudice, there will be found among the mass of the British electors, taken generally over the kingdom, a capacity of judging of the fitness of their representatives, a distinct power of observing with attention their conduct in their high office; and they possess means also, collectively speaking, of making their own opinion heard and respected, when there is pressing occasion for it.

I do not mention this difference between the inhabitants of the two countries, as a reason for refusing to France the benefits of a free representation, but to shew, that, for some time at least, it cannot have the salutary effect upon the political horizon of that country which arises from the like institution in our own, where there exists an intimate and graduated connection between the representative and electors, a general diffusion of political knowledge, and a systematic gradation from the member of parliament to the lowest freeholder;—where, in short, there is a common feeling between the representative and his constituent, the one knowing the nature of the power delegated, as well as the other does that which he receives, and both, though differing in extent of information, having something like common views upon the same subject. It may be long ere this general diffusion of political information takes place in France, It will, however, follow, if time is allowed for it, by years of peace, and of that good order which promotes quiet and general discussion of political rights. A freeholder, who suffered free-quarters from pandours[22] and cossacks twice in one year, has scarce tranquillity of mind sufficient to attend to theoretical privileges and maxims of state. But if called upon repeatedly to exercise his right of suffrage, he will gradually begin to comprehend the meaning of it, and to interest himself in the conduct of the representative to whom he gives his voice. Thus, as freemen make a free constitution, so a free constitution, if not innovated upon, and rendered ineffectual, will in time create a general and wholesome freedom of spirit amongst those who have to exercise the privileges which it bestows. Did such a general feeling now exist in France, we should not have to apprehend the desperate results which may attend the struggle of two parties only intent upon their own factious interests—a nobility and clergy, on the one hand, eager to resume privileges inconsistent with general freedom, and on the other, a factious oligarchy of considerable talent and little principle, prepared to run the race of the Brissotins[23] in 1792, and to encounter all the risques with which it was proved to be attended.

To the dangers of this collision of steel and flint, is to be added that which arises from the quantity of tinder and touch-wood, which lies scattered around to catch and foster every spark of fire;—an army dishonoured and discontented, bands of royalists, half-organized soldiers, half-voluntary partizans, thousands whom Buonaparte had employed in his extended system of espionage and commercial regulation; hundreds, also, of a higher class, selected generally for talent, activity, and lack of principle, who have now lost their various posts, as Mauris, Prefets, Sous-prefets, Commis, and so forth—all of whom would find their interest in a civil war. And what will restrain the factious from pushing the crisis to this extremity? Only a jealous fear of the allies, whose occupation of the fortresses in the north of France will, in that case, prove her best security; or perhaps the slender chance, that the members of the representation may be wise enough to sacrifice their mutual feuds to the general weal, and remember that they are summoned to wage their contest with the arms of courtesy, and not to push political debate into revolutionary frenzy. I leave them, therefore, with a sincere wish that they may not forget, in the vehemence of their internal dissensions, the duty which they owe to abstracted public, which they may at pleasure involve in a civil war by their mutual violence, or save from that dreadful crisis by their temper and moderation.

You must not expect from me any general view of French manners, or habits of society; and it is the less necessary, as you will find ample means of forming your judgment in the very spirited and acute work of Mr John Scott[24], published during the preceding year. I am inclined to think, that while he has touched the French vices and follies with enough of severity, he may not in some instances have done full justice to the gallant, amiable, and lively disposition, by which, in spite of an execrable education, and worse government, that people are still widely distinguished from other nations on the continent. But the ingenious author had prescience enough to discover the latent danger of the royal government of 1814, when it was disguised and disowned by the members of that government themselves;

nor has he in these affairs omitted an opportunity to plead the cause of freedom, religion, and morality, against that of tyranny, infidelity, and licentiousness. I ought also to mention the travels in France in the years 1814–15, the joint production of two young gentlemen,[25] whose taste for literature is hereditary; and I am informed, that another ingenious friend, (Mr S——n of Edinburgh[26]) whose extreme assiduity in collecting information cannot fail to render his journal interesting, intends to give it to the public. To such works I may safely refer you for an ample description of Paris, its environs, public places, and state of manners.

I should willingly have endeavoured to form my own views of the state of French society, as well as of their politics; but the time has been altogether unfavourable, as the persons of fashion in Paris have either retired to the country, or live in strict seclusion from foreigners, upon principles which it is impossible not to respect. The strangers, therefore, who now occupy this capital, form a class altogether distinct from the native inhabitants, and seek for society among each other. It was very different, I am told, upon the former entry of the allied troops, which for some time the Parisians regarded more as a pacification than a conquest. The Russian and Prussian officers were then eagerly sought after, and caressed by the French nobility; and the allied monarchs, on entering the Parisian theatres, were received with the same honours as in their own. But this is all over. The last cast was too absolute for victory or ruin, and the dye has turned up against France. One class of Frenchmen lament the event of the war as a national misfortune; and even those who have the advantage of it, feel that, in its cause, progress, and conclusion, it will be

recorded as a national disgrace. 'You own yourself,' said
I to a lively French friend[27], a great anti-imperialist, as he
writhed his face and shrugged when he passed a foreign
officer, 'you own yourself, that they only treated your
countrymen as they have merited.'—'Very true—and the
man that is hanged has no more than his deserts—but I
don't like to look at the hangman.'

Amid this dereliction, you must not suppose that we
sojourners in Paris suffer solitude for want of good society.
The extended hospitality of the Duke of Wellington, and of
Lord and Lady Castlereagh, has afforded rallying points to
the numerous English strangers, who have an opportunity
of meeting, in their parties, with almost all the owners of
those distinguished names, which for three years past have
filled the trumpet of fame. Our minister, whose name will
be read with distinction in this proud page of our annals,
and to whose determined steadiness in council much of the
success of 1814 is unquestionably due, occupies the palace
of Pauline Borghese, now that of the British embassy. The
Duke of Wellington lives in a large hotel at the corner of
the Rue des Champs Elysees, furnished most elaborately
by some wealthy courtier of Napoleon. Among its chief
ornaments, is a very fine picture of the ex-emperor, and a
most excellent bust[28] of the same personage. It is a thing to
remember, that I have seen in that hotel, so ornamented,
the greatest and the bravest whom Europe can send forth
from Petersburgh to Cadiz, assembled upon the invitation
of the British General, and yielding to him, by general
assent, the palm of military pre-eminence. In mentioning
those whose attentions rendered the residence of the British
at Paris pleasant and interesting, I ought not to forget Lord
Cathcart, whose situation as ambassador to the Russian

court gave him opportunities of gratifying the curiosity of his countrymen, by presenting them to the emperor, who has of late played such a distinguished part in European history, and by making them known to such men as Barclay de Tolli, Platow, Czernicheff, and other heroes of Kalouga and Beresina,[29] where the spear of the mighty was first broken. Besides the notice of these public characters, my stay in Paris was made happy by the society of many friends, both in the civil and military departments. You know my inherent partiality for the latter class, when they add gentle manners and good information to the character of their profession; and I can assure you, that as there never was a period when our soldiers were more respected for discipline and bravery, so the character of the British officers for gallantry and humanity, for general information, and for the breeding of gentlemen, never stood higher than at the capture of Paris. In such society, whatever secret discontents might in reality exist, Paris was to us like a frozen lake, over whose secret and fathomless gulphs we could glide without danger or apprehension; and I shall always number the weeks I have spent here among the happiest of my life.

In a short time, it is imagined, the greater part of the foreign troops will be withdrawn towards their own countries, or the fortresses they are to occupy in guarantee. It will then be seen whether the good intentions of the king, and the general desire of the country for peace, will be sufficient to maintain the public tranquillity of France amid the collision of so many angry passions; and there will, at the worst, remain this consolation, that if this restless people should draw the sword upon each other, effectual precautions have been taken by the allies to prevent them from again disturbing the peace of Europe.

With the hope of speedily rejoining the beloved circle round the fire-side, and acting, in virtue of my travelled experience, the referee in all political disputes, I am ever your affectionate friend,

PAUL.

Notes to *Paul's Letters to His Kinsfolk*

Walter Scott could never resist peppering his prose with often unattributed references and quotations from the works of others. *Paul's Letters to His Kinsfolk* is no exception and includes one untranslated passage in Attic Greek, a language Scott himself admitted he was no master of. In the following notes I have attempted to supply author and source to all sixty-odd of these quotations and references, together with translations where necessary. All but the most obvious foreign and dialect words and phrases have been translated. The full names and dates of people mentioned in the text, together with explanations of contemporary, historical and other references that may no longer be as familiar, after two hundred years, as they were to the author and to his first readers, have also been supplied.

LETTER I: PAUL TO HIS SISTER MARGARET

1 *Seventhly*: refers to a head, or topic, of a sermon.
2 *gowans*: daisies.
3 **Merchant Abudah**: see *Tales of the Genii*, an oriental

pastiche published in 1764 by James Kenneth Ridley (1736–1765) writing as 'Sir Charles Morell'. The protagonist of the first tale, a wealthy merchant, is given a priceless talisman contained in a chest, which, despite his possessing the fifty keys to its fifty locks, proves impossible to open.

4   **Young Norval . . . tutor the Hermit:** see John Home (1722–1808), *Douglas*, a verse tragedy first performed 1756. It was based on a broadside ballad that began with the lines: 'My name is Norval. On the Grampian Hills / My father feeds his flocks; a frugal swain; / Whose constant cares were to increase his store, / And keep his only son, myself, at home. / For I have heard of battles, and I long'd / To follow to the field some warlike lord . . .'

5   *Tamen excute nullum*: see Ovid, *Ars Amatoria*, Book I, line 151, *Et si nullus erit pulvis, tamen excute nullum* – 'And if [no dust] fall, flick none off'.

6   **'too much of water had I, poor Ophelia':** see Shakespeare, *Hamlet*, Act IV, Scene VII.

7   **the principal street of our northern capital:** Princes Street, Edinburgh.

LETTER II: PAUL TO HIS COUSIN THE MAJOR

1   **Bergen-op-Zoom:** besieged by the French in 1747 during the War of the Austrian Succession and Paul refers to the Major as having assisted in its defence on that occasion.

2   **Coehorn:** Menno, Baron van Coehoorn (1641–1704), known as 'the Dutch Vauban' after his celebrated French contemporary and rival.

3   **The tower . . . mountain green:** see Thomas

Campbell (1777–1844), *Gertrude of Wyoming*, part III, verse xxv.

4 **As maids . . . puppy-dogs**: see Shakespeare, *King John*, Act II, Scene I.

5 **Lord Lyndoch**: Bergen-op-Zoom was the scene of a disastrous British defeat by the French on 8 May 1814. Sir Thomas Graham, 1st Baron Lynedoch, commanded an attack on the town which was driven off with the loss of four colours, and 2,100 out of 4,000 men.

6 **The fate of a Dutch officer . . . wounds he had received**: in later editions Scott attached the following note: 'I have since been informed, from unquestionable authority, that this officer was not ill-treated by the French. It is remarkable, that he had personally ventured into the town to ascertain the possibility of success, the day before the attack was made.'

7 **WER DA**: phonetic transcription of the Dutch phrase *wie er daar*: 'who goes there?'

8 **Fontenoy**: an action, 11 May 1745, in the War of the Austrian Succession, which resulted in a decisive defeat of Anglo-Dutch and Hanoverian forces by Louis XV's French.

LETTER III: PAUL TO HIS COUSIN PETER

1 **So though the Chemist . . . by the way**: see Abraham Coley (1618–1628), *The Mistress*, part 62, 'The Maidenhead', verse 4.

2 **Ormond and Clarendon**: James Butler, 1st Duke of Ormonde (1610–1688) and Edward Hyde, 1st Earl of Clarendon (1609–1674).

3 **Sir Charles Wogan**: (*c*.1685–1754) a Jacobite soldier, adventurer and man of letters. For a time he was a

favourite at the court of King Philip V in Madrid, from where he sent Spanish wine to Jonathan Swift in exchange for books.

4 **'By well-tried faith . . . holy ties'**: see Joseph Addison (1672–1719), *The Campaign: a poem, to His Grace the Duke of Marlborough* (1704), written to commemorate the Battle of Blenheim of that year.

5 **as of Ilion, *Intra maenia peccatur, et extra***: see Epistle 2 of Horace, *Iliacos intra muros peccatur et extra* – 'There is sin among the Trojan walls and beyond'.

6 **Cardinal Fesch**: Joseph Fesch (1763–1839), Prince of France, cardinal and diplomat, uncle of Napoleon Bonaparte.

7 *A bas la calotte!*: literally 'Down with the skullcap' (synecdochically: priest)

8 **Comte D'Artois**: Charles Philippe (1757–1836), younger brother of Louis XVI and Louis XVIII, was crowned King Charles X of France in 1824 and reigned until his abdication following the July Revolution of 1830.

9 **Democracy, according to Burke . . . ambition**: see Edmund Burke (1729–1797), 'The Tendency of Democracy to excess in the Exercise, and in the Desire, of Power', from *An Appeal from the New to the Old Whigs* – 'The democratic commonwealth is the foodful nurse of ambition.'

10 **'ride on the whirlwind . . . storm'**: see Addison, *The Campaign*.

11 **Duke of Otranto**: Joseph Fouché, Duc d'Otrante (1759–1820), was Napoleon's Minister of Police, the engineer of his abdication and of Louis XVIII's restoration in July 1815.

12 **Duke of Orleans**: Louis Philippe (1773–1850). A member of the house of Bourbon, he succeeded Charles X to the French throne following the July Revolution of 1830 and abdicated during the February Revolution of 1848.

LETTER IV: TO THE SAME

1 **Marmont**: Auguste Marmont, Duc de Raguse, Marshal of France (1774–1852).

2 **On parole at ———**: in 1814 there had been a large number of French officers, prisoners of war on parole, in Melrose and the adjoining villages (see *Life* IV, pp. 137–8).

3 *Henri Quatre*: Henri IV of France (1553–1610), known as 'Henri le Bon'.

4 **Burke says . . . 'according to the letter'**: see Edmund Burke (1729–1797), *Remarks on the Policy of the Allies with respect to France, begun in October, 1793*: 'Whoever claims a right by birth to govern [post-revolutionary France], must find in his breast, or must conjure up in it, an energy not to be expected, perhaps not always to be wished for, in well-ordered states. The lawful prince must have, in everything but crime, the character of a usurper. He is gone, if he imagines himself the quiet possessor of a throne. He is to contend for it as much after an apparent conquest as before. His task is to win it; he must leave posterity to enjoy and to adorn it. No velvet cushions for him. He is to be always (I speak nearly to the letter) on horseback. This opinion is the result of much patient thinking on the subject, which I conceive no event is likely to alter.' (*Works* III, p. 450)

5 **'Sans doute . . . un bien chetif animal.'**: 'Without doubt
. . . But yes . . . Assuredly, Sir, he is born French . . .
Ah, agreed – but after all . . . it has to be admitted, that
a King who cannot mount a horse is a feeble creature.'

6 **Ney**: Michel Ney, Marshal of France, Duc d'Elchingen,
Prince of the Moscowa (1769–1815). His red hair and
florid complexion gave him the nickname *le Rougeaud*.
Napoleon called him 'the bravest of the brave'. Tried
for treason following the restoration of Louis XVIII,
he was executed by firing squad in a corner of the
Luxembourg Gardens on 7 December.

7 **'Enfeebled by age . . . lead'**: signed at Frankfurt
on 15 April 1815, Louis XVIII's proclamation to
the French nation was translated in the *Morning Post*
three days later: 'Broken down by age, and by the
misfortunes of twenty-five years, I cannot say to them
as my grandfather [Louis XV] did, rally under my
white plume, but I shall follow them closely to the
field of honour.'

8 **Duke d'Angouleme**: Louis Antoine (1775–1844) was
the eldest son of Charles Philippe, Comte d'Artois,
who succeeded his brother Louis XVIII, as Charles X.
The Duc d'Angoulême was the last dauphin of France,
cheated of succession to the throne by the terms of his
father's abdication during the 1830 Revolution. For
the last fourteen years of his life he styled himself the
legitimist pretender, Louis XIX.

9 **Duke de Berri**: Charles Ferdinand d'Artois (1778–
1820) was the youngest son of the future Charles X.
He was fatally stabbed by a Bonapartist assassin as he
left the Paris Opéra.

10 **Labedoyere**: General Charles Angelique François

Huchet de La Bédoyère (1786–1815). Napoleon's aide-de-camp during the Waterloo campaign. He was executed for treason on 19 August. Scott wrote of it to his wife: 'I saw a sort of bustle in the Tuilleries . . . I saw the king's gardes de corps all mounted to attend his coach, he came out with his handkerchief at his eyes & I understood Made. De Labedoyere whose husband was the first to desert with his regt. to Bony had thrown herself at his feet to beg for mercy for her husband. The King answerd that if the crime had been against himself alone he would have forgiven it but justice & the safety of the kingdom demanded an example. I next heard that Labedoyere was to be shot in the Champ de Mars. I went to see the ceremony but Messrs. the National Guard would not let me pass. I heard however a volley & learnd that this fellow who set the first example of treason was no more.' (*Letters* XII, pp. 143–4)

11 **The earthquake . . . breath of life**: see George Gordon Lord Byron (1788–1824), 'Ode to Napoleon Buonaparte'.

12 *qui timeri . . . odisse incipient*: see Tacitus, *Agricola*, 32.2., 'they who have ceased to fear will begin to hate'.

13 **Murat**: Napoleon Bonaparte's brother-in-law, Joachim-Napoleon Murat (1767–1815), Marshal of France, Prince of the Empire, Grand Duke of Berg and Clèves, King of Naples and the Two Sicilies. His Neapolitan army was routed by the Austrians at the battle of Tolentino on 3 May 1815. After Napoleon's fall he attempted to regain the throne of Naples but was arrested and tried for treason by his successor, Ferdinand IV. He was executed by firing squad in Calabria.

14 **Eugene Beauharnois**: Eugène Rose de Beauharnais (1781–1824), son of Joséphine Tascher de la Pagerie, and stepson of Napoleon.

15 **Madame Maret, Duchess of Bassano**: the wife of Hugues Bernard Maret, Napoleon's Foreign Minister and editor of the *Moniteur Universelle*.

16 **Caffé Montaussier**: '[one] of the . . . most remarkable temples of dissipation . . . the Café Montausier [is] devoted to the fair sex. [It] is fitted up in the guise of a theatre where music, singing and theatrical pieces are given; you pay nothing for admission, but are expected to call for refreshment . . . There is a very pretty graceful girl who attends here . . . She is full of wit and repartee; but her answer to all those who attempt to squeeze her hand and make love to her is always: *"Achetez quelque chose."*' (Major W. E. Frye, *After Waterloo*, pp. 61–2).

17 **Excelman's correspondence with Murat**: a letter from General Rémi Joseph Isidore Exelmans (1775–1852) pledging allegiance to the King of Naples was published in the *Morning Post* on 25 January 1815. At his court martial in Lisle he was charged with having 'kept up a correspondence with the enemy . . . while he was employed in the character of Inspector-General of the Cavalry in the First Military Division . . . with the enemy, because [Louis XVIII] has not recognised JOACHIM MURAT as King of Naples.' This was supposed to constitute an act of treason and espionage. He was acquitted. During the Waterloo campaign he fought at Ligny and at Wavre and in the defence of Paris.

18 **proclamation, issued at Lyons**: 'Soldiers: Come and range yourselves under the banners of your chief . . .

Victory shall march at a charging step; the eagle, with the national colours, shall fly from steeple to steeple, till it reaches the towers of Notre Dame. Then you will be able to show your scars with honour; then you will be able to boast of what you have done; you will be the liberators of your country! . . . you will each of you be able to say with pride, "And I also made part of that grand army which entered twice within the walls of Vienna, within those of Rome, of Berlin, of Madrid, of Moscow, and which delivered Paris from the stain which treason and the presence of the enemy had imprinted upon it."' (15 March 1815)

19 **Treaty of Paris**: signed 30 May 1814.

20 **a shameless charlatan, as one author expresses it**: unidentified.

21 **Maria Louisa and her son**: (1791–1847) daughter of Francis I of Austria, Napoleon's second Empress and the four-year-old Napoleon François Joseph Charles Bonaparte, Prince Imperial, King of Rome, Prince of Parma (1811–1832).

22 **Say, were ye tired . . . blood shall flow**: see Thomas Chatterton, 'Bristowe Tragedy; or, The death of Sir Charles Bawdin', verses xlvi and xlvii.

23 *Paix au dela du Rhin*: peace beyond the Rhine.

24 **Carnot**: Count Lazare Nicholas Marguerite Carnot (1753–1823), Napoleon's Minister of the Interior during the Hundred Days.

25 **Ghent**: the exiled Louis XVIII held court in the Belgian city at the Hotel d'Hane Steenhuyse during the Hundred Days.

26 **La Vendee**: The French *departement* of La Vendée was on the west coast south of Brittany.

27   *Vis inertiae*: resistance to change.

28   *tetes-du-pont*: bridgeheads.

LETTER V: PAUL TO THE MAJOR

1   **Bunker's-hill**: in addition to his participation in the War of the Austrian Succession, the Major is supposedly a veteran of the American War of Independence and of the engagement at Bunker Hill on 17 June 1775. Major John Scott was six years old at the time.

2   **skirmish at Rimini**: there was no fighting at Rimini during the Italian campaign of April and May 1815, although two minor clashes occurred twelve miles to the north-west and about twenty-two to the south-east of that town. The campaign effectively ended on 3 May with the rout of Murat's Neapolitan army at Tolentino.

3   **Blucher**: Gebhard Leberecht von Blücher, Prince of Wahlsatt (1742–1819). Prussian Field Marshal.

4   *Cedant arma togae*: see Cicero, *De Officiis*, Book I, xxii, 77 – 'Yield, ye arms, to the toga', i.e. military to civil power.

5   **Vandamme . . . General Girard**: General Dominique-Joseph René Comte Vandamme (1770–1830) and General Jean Baptiste Girard, Duc de Ligny (1775–1815). Girard was ennobled by Napoleon on the field at Ligny, 16 June, but was fatally wounded shortly afterwards.

LETTER VI: PAUL TO MAJOR ——, IN CONTINUATION

1   **Joseph II**: the Holy Roman Emperor (1741–1790).

2 **Prince of Orange**: Willem Frederik George Lodewijk (1792–1849).

3 *'Come to me and I will give you flesh'*: at Waterloo Kenneth MacKay of Tongue, a piper in the 79th Cameron Highlanders, played the *pibroch* 'Cogadh no Sith' (War or Peace) as his regiment was under attack by French cuirassiers. The Cameron clan's battle cry was, 'Come you sons of hounds and I will give you flesh.' This in turn presumably derived from 1 Samuel, 17:44, 'And the Philistine said to David, Come to me, and I will give thy flesh unto the fowls of the air, and to the beasts of the field.'

4 **Sir Thomas Picton**: Lieutenant General Sir Thomas Picton (1758–1815) commanded the 5th Infantry Division at Waterloo where he was shot through the head. He was the highest ranking fatality of the battle on the Allied side.

5 **Duke of Brunswick**: Frederick William, Duke of Brunswick-Wolfenbüttel (1771–1815), a German prince who succeeded to the title on the death of his father at the Battle of Jena in October 1806. He himself was killed at Quatre Bras on 16 June.

6 **'gay in the morning as for summer-sport'**: see John Home (1722–1808), *Douglas* (1756), Act I, Scene I – 'Gallant in strife, and noble in their ire, / The battle is their pastime. They go forth / Gay in the morning, as to the summer's sport: / When evening comes, the glory of the morn, / The youthful warrior is a clod of clay.'

7 **'Circumstantial Details of the Battle of Waterloo'**: one of the earliest books about the battle, published 24 August 1815, by John Booth.

8 **Account of the Battle of Leipsic . . . Eye-Witness**:

Scott was probably referring to an account published in 1814 and translated from the German: *A narrative of the battle of Hanau, and other events connected with the retreat of the French army from Leipzig to the Reine: forming a continuation of the narrative of the battles of Leipzig. By an Eye-Witness.*

9 **General Maitland**: Major General Peregrine Maitland (1777–1854) commanded two battalions of the Grenadier Guards at Waterloo. He led the advance against Napoleon's Old Guard in the closing moments of the battle, following Wellington's order: 'Now, Maitland, now's your time!'

10 **Colonel Macara**: Lieutenant Colonel Sir Robert Macara (1759–1815) commanded the 42nd (or Royal Highland) Regiment of Foot.

11 **'Today for revenge, and tomorrow for mourning'**: a century earlier, at the battle of Sheriffmuir, 13 November 1715, Jacobite rebels attacked the British forces of John Campbell, 2nd Duke of Argyll, to the rallying cry of, 'Revenge to-day, mourning tomorrow!'

12 **Colonel Cameron**: Scott paid further tribute to John Cameron (1771–1815) in *The Field of Waterloo*, stanza XXI, and in 'The Dance of Death', verse II: 'Brave Cameron heard the wild hurra / Of conquest as he fell.' His monument in Kilmallie Cemetery, Lochaber, Argyllshire, bears an inscription written by Scott which contains the words: 'With a spirit that knew no fear and shunned no danger, he accompanied, or led, in marches, sieges, in battles, the gallant 92nd regiment of Scottish Highlanders, always to honour, almost always to victory.' (Robert Monteith, *A Collection of Epitaphs and Monumental Inscriptions: Chiefly in Scotland*, 1834, p. 347)

LETTER VII: PAUL TO MAJOR ——, IN CONTINUATION

1 **Bulow**: Friedrich Wilhelm Freiherr von Bülow, Graf von Dennewitz (1755–1816).

2 **queen martyred . . . disgrace as a bondsman**: Duchess Louise of Mecklenburg-Strelitz, Queen Consort of Prussia (1776–1810). In 1807 following her country's disastrous defeat at the Battle of Jena, she pleaded in vain with Napoleon on behalf of her husband, Frederick William III, for favourable peace terms. Her premature death three years later, aged thirty-four, prompted the French Emperor to remark, 'The King has lost his best minister.'

3 **Stern look'd . . . yet to kill**: see Dryden's translation of Boccaccio's *Theodore and Honoria*, lines 193–4.

4 **second corps commanded by Girard**: Scott was misinformed. Lieutenant General Jean-Baptiste Drouet, Comte d'Erlon (1765–1844) commanded the 2nd Corps. The Emperor's order to attack St Armand was countermanded by Marshal Ney who ordered them to Quatre Bras. After an afternoon of futile marching and countermarching, night fell without the 2nd Corps having fired a shot.

5 **Thielman . . . Grouchy**: General Johann Adolf von Thielmann (1765–1824), commander of the Prussian III Korps, would defend the town of Wavre against the superior French forces of Marshal Emmanuel de Grouchy (1766–1847), keeping them occupied while the rest of the Prussian army marched west to tip the balance against Napoleon at Waterloo.

6 **Earl of Uxbridge**: Henry Paget (1768–1854) commanded the British Cavalry Corps. Wounded in the

dying moments of the battle, he is supposed to have said to the Duke of Wellington: 'My God, sir. I've lost my leg.' To which the Duke replied: 'My God, sir. So you have.' Shortly thereafter he was elevated by the Prince Regent to 'the name, stile, and title of Marquess of Anglesey'.

7   **Account of the Battle . . . British Officer on the Staff**: published in 1815, it included 'an appendix containing the British, French, Prussian, and Spanish official details, etc.'.

8   **Colonel Carmichael Smith**: James Carmichael Smyth (1779–1838) commanded the Corps of Royal Engineers.

9   **Sir William de Lancey**: Colonel Sir William Howe De Lancey (1778–1815) was Wellington's Deputy Quartermaster-General. He was struck in the back by a spent cannonball which detached his ribcage from his spine. Nursed by his young wife Magdalene, he survived for six days. Her memoir, *A Week at Waterloo*, edited by Major B. R. Ward, was published in 1906.

10 **Planchenoit**: the English press had reprinted reports received in Paris that Napoleon had spent the night before the battle at headquarters in the village of 'Plancheny'. It was, in fact, at Le Caillou.

11 **Bourmont and other officers**: on 14 June 1815 General of Division Louis-Auguste-Victor, Comte de Ghaisnes de Bourmont (1773–1846) deserted from Napoleon's army and surrendered to the Prussians, taking with him his staff and an escort of lancers. He was able to divulge Napoleon's campaign plans but little that the Prussians did not already know.

12   *Je les tiens donc ces Anglois*: 'So, now I've got these English.'

13   **Jerome, the ex-king of Westphalia**: Napoleon's youngest brother (1784–1860).

14   **'*Il rit bien, qui rit le dernier*'**: he laughs best that laughs last.

15   **Mareschal Ney's letter to Fouché**: Ney's letter to the Minister of Police defending his conduct at Quatre Bras and Waterloo against 'false and defamatory reports' was written in Paris and dated 26 June 1815. According to John Scott of Gala, the text was published in Paris as a pamphlet and 'was in everybody's hands' (*Journal*, p. 108). The *Caledonian Mercury* published a translation on 17 July.

16   **'Never a man's thought . . . Major'**: see Shakespeare, *Henry IV Part 2*, Act II, Scene II.

17   **Within these forty hours . . . said so**: see Shakespeare, *Henry VIII*, Act III, Scene II.

18   **Buonaparte's bulletin**: a dispatch was published in Paris on 20 June. It began: 'The French armies have again immortalised themselves on the plains of Fleurus.' It claimed that 1,700 prisoners had been taken at Charleroi, while at Quatre Bras 'a British division of 5 or 6000 Scotch was cut to pieces [and] we have not seen any of them prisoners . . . Their loss is said to be 50,000 men' ('Paris Papers', *Morning Chronicle*, 26 June 1815).

LETTER VIII: TO THE SAME

1   *point d'appui*: point of support.

2   **a French officer of cuirassiers**: Scott is perhaps mistaken. A French officer of cuirassiers did desert but it was towards the end of the day and he warned that the Imperial Guard was about to attack.

3　**Lord Hill**: Lieutenant General Lord Rowland Hill (1772–1842) commanded the Duke of Wellington's II Corps.

4　**An officer of engineers**: unidentified.

5　**Soult**: Nicholas Jean de Dieu, Duc de Dalmatia (1769–1851), Napoleon's Chief of Staff during the Waterloo campaign.

6　**Col. M'Donell . . . Glengarry**: Lieutenant Colonel James Macdonell of the Coldstream Guards (1781–1857). He was the third son of Duncan Macdonell of Glengarry.

7　**Don Miguel Alava**: Miguel Ricardo de Álava y Esquivel (1770–1843). The Duke of Wellington's Spanish military attaché and aide-de-camp during the Peninsular War and at Waterloo.

8　**the picked regiments of 1795**: The English parliament passed legislation enabling an expansion of the army from 45,000 to 120,000 regular soldiers, 56,000 militia and 40,000 men to defend Ireland and the West Indies and plantations, 'exclusive of fencibles and volunteers, foreign troops in British pay, and embodied French emigrants'. To achieve this goal, the sum of £27,540,000 was to be raised by taxation. Objections were voiced by the Whigs that the improved efficiency and expansion of the militia would 'increase the influence and patronage of ministers, and . . . place the whole military strength of the kingdom under their immediate direction; a step which was evidently preparatory to the complete establishment of arbitrary power.' Such objections were over-ruled. (Robert Bisset, *History of the Reign of George III*, vol. VI, pp. 26–7)

9   **German Legion**: the King's German Legion was a unit of the British army formed in 1803 from Hanoverian troops. It was disbanded in 1816.

10   **Sir John Elley**: Lieutenant Colonel Sir John Elley of the Royal Regiment of Horse Guards (1764–1839).

11   **Shaw . . . of the Life-Guards**: stories abounded of Shaw's prowess in the battle. The painter Benjamin Robert Haydon was thrilled by one eye-witness account: 'a Cuirassier gave point at him, Shaw parried the thrust, and before the Cuirassier recovered Shaw cut him right through his brass helmet to the chin, "and his face fell off him like a bit of apple."' (*Correspondence & Table Talk*, vol. II, p. 271)

12   **Major Norman Ramsay**: (1782–1815) commanded 'H' Troop of the Royal Horse Artillery north of Hougoumont. Killed at an early stage of the battle, he was buried on the field but his body was brought back to Scotland three weeks later by his father who had lost three sons in eight months.

13   **'ought to have thought of it . . . every thing at once'**: Wellington spoke of this later: 'We should not have lost La Haye Sainte,' he told Lord Fitzroy, 'if there had only been a wicket behind to let in ammunition. But the French kept up such a fire on the front, that we could not supply it from that quarter.' On another occasion he took full responsibility for the oversight: 'No – in fact it was my fault, for I ought to have looked into it myself.' (Philip Henry Stanhope, *Notes of Conversations with the Duke of Wellington*, 3rd edition, 1889, pp. 220 and 245)

14   **Sir Alexander Gordon**: (1786–1815) 3rd Foot Guards, died at Wellington's headquarters in the early hours of 19 June after having his leg amputated in the field.

15 **Lieutenant-Colonel Canning**: Charles Fox Canning (1782–1815). His memorial tablet in the church at Waterloo reads: 'Near his great chief, on many a trying day / He braved each peril of the deadly fray / And when on Waterloo's ensanguined plain / He fell in glory 'midst the glorious slain / Unmoved by aught to selfish minds allied / "Thank Heaven! My Leader lives" he said and died.'

16 **Count Lobau**: Georges Mouton, Comte de Lobau (1770–1838), commanded the VI Infantry Corps during the defence of Plancenoit at Waterloo.

17 **the Prussian rear (commanded by Tauenzein)**: Scott is mistaken. General Bogislav Friedrich Emanuel von Tauentzien (1760–1824) commanded the Prussian VI Korps, which took no part in the Waterloo campaign. Wavre was defended by General Thielmann (see p. 317, note 5).

18 **There thou shouldst be . . . Seems bruited**: see Shakespeare, *Macbeth*, Act V, Scene XIII.

19 **General Frederick Adam**: (1781–1853) wounded at Waterloo. See letter XI, note 15.

20 **'*Ils sont meleés ensemble!*'**: they are mixed together.

21 **Captain Campbell**: General Adam's aide-de-camp was Scott's guide across the battlefield on 9 August. See below.

22 **Gneisenau**: August Neidhardt von Gneisenau (1760–1831) was Blücher's Chief of Staff.

23 ***Quoi! tu n'es pas mort?***: a French lancer greeted the wounded and helpless Sir Frederick Cavendish Ponsonby thus before stabbing him in the back. Ponsonby was trampled on and plundered by French and Prussian soldiers and lay all night on the battlefield

wounded in seven places, but survived to tell his story.

24 **Ponsonby**: Major-General Sir William Ponsonby (1772–1815) was killed by Polish lancers at Waterloo when his horse became stuck in a heavily ploughed field. He was no relation to Sir Frederick Cavendish Ponsonby.

25 **Duhesme**: General Comte Guillaume Philibert Duhesme (1766–1815) commanded the Young Guard in the defence of Plancenoit where he was mortally wounded. The 'Homeric' death attributed to him by Scott was widely believed but apocryphal. He was, in fact, lodged in the inn at Genappe and treated by Blücher's personal physician before succumbing to his wounds some days later.

26 **Friant**: General Louis Friant (1758–1829) commanded the Grenadiers of the Old Guard at Waterloo where he was wounded. Scott is mistaken in thinking him killed.

27 κάτθανε καὶ Πάτροκλος, ὅ περ σέο πολλὸν ἀμείνων: 'Patroclus also died, and he was better far than you.' (*Iliad*, book 21, line 107) Himself 'no Grecian', Scott asked his friend William Erskine for the Greek text of this quotation. 'The line occurs where Achilles is intreated for mercy by some poor Devil a son of Priam if I recollect right in his first carnage after Patroclus' death,' he wrote. 'Will you mark it in very legible Greek Characters on a separate slip of paper & inclose it to me.' (*Letters* IV, p. 148)

28 **General Cambrone**: Pierre Jacques Cambronne (1770–1842) is said to have greeted the invitation to surrender with the single word: '*Merde!*'

LETTER IX: PAUL TO HIS SISTER MARGARET

1 **I should recollect how many descriptions have already appeared**: the catalogue of the British Library lists over forty works – including Scott's own *Field of Waterloo*, along with other poems, songs, arrangements for pianoforte, sermons, works in French, German, Spanish, Italian and Welsh, as well as numerous 'Authentic Narratives' – published during the remaining six months of 1815, prior to the appearance of *Paul's Letters to His Kinsfolk* in early January 1816. To these can be added a much greater number of accounts published in the press.

2 **pococurantés**: indifferent people (derived from the Italian *poco* and *curante*: little caring).

3 **John Lacoste**: Jean Baptiste La Coste. Pryse Lockhart Gordon, a half-pay Major resident in Brussels, who accompanied Scott and his companions on their tour of the field, was sceptical about La Coste's story and claimed he had been in a safe hiding place ten miles away for the whole day. (See *Personal Memoirs, or reminiscences of men and manners at home and abroad, during the last half century, with occasional sketches of the author's life, etc.*, published London 1830.) However, Napoleon himself is known to have spoken of his guide in conversation with William Warden, surgeon of *HMS Northumberland*, on St Helena, which gives credence to at least the broad outline of La Coste's account. (See *The Times*, 28 November 1816.)

4 *Vainqueur de Vainqueur de la terre*: conqueror of the conqueror of the earth. The phrase occurs in a letter of 7 February 1755 to Lord Chesterfield from Samuel Johnson.

5   **promise of making his fortune**: Napoleon had told La Coste when he engaged him as guide on the morning of the battle: 'that if he [Bonaparte] succeeded, his recompense should be a hundred times greater than he could imagine'. Following the battle he was dismissed with a single Napoleon for his trouble.

6   **The extent was so limited**: the opposing armies occupied an area measuring two-and-a-half miles from one ridge to the other, by three miles from east to west, and the actual fighting was confined to a front just two miles long. This meant that some 200,000 men, 60,000 horses and 537 guns were in action on a piece of land measuring five square miles.

7   **Rank rush'd on rank . . . the fire reposed**: the precise source for this quotation has not been traced. However, the couplet may have been adapted by Scott from William Sotheby (1757–1833), *The Battle of the Nile, a poem* (1799), in which the second line and a variant on the first are to be found: 'The signal flam'd, around a host enclos'd / The thunder ceas'd not, nor the fire reposed; / Fleet clash'd on fleet; on lightning, lightning stream'd; / Beneath the blaze the crimson billow gleam'd'.

8   **Around them . . . lair of dying men**: see Joanna Baillie (1762–1851), *Ethwald: a Tragedy*, Part Second, Act II, Scene I.

9   **studied at Leyden**: founded in 1575, the University of Leyden is the oldest in the Netherlands.

10 **forty thousand . . . much higher**: the combined Anglo-Allied and Prussian dead and wounded numbered some 22,000; estimates of French losses range from 22,000 to 31,000.

11 **one of the heroes of the day**: Scott was escorted across the field by Captain Robert Preston Campbell of the 7th Foot (see above). Campbell is said to have had the distinction of firing the last shot of the battle, a French gun captured by his regiment and turned on the retreating enemy.

12 **like Shakspeare's mulberry-tree**: supposedly planted by Shakespeare in the grounds of New Place, Stratford-upon-Avon, the tree was cut down in 1756 by the Reverend Francis Gastrell who had become tired of visitors asking to see it. In 2013 a tea caddy carved from the wood was sold at Christy's for £13,000.

13 **A relique . . . given me by a lady**: Pryse Lockhart Gordon writes as follows: '. . . the most precious memorial was presented to him by my wife – a French soldier's book, well stained with blood, and containing some songs popular in the French army, which he found so interesting that he introduced versions of them in his Paul's Letters; of which he did me the honour to send me a copy, with a letter, saying, "that he considered my wife's gift as the most valuable of all his Waterloo relics."' (*Personal Memoirs*, quoted *Life*, p. 59.) John Scott of Gala attributed the songs to Hortense Eugénie de Beauharnais, Napoleon's stepdaughter.

14 **one of our Scottish men of rhyme**: a sly reference by Paul to Scott himself.

15 *sirventes* and *lais*: medieval verse forms.

LETTER X: PAUL TO ——, ESQ. OF ——

1 **land of Goshen**: the fertile region of Egypt where Joseph settled his family: 'And thou shalt dwell in the

land of Goshen . . . thou and thy children, and thy children's children, and thy flocks, and thy herds, and all that thou hast.' (Genesis 46:10)

2   *revenons à nos moutons*: the phrase originated in an anonymous fifteenth-century play called *La Farce de Maître Pathelin*, and subsequently became a French figure of speech. Literally: let us return to our sheep; figuratively: let us get back to the subject at hand.

3   **a navy at Antwerp**: this port, at the mouth of the river Scheldt, would have given a French naval force effective control of the Channel and a strategic base for invading England.

4   **bombardment by Sir Thomas Graham**: prior to his disastrous attack on Bergen-op-Zoom, General Thomas Graham, 1st Baron Lynedoch (1748–1843), took part in the failed Anglo-Prussian operation in February 1814, during the blockade of Antwerp.

5   **small fascine-battery**: a defensive structure made from 'fascines' – bundles of brushwood.

6   **alienation of the Tyrol from Austria**: under the terms of the Peace of Pressburg, signed with France after defeats at Ulm and Austerlitz, Austria ceded Tyrol to Bavaria.

7   **'Care I for the limbs, the thewes, the sinews of a man – Give me the spirit!'**: see Shakespeare, *Henry IV Part 2*, Falstaff to Justice Shallow, Act III, Scene II.

8   **partition of Poland**: successive partitions – in 1772, 1793 and 1795 – between Russia, Prussia and Austria resulted in the effective elimination of Poland as a sovereign state for 123 years.

9   **Philip the Second**: (1527–1598) King of Spain.

He became Lord of the Seventeen Provinces of the Netherlands in 1555.

10   **Archbishop of Liege**: in later editions Scott attached a footnote: 'I take this opportunity to announce the correction of a very gross error in the first edition of these Letters, where the name of the Bishop of Liege had, through misinformation, been inserted for that of the Bishop of Ghent. The extent of this mistake, which I deeply regret, will be best understood by the following extract from a letter, in which it is pointed out and corrected. The authority of the writer is beyond dispute, and Paul readily admits the inaccuracy of his notes, though taken upon the spot.' The letter referred to contains the following: 'The Bishop of Liege was never an adherent or ally of Bonaparte. On the contrary, driven from his . . . bishopric . . . he took refuge at Ratisbone . . . where he has never ceased to enjoy the respect of those who were most opposed to the views of the usurper . . . It would have been impossible for the Bishop of Liege to have issued a pastoral letter, not only of the nature in question, but of any kind whatever; because, though still styled Bishop, he has in effect no diocese, that of Liege having been abolished during the French occupancy. I should conceive the prelate whose name ought to have been cited in this part of the work, to be the Bishop of Ghent, to whom all that has been erroneously attributed to the Prince-Bishop of Liege will exactly apply . . .' The writer of the letter is not identified.

11   **chef-d'oeuvre of Rubens, the Descent from the Cross**: see introductory essay, p. 6.

12   *swamy*: originally a Hindu idol, used here generically for any religious image.

13   **palace of Lacken**: the Palace at Laeken, just north of Brussels, was the former summer residence of the governors of the Hapsburg Netherlands, now occupied by the Belgian Royal Family. Anticipating an early victory, Napoleon had a proclamation 'to the Belgians and Inhabitants of the left Bank of the Rhine', printed before he left Paris, post-dated 17 June 1815 and signed 'At the Imperial Palace of Lacken'. Bundles were found in his campaign coach, abandoned during the retreat after Waterloo.

14   **'Entire affection scorned nicer hands'**: see Edmund Spenser (1552/3–1599), *The Faerie Queene*, Book 1, Canto 8, Stanza 40.

15   **Baron Trenck**: Friedrich Freiherr von der Trenck (1726–1794). Prussian officer, adventurer and author. While serving as an orderly officer to Frederick the Great, he was wrongly accused of spying for Austria and imprisoned in the fortress of Gatz, where, on the king's orders, his own gravestone served as the only seat. He escaped but was later recaptured and confined in the citadel at Magdeburg for ten years in heavy manacles and chains to prevent further flight. He was finally released in 1763. *The Memoirs of Frederick Baron Trenck, Written by Himself* was published in English translation in 1788.

16   **as Anstey says, 'so clumsy and clunch'**: see Christopher Anstey (1724–1805), 'An Election Ball in Poetical Letters from Mr Inkle, a Freeman of Bath, to his wife at Gloucester'. The verse satire contains the lines: 'In pudding there's something so clumsy

and clunch, / And something so filthy so stinking in punch.'

LETTER XI: TO THE SAME

1 **General Rey**: the garrison commandant at Valenciennes was a Général Roy.

2 **French loyalist officer named Gordon**: the incident was reported, with variations, in the *Morning Chronicle*: he was 'arrested and shot upon the glacis of the fortress' (13 July 1815). Then in the same paper, twelve days later: 'He was allowed to approach, and when he was within musket shot he was fired at and fell. His dead body was then seized and cut in a thousand pieces' (25 July 1815). The officer's name was Lauriston.

3 **Sully**: Maximilien de Béthune, Duc de Sully (1560–1641), grand commissioner of highways and public works, superintendent of fortifications and grand master of artillery under Henri IV of France.

4 **'winds round . . . hill of vines'**: see Coleridge's translation of *The Piccolomini*, Act I, Scene IV, the second play of the Wallenstein trilogy by Friedrich Schiller (1759–1805).

5 **stoical virtue of a Brutus**: as leader of the revolt that overthrew Tarquin, the last king of Rome, Lucius Iunius Brutus is regarded as the founder of the Roman Republic, and greatly respected for his stoicism in having his own sons put to death for subsequently plotting against the state. He was claimed as ancestor by the family of Marcus Iunius Brutus, one of the assassins of Julius Caesar.

6 **Louis XI**: (1423–1483) responsible for uniting France after the Hundred Years War and establishing the

style of French monarchy that would last until the Revolution, Louis was called, variously, 'the Prudent', 'the Cunning', and 'the Universal Spider'. He figures prominently as an unmitigated villain in Scott's 1823 novel *Quentin Durwood*.

7   **civil wars of the League**: the conflict known variously as the Nine Years War, the War of the Grand Alliance, and the League of Augsberg War (1688–97). It was fought between Louis IV and the Holy Roman Emperor allied with the Electors of Bavaria, Palatinate and Saxony, and the kings of Sweden and Spain to prevent French expansion into the Low Countries.

8   *noblesse campagnarde*: landed nobility.

9   **Crummie**: Scottish dialect for cow, originally one with a crumpled horn.

10 *Grieve*: farm overseer.

11 *Das ist gut – sehr wohl*: That is good – very well.

12 **'Who is he . . . let that pass'**: see *Beggars Bush* by Francis Beaumont and John Fletcher, Act II, Scene I.

13 **Sultan Mahmoud's owls**: Sultan Mahmoud Subuktekin, King of Persia, brought great desolation to his realm until persuaded to mend his ways. His vizier, Khasayas, told the Sultan that he understood the language of birds, and reported that he had heard two owls talking about him. One owl had a son, the other a daughter. The son's father agreed to a marriage between their two children on condition that the daughter be provided with a dowry of fifty ruined villages. The daughter's father happily agreed and promised not fifty but 500, adding: 'God grant a prosperous long life to the sultan Mahmoud, and as long as he continues King of Persia, we shall never

want destroyed villages!' Sultan Mahmoud 'did not want penetration'. He rebuilt the villages and cities 'and afterwards thought of nothing but the good of his people'. See 'The Fable of the Owls', in Henry Weber's *Tales of the East*, (Edinburgh, John Ballantyne & Co.: 1812) vol. 3, p. 193.

14 **'Amazement in his van . . . Solitude behind'**: see Thomas Gray (1716–1771), opening verse of *The Curse upon Edward*.

15 **my friend General A——**: Major-General Frederick Adam, wounded at Waterloo and 'who could not as yet mount on horseback'. (*Life*, p. 57)

16 **'O noble thirst! . . . drink all'**: see William Congreve (1670–1729), *The Mourning Bride*, Act V, Scene II.

17 **frontispiece of Lily's grammar**: *A Short Introduction of Grammar* by William Lily (*c*.1468–1522), first headmaster of St Paul's Cathedral School, became, by edict of Henry VIII, the standard Latin primer taught in British grammar schools throughout the sixteenth and seventeenth centuries. Revised editions continued to be used as late as the mid-nineteenth century. The frontispiece showed pupils sitting under the Tree of Knowledge.

18 **Chantilly . . . princely family of Condé**: the title Prince of Condé was assumed in the mid-sixteenth century by Louis de Bourbon, uncle to Henri IV of France, and borne by his male descendants. The Château de Chantilly was home to the most celebrated representative, known for his military prowess as 'Le Grand Condé' (1621–1686).

19 **Yorick and La Fleur**: see Laurence Sterne (1713–1768), *A Sentimental Journey Through France and*

Italy (published 1768). The Reverend Mr Yorick is the narrator, La Fleur the young Frenchman who accompanies him as servant.

20 **King of Brobdignag . . . Houyhnhnms**: refers to the countries of giants and horses in parts two and four of *Gulliver's Travels* by Jonathan Swift (1667–1745).

21 **Henry de Bourbon, seventh Prince of Condé**: (1710–1740). The large fountain in the Chantilly stables was designed by André Le Nôtre (1613–1700).

22 **Sarmatian partizans**: an Iranian people flourishing from about the fifth century BC to the fourth century AD. Their territory corresponded to modern Ukraine, Southern Russia and the north-eastern Balkans around Moldova. Scott is presumably referring to the Prussians figuratively as barbarians.

23 **'*Et pourtant . . . mauvaise compagnie*'**: 'And yet, my friend, if it were not for those people there!' [Paul's unfinished sentence implies that without the Prussians France would not have been rid of Napoleon.] 'Ah yes, Monsieur, without them we would perhaps never have seen our good Duke [of Bourbon] again. Assuredly that is a welcome return – but I must admit that he has come back in rather bad company.'

24 **'*Dans sa pompe élégante . . . âge embelli*'**: 'In her elegant pomp, admired Chantilly / From hero to hero, from age to age embellished.' See Jacques Delille (1738–1813), *Les Jardins, ou L'Art d'Embellir Les Paysages* (1782).

25 **'in which he of Gath . . . and all'**: see William Cowper (1731–1800), *The Task*.

LETTER XII: PAUL TO HIS SISTER

1   **Place de Louis Quinze**: designed by Ange-Jacques Gabriel (1698–1782) in 1755 and named in honour of the reigning king. It was renamed 'place de la Révolution' after 1790 and it was there that Louis XVI was guillotined in 1793. In 1795, under the Directory, it became the place de la Concorde. With the Bourbon restoration of 1814 it reverted to its original name. Following the July Revolution of 1830 it became the place de la Concorde again.

2   **Temple of Victory . . . Temple of Concord**: L'église Sainte-Marie-Madeleine, or La Madeleine, at the end of the rue Royale, dominates the northern vista from the place de la Concorde. Construction began in 1763 but only the portico and foundations had been finished by the start of the revolution in 1789. Napoleon continued the work, intending it to be rededicated as the *Temple de la Gloire de la Grande Armée*. Following the Bourbon restoration work continued, but it was not finally consecrated as a church until 1842.

3   **large hotel . . . Duke of Wellington**: the Hôtel de la Reynière was previously owned by the General Andoche Junot, Duc d'Abrantes (1771–1813).

4   **Bridge of Jena**: pont d'Iéna was built 1809–13 to commemorate the French victory over the Prussians in 1806.

5   **Venetian Horses**: the *Quadriga* of St Mark's Basilica would be removed from the Arc du Carrousel on 30 September 1815 and returned to Venice.

6   **gourd of the prophet**: the plant that afforded shade to the prophet Jonah in front of Nineveh (Jonah 4:6–11).

7   **fable of the Seven Sleepers**: seven Christian youths are said to have hidden in a cave in Ephesus to escape persecution during the reign of the Roman Emperor Decius, fallen asleep and awoken 180 years later during the reign of the Christian Theodosius II.

8   *Le Char le tient*: the Chariot holds him.

9   **statue of Buonaparte**: the statue was in fact melted down. Canova's colossal marble nude of Bonaparte, however – rejected by the Emperor as being 'trop athlétique' – was found covered up in the Louvre. It was this that the British government bought for 66,000 francs and presented to the Duke. It now stands in the stairwell at Apsley House.

10 **elephant**: the permanent bronze statue was never cast. The plaster model remained on the site until its demolition in 1846.

11 **N.'s . . . H.'s and B.'s**: from the initial of 'Napoleon' to those of 'Bourbon' and 'Henri IV', first and most revered of the Bourbon kings, responsible for constructing the *pont Neuf* and for adding the *Grande Galerie* to the Louvre.

12 **Lord Chesterfield . . . Fleet-ditch**: Philip Stanhope, 4th Earl of Chesterfield (1694–1773), statesman and man of letters. A tributary of the Thames flowing through Clerkenwell, the river Fleet, was for centuries little more than a sewer. It is now entirely underground.

13 **'no snug lying in the abbey'**: see Richard Brinsley Butler Sheridan (1751–1816), *The Rivals*, Act V, Scene II.

14 **Mirabeau . . . Marat**: Honoré Gabriel Riqueti, Comte de Mirabeau (1749–1791); Jean Paul Marat (1743–1793).

LETTER XII: THE SAME TO THE SAME

1 *schako*: a tall, cylindrical, military-style hat. Scott mistakenly gives it as '*schakos*' in the first edition.

2 **Mons. Le Noir**: Alexandre Lenoir (1761–1839).

3 *incivisme*: a lack of public spiritedness.

4 **Sçavans**: archaic form of 'savants' or scholars. *Le Journal des Sçavans*, the earliest scholarly periodical in Europe, was first published in Paris, 1665, and ceased publication during the French Revolution in 1792. It reappeared briefly in 1797, and regularly from 1816, as *Le Journal des Savants*.

5 **Clovis and Pharamond**: Pharamond or Faramund (*c*.370–427) and Clovis I (*c*.466–511), kings of the Franks.

6 **Abelard and Heloïse . . . Boileau**: the tombs of Abelard (1079–1142) and Héloïse (*c*.1090–1164), and those of Molière (1622–1673), La Fontaine (1621–1695) and Boileau (1636–1711), are now to be found in Père Lachaise. The tomb of Descartes (1596–1650) is in the Abbey of Saint-Germain des Près.

7 **'Torn from their destined page . . . heroic deed'**: see John Ferriar (1761–1815), 'Illustrations of Sterne', line 121. Ferriar was a Scottish physician and poet.

8 **a Grainger**: James Granger (1723–1776) published a *Biographical History of England* (1769), which included blank pages enabling the owner to paste in illustrations cut from other books.

9 ***Omnis Thais Thaida olet***: more correctly, *omnia cum fecit, Thaida Thais olet* – 'But when all's done Thais smells of Thais.' See Martial, *Epigrams* (VI: 93: 12).

10 **corregidor of Leon . . . Captain Rolando's subterranean mansion**: see Alain-René Lesage

(1668–1747), *Adventures of Gil Blas of Santillane*. The description of Captain Rolando's underground hideout is to be found in Book 1, chapter IV. In chapter XII the *corregidor*, or town magistrate, relieves Gil Blas of the portion of the gang's booty he has escaped with.

11 **'Ye have taken away my gods . . . what aileth me?'**: see Judges 18:24.

12 **burning of Don Quixote's library**: see Miguel de Cervantes (*c*.1547–1616), *Don Quixote*. Following chapter VI, entitled 'Of the great and pleasant Inquisition held by the Priest and the Barber over our ingenious gentleman's library', Don Quixote's books are burnt in the courtyard by his housekeeper.

13 **group of drinking boors**: subject matter of the seventeenth-century Dutch genre painter Jan Steen (1626–1679) who specialised in tavern scenes.

14 **Dalilahs . . . similar flourishes in poetry**: see John Dryden (1631–1700), the preface 'containing a Parallel betwixt Painting and Poetry' to his translation of *De Arte Graphica* by C. A. Du Fresnoy: 'All I can say for those passages, which are, I hope, not many, is, that I knew they were bad enough to please, even when I writ them. But I repent of them among my sins; and if any of their fellows intrude by chance in my present writings, I draw a stroke over all those Dalilahs of the theatre, and am resolved I will settle myself no reputation by the applause of fools.'

15 **Mention the force . . . extremely fine**: see John Gay (1685–1732), 'An Epistle to the Right Honourable William Pulteney, Esq.', lines 115–20. From *Poems on Several Occasions* (1720).

16 **David**: Jacques-Louis David (1748–1825).

17 **Apollo Belvidere**: marble Roman copy of a Greek bronze. Following its discovery in the late fifteenth century it was displayed in the courtyard of the Belvedere Palace in the Vatican.

18 **as Poins says . . . I could pity them**: Scott misremembers. After playing a joke on Falstaff, it is Prince Hal who says to Poins: 'Were't not for laughing, I should pity him.' See Shakespeare, *Henry IV Part 1*, Act II, Scene III.

19 **Borghesé pictures . . . life of Mary de Medicis**: in 1807 Napoleon put pressure on his brother-in-law, Camillo Filippo Ludovico Borghese, to sell a portion of his sculpture collection to the French state at well below the market price. No pictures were included in the deal, however. Rubens's twenty-two gigantic canvases celebrating the life of Henri VI's queen are now in the Louvre.

20 **Malmaison**: seven miles west of Paris, the chateau was, in 1815, the home of Josephine's daughter, the Princess Hortense. Following his abdication and departure from the Élysées Palace, Napoleon spent four days at Malmaison with his entourage before leaving for the west coast.

21 **Canova**: Antonio Canova (1757–1822) was commissioned by Pope Pius VII to negotiate and oversee the restitution of works from the Louvre belonging to the Vatican.

LETTER XIV: PAUL TO THE MAJOR

1 **Baron Muffling**: Friedrich Karl Ferdinand Freiherr von Müffling (1775–1851). Wellington's Prussian liaison officer during the Waterloo Campaign.

2 **a certain general renowned in song**: General Sir John Cope (1690–1760) was the commander of British forces routed by Charles Edward Stuart's highlanders at Prestonpans, north of Edinburgh, at daybreak on 21 September 1745. This battle forms the climax to Scott's *Waverley*. Cope reported the disaster in person to the garrison at Berwick-on-Tweed, a humiliation relished in Adam Skirving's Jacobite ballad 'Hey Johnnie Cope, are ye wauking yet?', which includes the couplet: 'Now Johnnie, troth ye werena blate [shy] / Tae come wi' news o' your ain defeat.'

3 **Long Parliament**: summoned by Charles I in November 1640, its members pushed through legislation forbidding its dissolution without parliamentary consent. It was the 'Rump' of the Long Parliament that ordered the execution of the King in 1649. Ousted by Cromwell in 1653 it was briefly recalled after his death and finally voted to dissolve itself in 1660.

4 **Federés**: revolutionary militia.

5 **Lucien**: Lucien Bonaparte (1775–1840) had dissolved the upper and lower Chambers by force during the *coup d'état* of 9 and 10 November 1799 – *18 Brumaire* in the French republican calendar – and established his elder brother as First Consul.

6 **infant son**: Napoleon François Joseph Charles Bonaparte, Prince Imperial, King of Rome, Prince of Parma (1811–1832) was four years old and lived in Austria with his mother, the estranged Empress Marie-Louise. He had been proclaimed Emperor of the French in 1814, aged three, when his father abdicated for the first time. Then he retained the title Napoleon II for just a week. In 1815 his reign would last a fortnight.

7　**Labedoyere bullied in vain**: The twenty-nine-year-old General harangued the Chamber of Peers during a debate about the succession on 23 June: 'Napoleon abdicated in favour of his son, his abdication is one and indivisible. If his son is not recognised, is not crowned, I say that Napoleon did not abdicate, that his declaration should be null and void . . . If [you] reject Napoleon II, the Emperor has but to unsheath the sword again to surround himself with brave men who . . . will follow him once again with the cry of *"vive l'Empereur!"* And when you see that, do not complain of civil war: it is you who will have caused it with your creeping treachery!' (Reported in *Morning Chronicle*, 28 June 1815.)

8　**'While they sit . . . of making laws'**: see Jonathan Swift (1667–1745), *A Character, Panegyric, and Description of the Legion Club* (1736).

9　**Mons. Garnier**: Jacques Garnier, known as Garnier de Saintes (1755–1818).

10　**Abbess of Andouillets**: see Laurence Sterne (1713–1768), *The Life and Opinions of Tristram Shandy*, vol. VII, ch. 25, in which the Abbess tries to drive her mules by using the muleteer's coarse expressions, 'bouger' and 'fouter' (*bougre* and *foutre*). She avoids the venial sin of swearing by uttering only the first syllable in each case, her novice Margarita supplying the second. The attempt is unsuccessful.

11　**like the Duke of Buckingham**: see Shakespeare's *Richard III*, Act III, Scene VI.

12　**Merlin of Douai**: Philippe-Antoine Merlin de Douai (1754–1838). He voted for the execution of Louis XVI and proposed the so-called 'Law of Suspects', which severely curtailed individual freedom during the Reign of Terror. He was exiled after the second Bourbon restoration.

13 **Regnault de St Jean d'Angely**: Michel Louis Étienne Renaud de Saint-Jean d'Angely (1761–1819), Secretary of State, he was the first of Napoleon's councillors on 21 June 1815 to suggest his only course was abdication.

14 **Boulay de la Meurthe**: Antoine Jacques Claude Joseph, Comte Boulay de la Meurthe (1761–1840).

15 **peer . . . St Stephen's**: reference to the cry, 'I spy strangers!', of a member of the House of Commons on noticing a Peer or other unauthorised person in the Chamber. St Stephen's chapel, Westminster, was used for sittings of the Commons until it was destroyed by fire in 1834.

16 **Davoust . . . defence of Hamburgh**: Louis Nicholas Davout, Duke of Auerstädt, Prince of Eckmühl (1770–1823) defended the fortified port city of Hamburgh from 24 December 1813 until 12 May 1814.

17 **Prince-Marshal**: i.e. Blücher.

18 **Congreve's rockets**: the invention of Sir William Congreve (1772–1828).

19 **Massena**: Marshal André Masséna, Duke of Rivoli, Prince of Essling Masséna (1758–1817).

20 **'Where the flesh'd soldier . . . wide as hell'**: see Shakespeare, *Henry V,* Act III, Scene III.

21 **'Should not I spare Nineveh . . . also much cattle'**: Jonah 4:11.

22 **Tilly . . . Magdeburg**: during the Thirty Years War, Johann Tserclaes, Count of Tilly (1559–1632), commanding the forces of the German Catholic

League, allied to the Holy Roman Emperor, laid siege to and plundered the Protestant city of Magdeburg. In the massacre that followed only 5,000 of its 30,000 citizens were left alive.

23 **Edinburgh Volunteers**: Royal Edinburgh Volunteer Light Dragoons. See introductory essay, pp. 4–5.

24 **Mareschal M'Donald, Duke of Tarentum**: Marshal of France, Étienne Jacques Joseph Alexandre MacDonald, Duke of Taranto (1765–1840).

25 **Moreau**: General Jean Victor Marie Moreau (1763–1813).

26 **battle of Novi**: 15 August 1799.

27 **our affair . . . of 1745**: the Jacobite Rebellion, setting for *Waverley* (1814).

28 **splendid review**: see general introduction, p. 11.

29 **devouring cannibal . . . voyages of Aboulfouaris**: see Henry Weber, *Tales of the East*, vol. 2. Aboulfouaris, 'The Great Voyager', reminiscent of Sinbad, tells of rescuing a monstrous naked man from the sea who demands food and proceeds to eat all the provisions of the ship. The crew try to throw him back overboard but he resists and proves invulnerable to their cutlasses. Powerless, they wait to catch him unawares when he falls asleep but 'The cruel wretch, guessing our design, told us he never slept; that the great quantity of victuals he eat repaired the wearisomeness of nature and supplied the want of sleep.' Eventually a gigantic *roc* swoops down and plucks him from the deck. A vicious fight ensues and the monstrous man and bird kill one another.

30 **The Order of Faith and Honour**: unidentified.

31 **They are but warriors . . . painful field**:

Shakespeare, *Henry V,* Act IV, Scene III.

32   **Castle of Vincennes**: Charles V's fourteenth-century fortress on the eastern outskirts of Paris.

33   **Caliph Vathek**: William Beckford's Gothic novel *Vathek* was published in Lausanne in 1807. The hall referred to is encountered towards the end: '. . . a place which, though roofed with a vaulted ceiling, was so spacious and lofty, that at first they took it for an immeasurable plain. But their eyes at length growing familiar to the grandeur . . . discovered rows of columns and arcades, which gradually diminished, till they terminated in a point radiant as the sun when he darts his last beams athwart the ocean.'

34   **battlepiece by Salvator**: Salvator Rosa (1615–1673) was noted for his rocky landscapes, his scenes of the Hundred Years War and of witchcraft. His 'celebrated picture of the Witch of Endor' particularly impressed Scott in the Louvre. He was also impressed by 'a battle-piece . . . representing an attack of cavalry on a bridge, remarkable for its spirit and force', by Philips Wouwerman (1619–1668) rather than Salvator (*Journal*, p. 159).

35   **battle of Issy . . . 2nd of July**: the last engagement – between General Ziethen's Prussian I Korps and the French III Corps commanded by General Vandamme – before the capitulation of Paris. Scott mistakenly dates it June rather than July.

36   **Ha! Majesty . . . is set on fire**: Shakespeare, *King John*, Act II, Scene I.

37   **Colonel Francis Hepburn . . . Lieutenant-Colonel Home**: Hepburn (1779–1835), Alexander George Woodforde (1782–1870), James Macdonell

(1781–1857). *The Waterloo Roll Call* (2nd edition, 1904) has the following note relating to Lieutenant-Colonel Francis Home: 'Gained distinction in the defence of Hougoumont, and succeeded Col. Macdonell (who was wounded) in the command *within* the building late in the afternoon of Waterloo Day.'

LETTER XV: PAUL TO THE REVEREND MR ——, MINISTER OF THE GOSPEL AT ——

1 **old Dame of Babylon**: 'And upon her forehead was a name written, MYSTERY, BABYLON THE GREAT, THE MOTHER OF HARLOTS AND ABOMINATIONS OF THE EARTH' (Revelation 17:5). Presbyterianism taught that the 'Whore of Babylon' represented the Roman Catholic Church. See also, Scott's Covenanter, Mr Gifted Gilfillan's remark: 'the muckle harlot, that sitteth upon seven hills, and drinketh the cup of abomination.' (*Waverley*, ch. 36)

2 **the *Nineteenthly* of an afternoon's sermon**: compare the *Seventhly* on p. 305 (Letter I, note 1). The *nineteenthly* is presumably a head or topic at the end.

3 *pavé*: i.e. figuratively relegated to the pavement.

4 **Giant Pope . . . Giant Pagan**: see John Bunyan (1628–1688) *The Pilgrim's Progress*. 'I espied a little before me a cave, where two giants, *Pope* and *Pagan*, dwelt in old time, by whose Power and Tyranny the Men whose bones, blood, ashes, &c. lay there, were cruelly put to death . . . *Pagan* has been dead many a day, and as for the other, though he be yet alive, he is by reason of age, and also of the many shrewd brushes that he met with in his younger days, grown so crazy

and stiff in his joints, that he can now do little more than sit in his Cave's mouth, grinning at Pilgrims as they go by, and biting his nails, because he cannot come at them.'

5   **the year X**: 23 September 1801–22 September 1802 in the French Republican Calendar.

6   **Edict of Nantes**: signed by Henry IV of France in 1598, it granted civil rights to Calvinist Protestants or Huguenots. Its revocation at Fontainbleau by Louis XIV in 1685 led to widespread religious intolerance and persecution.

7   **Clement Marot . . . *belle Endormie***: French poet Clément Marot (1496–1544) translated the Psalms into vernacular French, a form more congenial to Protestant congregations than Latin. 'Awake, Sleeping Beauty' was a popular eighteenth-century French song.

8   **Calvinistic heroes of moor and moss**: the signatories of the National Covenant of 1638 rejecting James VI's *Book of Common Prayer*. To escape persecution the 'covenanters' held their religious services in the open air in remote country areas.

9   **'arose the song . . . the breeze-borne note'**: see James Grahame (1765–1811), *The Sabbath*.

10 **parable of Lord Shaftesbury . . . be spoken for?'**: Anthony Ashley-Cooper, 1st Earl of Shaftesbury (1621–1683). 'We have a little sister, and she hath no breasts: what shall we do for our sister in the day when she shall be spoken for?' (Song of Solomon 8:8)

11 **Dom-Daniel**: a hall at the bottom of the sea haunted by evil magicians and spirits, first mentioned in *Arabian Tales; Being a Continuation of the Arabian Nights Entertainments. Consisting of One Thousand and*

One Stories, Told by the Sultaness of the Indies (1793), 'translated' by Denis Chavis and Jacques Cazotte. Robert Southey (1774–1843) features it in his oriental epic poem *Thalaba the Destroyer* (1801).

12 **E O tables**: an early form of roulette popular in England during the 1770s and prohibited by legislation in the early 1780s. It was played by dropping a ball into a spinning wheel divided into forty sections, half marked 'E' and half 'O': Even and Odd.

13 **Joanna Southcote**: (1750–1814) English mystic and prophetess who claimed to be the woman spoken of in the Book of Revelation (12:1) 'clothed with the sun, and the moon under her feet, and upon her head a crown of twelve stars'. At the age of sixty-four she claimed to be pregnant with the new Messiah whose date was fixed for 19 October 1814.

14 **Baron Swedenborg**: Emanuel Swedenborg (1688–1772) Swedish scientist, philosopher and, for the last twenty-eight years of his life, theologian and mystic.

15 **Wallenstein . . . And plunges in unfathomable ruin'**: the lines come from Coleridge's translation of the third play in Schiller's trilogy, *The Death of Wallenstein*, Act IV, Scene II.

LETTER XVI: PAUL TO HIS COUSIN PETER

1 **'*Ou veux tu . . . Imbecille*'**: 'Where do you want me to go, Traitor?' 'Where you like, Imbecile.'

2 **Shaftesbury and Sunderland**: Anthony Ashley Cooper, 1st Earl of Shaftesbury (1621–1683), and Sir Charles Spencer, 3rd Earl of Sunderland (1675–1722). During the English Civil War Shaftesbury fought on the Royalist side first, then went over to the Parliamentary

NOTES TO PAUL'S LETTERS TO HIS KINSFOLK

side. He was one of a Parliamentary delegation that invited Charles II to return to England. Sunderland held high office under George I but in later life was implicated in a plot to restore the House of Stuart.

3 *Dictionnaire des Girouettes*: published in Paris, 1815, the 'Dictionary of Weathervanes' had as frontispiece an allegorical engraving showing a much-decorated official signing documents on the turning sails of a windmill. Underneath was a quotation from the Persian poet Saadi: 'If the plague was giving pensions, the plague would still find flatterers and servants.' Below this was a Latin phrase: *verba volant scripta manent* – words fly, writing remains.

4 **Duke of Wellington . . . Castlereagh**: it is generally believed that Fouché colluded with the English throughout his last term in office as Napoleon's Minister of Police during the Hundred Days, and that he was responsible for passing to Wellington the detailed account of the strength and disposition of the French army circulated to the allies on 16 May 1815.

5 **Talleyrand**: Charles Maurice de Talleyrand-Périgord (1754–1838), Napoleon's former Foreign Minister, chief French negotiator at the Congress of Vienna in 1814 and instrumental in the restoration of Louis XVIII.

6 *Royalistes purs et par excellence*: royalists through and through.

7 **two or three principal criminals . . . all the rest**: Louis XVIII's proclamation at Cambrai on 28 June had promised an amnesty to 'misled Frenchmen' for their conduct during the Hundred Days. There were, however, to be exemptions. On 26 July the

Moniteur Universal published a list of fifty-seven individuals. Thirty-eight of these, who had rallied to Bonaparte *after* the King's departure from France on 23 March, were ordered to leave Paris within three days and placed under surveillance in the provinces pending a decision by the legislature. The fate of the other nineteen was to be more clear-cut. These, who had actively participated in the violent overthrow of royal authority *before* 23 March, were to be tried for treason. Only three of the proscribed individuals were executed: La Bédoyère, Ney and General Mouton-Duvernet who was shot at Lyons on 27 July. A few were tried and acquitted, the rest escaped abroad.

8 **Duc d'Enghien**: the royalist martyr was executed by firing squad at the Château de Vincennes in March 1804, allegedly on charges trumped up by First Consul Bonaparte.

9 **King Phys. and King Ush.**: see George Villiers, the Duke of Buckingham (1628–1687), *The Rehearsal*.

10 **one of the king's proclamations**: it was made at Cambrai, 28 June 1815: 'I hasten . . . to place myself . . . between the Allied and the French armies, in the hope that the feelings of consideration of which I may be the object may tend to their preservation. This is the only way in which I have wished to take part in the war. I have not permitted any prince of my family to appear in foreign ranks, and have chained in the courage of those of my servants who had been able to range themselves around me.' Reported in *The Times*, 4 July 1815.

11 **Edward I . . . victory at Dunbar**: Edward invaded Scotland in 1296 ostensibly to wrest control from the

council of nobles that had effectively deposed John Balliol, King of Scots. Following the battle of Dunbar, Edward claimed the Scottish throne, established a Scottish Parliament at Berwick to govern in his name and removed the Stone of Scone to England.

12 **Exclusion Bill**: introduced in May 1679, the Bill was intended to exclude Charles II's brother and heir presumptive, James, Duke of York, from succeeding to the throne on the grounds that he was a Roman Catholic. It was opposed by the Tory Party while the Bill's supporters would later become known as the Whig Party. Attempts to pass it resulted in successive dissolutions of Parliament over the following two years before the 'Exclusion Crisis' was finally brought to an end and the Bill defeated by the House of Lords in 1681.

13 **Huningen**: the Allies' failed blockade of the garrison town of Hüningen in Alsace-Lorraine began on 21 December 1813 and continued until 15 April 1814, even though Paris had fallen in March and Napoleon had abdicated for the first time on 11 April. Louis XVIII did not arrive to take possession of his throne until 3 May.

14 **Napoleon's present place of exile**: St Helena was 5,000 miles from Europe; 1,800 miles from the coast of South America and 1,200 miles from Africa. 'At such a distance and in such a place', the British Prime Minister, Lord Liverpool, declared, 'all intrigue would be impossible, and, being withdrawn so far from the European world, he would be very soon forgotten.' (Liverpool to Castlereagh, 21 July 1815)

15 **we have but scotched the snake, not killed him**: see Shakespeare, *Macbeth*, Act III, Scene IV.

16   **their tears . . . rejoicings his return**: compare
      Louis XVIII's Proclamation to the French People
      issued at Cambrai, 28 June 1815: 'I promise . . . to
      pardon misled Frenchmen, all that has passed since
      the day when I quitted Lille, amidst so many tears, up
      to the day when I entered Cambrai, amidst so many
      acclamations.' Reported in *The Times*, 4 July 1815.

17   *Wittenagemot*: deriving from the Old English for
      'meeting of wise men', this was a sort of Anglo-Saxon
      parliament – an assembly of English noblemen, both
      secular and ecclesiastical, operating from the late sixth
      to the eleventh century, and whose primary function
      was to advise the king.

18   **Costard . . . that did amount**: see Shakespeare,
      Love's Labours Lost, Act V, Scene II.

19   **idle dreamer . . . the streamer**: see Matthew Prior
      (1664–1721), *Alma; or, The Progress of the Mind. In Three
      Cantos. Canto 1.*

20   **like Fabius**: Quintus Fabius Maximus Verrucosus
      (*c.*280–203 BC) was a Roman dictator and general.
      Believing that Hannibal could not be defeated in
      a pitched battle, he held back from confrontation
      and conducted a campaign of attrition against the
      Carthaginian commander, thereby earning himself an
      additional name: 'Cunctator' – the Delayer.

21   **National Representatives**: in the state of emergency
      following the defeat at Waterloo, and to prevent
      Napoleon seizing dictatorial power, the Chamber of
      Representatives had declared itself *en permanence*, any
      attempt to dissolve it constituting an act of treason.
      This state of permanence was, however, shortlived.
      With the restoration of Louis XVIII the Chamber was

dissolved and in October 1815 a new assembly – the Chamber of Deputies – was elected, dominated by ultra-royalists determined to undo the effects of the Revolution and re-establish the *ancien régime*. Louis XVIII, recognising such a policy as unobtainable, called this far from conciliatory body *la Chambre introuvable*.

22 **free-quarters from pandours**: refers to the billeting of Croatian infantrymen in the pay of the Austrian army – figuratively: robbers.

23 **Brissotins**: members of a moderating political faction led by Jacques-Pierre Brissot in the Legislative Assembly of the National Convention during the French Revolution. They were also known as 'Girondists' because the most prominent members were Deputies from the *département* of the Gironde in south-western France. Their mass execution in 1793 marked the beginning of the Terror.

24 **work of Mr John Scott**: *A Visit to Paris in 1814: being a review of the moral, political, intellectual and social condition of the French Capital* by John Scott, Editor of *The Champion* newspaper, was published by Longman, Hurst, Rees, Orme and Brown early in 1815. A second edition, 'corrected, and with a new preface referring to late events' was published 7 September the same year. The author paid a second visit, during the allied occupation, and wrote *Paris revisited, in 1815, by way of Brussels: including a walk over the field of battle at Waterloo*, published 1816.

25 **the joint production of two young gentlemen**: *Travels in France during the years 1814–1815: Comprising a residence at Paris, during the stay of the allied armies, and*

at Aix, at the period of the landing of Bonaparte, published 1815, had three authors: Sir Archibald Alison, William P. Alison and John Hope. A second volume was by Alexander Fraser Tytler.

26   **Mr S——n of Edinburgh**: *A Visit to Flanders, in July, 1815, being chiefly an account of the Field of Waterloo, etc.* by 'James Simpson, Advocate' was published later that year.

27   **a lively French friend**: presumably the traveller and archaeologist, Jean-Baptiste Le Chevalier, Scott's guide throughout his stay in Paris.

28   **a very fine picture of the ex-emperor, and a most excellent bust**: the painting was by François-Pascal-Simon Gérard (1770–1837). 'It was a kit-cat, or three quarter's picture . . . the dress green, with white facings, and the usual decorations worn by the original: – the colour of the countenance was of a pale hue, and the remarkable expression of the eye delineated with much force. It was . . . reckoned the best likeness that had ever been taken of Napoleon.' (*Journal* p. 129) James Simpson wrote of the same occasion: 'One of the most striking and significant features of the scene was the appearance of a portrait of Napoleon, which had been recently finished for Junot; and was left leaning against a wall in one of the rooms. The Duke, with true magnanimity, had allowed the picture to remain; so that the fallen emperor also seemed to form part of the company. I saw the King of Prussia and one or two other personages, whose fates had been strangely connected with his, stand for a few seconds before the portrait, and a few remarks on the fidelity of the likeness.' (*Paris After Waterloo*, pp. 195–6)

29   **Barclay de Tolli . . . Beresina**: Field Marshal Michael
      Andreas Barclay de Tolly (1761–1818), commander in
      chief of the Russian army, was a descendant of the
      Scottish clan Barclay. The Cossack chief, or Hetmann,
      Count Matvei Ivanovich Platov (1751–1818), 'a great
      favourite' of Scott's from his reading of the Russian
      campaign, was in turn especially attentive to the writer
      in Paris. Napoleon's retreat from Moscow was along
      the Kaluga Road, and fighting at the river Beresina
      further west took place over three days in November
      1812. General A. Chernyshev (1785–1857) fought at
      Austerlitz and Freidland, and used highly effective
      guerrilla tactics against the retreating French army.

The Field of Waterloo, a Poem

Introduction

Scott told James Ballantyne that 'he had never felt awed or abashed except in the presence of one man – the Duke of Wellington'. And when Ballantyne suggested that he had perhaps impressed the Duke also – as a great poet and novelist – Scott was self-deprecating: 'What would the Duke of Wellington think of a few *bits of novels*, which perhaps he had never read, and for which the strong probability is that he would not care a sixpence if he had?' Whatever – if anything – he thought of Scott as a writer, Wellington was 'most distinguishingly civil' at their first meeting shortly after the writer's arrival in Paris:

At supper I had the honour of sitting next the Duke by special invitation & he told me all I could ask him about his campaigns & particularly about the Battle of Waterloo – he is the most plain & downright person you ever knew. [1]

---

[1] Scott to his wife, postmarked 28 August, *Letters* XII, p. 143.

It would have been surprising if, during that conversation or some time later, Scott had not asked His Grace's permission to dedicate to him the poem he was then composing about the battle. The Duke's refusal of such an honour would not have indicated his approval or otherwise of Scott's poetry, only his distaste for such attentions. In the months and years following the battle many an author of a 'Memoir', 'True Account' or 'Accurate Narrative' of Waterloo would write begging for the effective endorsement of the Duke's name on its dedication page. Each would receive an identical reply:

> I have long felt myself under the necessity of declining to give my consent that any work should be dedicated to me, with the contents of which I am not previously acquainted; and you will readily believe, that I feel this necessity in a stronger degree in regard to a History of the Battle of Waterloo, than I should do upon any other subject.[2]

And it was presumably for this reason that Scott had to settle for dedicating his poem to the Duke's wife instead, addressing her by the title she had just acquired following the King of the Netherlands' elevation of her husband to the Dutch aristocracy: 'Her Grace the Duchess of Wellington, Princess of Waterloo'.

The poem was published in late October. 'It is not so good as I wish it,' Scott told a friend. 'But after repeated trials it is as good as I can make it.'[3] After the dedication page came a disclaimer in which he apologised for any 'imperfections'

---

[2] 'Original Letters from the Duke of Wellington, Respecting the Battle of Waterloo', *Canterbury Magazine*, October 1834.

[3] Scott to John B. S. Morritt, 2 November 1815, *Letters* IV, p. 111.

in the poem, explaining that it had been 'composed hastily' and at a time when 'the Author's labours were liable to frequent interruption'. Its unassailable vindication was the urgency with which it had been written and published: 'for the purpose of assisting the Waterloo Subscription'. The two considerations of hurried writing and charitable intent attracted a particularly favourable notice in *La Belle Assemblée*, a London periodical rejoicing in the subtitle *Bell's Court and Fashionable Magazine Addressed Particularly to the Ladies*. The anonymous correspondent declined to offer criticism of 'a work above all praise, both for its own peculiar merit, and the benevolent purpose for which it was written' and then declared that 'if the hasty productions of Mr Scott are thus replete with poetic excellence and interest, we may venture to affirm he need never bestow much time and labour in the charming productions which issue from his pen'.

Opinion elsewhere seems to have split along political lines. The Tory *Morning Post* withheld criticism, and confined itself to featuring short excerpts from the poem. Not so the Whig-aligned *Morning Chronicle*. Scott had anticipated that *The Field of Waterloo* would 'give offence to [his] old friends the Whigs by not condoling with Bonaparte'.[4] So it proved, although no mention was made of the poet's unfavourable assessment of Napoleon: his ruthless ambition, his flight from the field, his failure to take the honourable course of dying with his men, 'Abhorr'd – but not despised'.[5] Instead, the *Chronicle* contrived a test of the poem's literary worth by first converting an extract into prose and then back into verse. It concluded, 'the rich imagery, the pathos of genuine

---

[4] Scott to John B. S. Morritt, 2 October 1815, *Letters* IV, p. 100.
[5] Stanza XIII, line 38.

poetry must certainly lose much by being turned into prose, but what appears in that shape, stupid flat nonsense, cannot be good or beautiful in poetry'.[6]

A fortnight later, the *Morning Post* carried a joke subsequently taken up in a number of other newspapers: 'Some ill-natured critics assert, that WALTER SCOTT has *fallen* in *"the field of Waterloo"*'.[7] The *Morning Chronicle* followed its formal analysis by printing an ode of its own, attacking the poems of Scott in general, his latest in particular:

> WALTER SCOTT! – WALTER SCOTT!
> How hard is his Lot
> Who is doom'd to read over thy rhymes?
> Such goblins! – such frights!
> Such sieges! – such fights!
> Such customs! – such manners! – such times!
>
> Then comes Waterloo
> With a *holloa bellou*!
> Of Legions disabled and slain;
> But you not content
> With the blood they have spent,
> Will *mangle* them over again.[8]

Generally regarded as inferior to most of Scott's other work, the poem's very subject matter invited comparison with his already celebrated climactic battle scenes – with that of Bannockburn in *The Lord of the Isles*, published in

---

[6] 3 November 1815.
[7] 17 November 1815.
[8] 4 December 1815.

January 1815, and particularly with that of *Marmion: A Tale of Flodden Field* seven years earlier. The most succinct and famous of the squibs thrown at *The Field of Waterloo* has a final, seldom quoted couplet that makes the unfavourable comparison with the earlier poem clear:

> How prostrate lie the heaps of slain
> On Waterloo's immortal plain!
> But none by sabre or by shot,
> Fell half so flat as WALTER SCOTT
>
> Yet who with magic spear or shield
> E'er fought like him on Flodden Field.[9]

Modern readers, however, should attempt to approach it with an open mind. It does not suffer today from the same comparisons made in 1815, Scott's poetry being read now more seldom even than his prose. It certainly possesses an advantage – for those reading it in 2015 as opposed to that more leisured and patient readership for whom Scott was writing two centuries ago – in being comparatively short. *Marmion* runs to well over 300 pages, *The Lord of the Isles* to 275, with a further 168 pages of the author's notes. *The Field of Waterloo* can be read at a sitting. Perhaps it also benefits, in economy and immediacy, from the speed at which it was composed. It takes just three of its twenty-three stanzas to get us from the forest of Soignes, through the village of Waterloo and, a mile further, to the top of the slope overlooking the battlefield, during a hot day such as that on which Scott himself first saw it. The following three

---

[9] Anonymous, 'Epigram on Scott's Waterloo', *Monthly Repository of Theology and General Literature*, March 1816.

stanzas, like those preceding, are written in the present tense, the poet, as it were, taking the reader by the arm and pointing out this or that detail of the terrain as it appeared to him on 10 August 1815, relating each to the action only seven weeks earlier:

> . . . that line so black
> And trampled, marks the bivouack,
> Yon deep-graved ruts the artillery's track,
>   So often lost and won;
> And close beside, the harden'd mud
> Still shows where, fetlock-deep in blood,
> The fierce dragoon, through battle's flood,
>   Dash'd the hot war-horse on.

This sixth stanza culminates in a passage that only a man who had stood close to a fresh, thinly covered mass grave in the heat of summer could have written:

> And feel'st thou not the tainted steam,
>   That reeks against the sultry beam,
>   From yonder trenched mound?
> The pestilential fumes declare
> That Carnage has replenish'd there
>   Her garner-house profound.

Having been drawn by Scott this far into his narrative, today's reader is unlikely to find the remaining seventeen stanzas either tedious or lacking in dramatic and emotional power. *The Field of Waterloo*, like any rhythmical poem, is most effectively read aloud and the four-foot lines of its tetrameter can take us at a brisk canter to the finish. True, the smart clip of that rhythm is brought to an abrupt plod with the six Spenserian stanzas of Scott's 'Conclusion'. This shift from eight to ten syllables per line, and an extra two in the ninth line of each stanza, slows the pace considerably and might seem, to modern taste, at best an anticlimax, at worst a ponderous makeweight to be passed over with little loss. It should, however, be read; and read as Scott intended: sonorously addressed to the 'Stern tide of human Time', summing up the long period of warfare ended by Napoleon's defeat with an elegiac meditation on history, peace and the moral legacy of carnage.

THE

FIELD

OF

WATERLOO;

A POEM.

BY

WALTER SCOTT, Esq.

Though Valois braved young Edward's gentle hand,
And Albret rush'd on Henry's way-worn band,
With Europe's chosen sons in arms renown'd,
Yet not on Vere's bold archers long they look'd,
Nor Audley's squires nor Mowbray's yeomen brook'd,—
They saw their standard fall, and left their monarch bound.

AKENSIDE.

EDINBURGH:

Printed by James Ballantyne & Co.

FOR ARCHIBALD CONSTABLE AND CO. EDINBURGH; AND
LONGMAN, HURST, REES, ORME, AND BROWN,
AND JOHN MURRAY, LONDON.

1815.

To
Her Grace
The
Duchess of Wellington,
Princess of Waterloo,
&c. &c. &c.

The following verses
are most respectfully inscribed
by
the author.

ADVERTISEMENT.

It may be some apology for the imperfections of this Poem, that it was composed hastily, during a short tour upon the continent, when the Author's labours were liable to frequent interruption. But its best vindication is, that it was written for the purpose of assisting the Waterloo Subscription.

THE FIELD OF WATERLOO.

Fair Brussels, thou art far behind,
Though, lingering on the morning wind,
 We yet may hear the hour
Peal'd over orchard and canal,
With voice prolong'd and measured fall,
 From proud Saint Michael's tower;
Thy wood, dark Soignies, holds us now,
Where the tall beeches' glossy bough
 For many a league around,
With birch and darksome oak between,
Spreads deep and far a pathless screen,
 Of tangled forest ground.
Stems planted close by stems defy
The adventurous foot—the curious eye
 For access seeks in vain;
And the brown tapestry of leaves,
Strew'd on the blighted ground, receives
 Nor sun, nor air, nor rain.
No opening glade dawns on our way,
No streamlet, glancing to the ray,
 Our woodland path has cross'd;
And the straight causeway which we tread,
Prolongs a line of dull arcade,

Unvarying through the unvaried shade
 Until in distance lost.

II.

A brighter, livelier scene succeeds;
In groupes the scattering wood recedes,
Hedge-rows, and huts, and sunny meads,
 And corn-fields glance between;
The peasant, at his labour blithe,
Plies the hook'd staff and shorten'd scythe:—
 But when these ears were green,
Placed close within destruction's scope,
Full little was that rustic's hope
 Their ripening to have seen!
And, lo, a hamlet and its fane:—
Let not the gazer with disdain
 Their architecture view;
For yonder rude ungraceful shrine,
And disproportion'd spire, are thine,
 Immortal WATERLOO!

III.

Fear not the heat, though full and high
The sun has scorch'd the autumn sky,
And scarce a forest straggler now
To shade us spreads a greenwood bough;
These fields have seen a hotter day
Than ere was fired by sunny ray.
Yet one mile on—yon shatter'd hedge
Crests the soft hill whose long smooth ridge
 Looks on the field below,
And sinks so gently on the dale,

That not the folds of Beauty's veil
    In easier curves can flow.
Brief space from thence, the ground again
Ascending slowly from the plain,
    Forms an opposing screen,
Which, with its crest of upland ground,
Shuts the horizon all around.
    The soften'd vale between
Slopes smooth and fair for courser's tread;
Not the most timid maid need dread
To give her snow-white palfrey head
    On that wide stubble-ground;
Nor wood, nor tree, nor bush are there,
Her course to intercept or scare,
    Nor fosse nor fence are found,
Save where, from out her shatter'd bowers,
Rise Hougoumont's dismantled towers.

IV.

Now, see'st thou aught in this lone scene
Can tell of that which late hath been?—
    A stranger might reply,
'The bare extent of stubble-plain
Seems lately lighten'd of its grain;
And yonder sable tracks remain
Marks of the peasant's ponderous wain,
    When harvest-home was nigh.
On these broad spots of trampled ground,
Perchance the rustics danced such round
    As Teniers loved to draw;
And where the earth seems scorch'd by flame
To dress the homely feast they came,

And toil'd the kerchief'd village dame
    Around her fire of straw.'—

V.

So deem'st thou—so each mortal deems,
Of that which is from that which seems:—
    But other harvest here
Than that which peasant's scythe demands,
Was gather'd in by sterner hands,
    With bayonet, blade, and spear.
No vulgar crop was theirs to reap,
No stinted harvest thin and cheap!
Heroes before each fatal sweep
    Fell thick as ripen'd grain;
And ere the darkening of the day,
Piled high as autumn shocks, there lay
The ghastly harvest of the fray,
    The corpses of the slain.

VI.

Aye, look again—that line so black
And trampled, marks the bivouack,
Yon deep-graved ruts the artillery's track,
    So often lost and won;
And close beside, the harden'd mud
Still shows where, fetlock-deep in blood,
The fierce dragoon, through battle's flood,
    Dash'd the hot war-horse on.
These spots of excavation tell
The ravage of the bursting shell—
And feel'st thou not the tainted steam,
That reeks against the sultry beam,

370

From yonder trenched mound?
The pestilential fumes declare
That Carnage has replenish'd there
    Her garner-house profound.

VII.

Far other harvest-home and feast,
Than claims the boor from scythe released,
    On these scorch'd fields were known!
Death hover'd o'er the maddening rout,
And, in the thrilling battle-shout,
Sent for the bloody banquet out
    A summons of his own.
Through rolling smoke the Demon's eye
Could well each destined guest espy,
Well could his ear in ecstacy
    Distinguish every tone
That fill'd the chorus of the fray—
From cannon-roar and trumpet-bray,
From charging squadrons' wild hurra,
From the wild clang that mark'd their way,—
    Down to the dying groan,
And the last sob of life's decay
    When breath was all but flown.

VIII.

Feast on, stern foe of mortal life,
Feast on!—but think not that a strife,
With such promiscuous carnage rife,
    Protracted space may last;
The deadly tug of war at length
Must limits find in human strength,

And cease when these are pass'd.
Vain hope!—that morn's o'erclouded sun
Heard the wild shout of fight begun
    Ere he attain'd his height,
And through the war-smoke volumed high,
Still peals that unremitted cry,
    Though now he stoops to night.
For ten long hours of doubt and dread,
Fresh succours from the extended head
Of either hill the contest fed;
    Still down the slope they drew,
The charge of columns paused not,
Nor ceased the storm of shell and shot;
    For all that war could do
Of skill and force was proved that day,
And turn'd not yet the doubtful fray
    On bloody Waterloo.

IX.

Pale Brussels! then what thoughts were thine,
When ceaseless from the distant line
    Continued thunders came!
Each burgher held his breath, to hear
These forerunners of havock near,
    Of rapine and of flame.
What ghastly sights were thine to meet,
When, rolling through thy stately street,
The wounded shew'd their mangled plight
In token of the unfinish'd fight,
And from each anguish-laden wain
The blood-drops laid thy dust like rain!
How often in the distant drum

Heard'st thou the fell Invader come,
While Ruin, shouting to his band,
Shook high her torch and gory brand!—
Cheer thee, fair City! From yon stand,
Impatient, still his outstretch'd hand
    Points to his prey in vain,
While maddening in his eager mood,
And all unwont to be withstood,
    He fires the fight again.

X.

'On! On!' was still his stern exclaim;
'Confront the battery's jaws of flame!
    'Rush on the levell'd gun!
'My steel-clad cuirassiers, advance!
'Each Hulan forward with his lance,
'My Guard—my chosen—charge for France,
    'France and Napoleon!'
Loud answer'd their acclaiming shout,
Greeting the mandate which sent out
Their bravest and their best to dare
The fate their leader shunn'd to share.
But HE, his country's sword and shield,
Still in the battle-front reveal'd,
Where danger fiercest swept the field,
    Came like a beam of light,
In action prompt, in sentence brief—
'Soldiers, stand firm,' exclaim'd the Chief,
    'England shall tell the fight!'

XI.

On came the whirlwind—like the last

But fiercest sweep of tempest blast—
On came the whirlwind—steel-gleams broke
Like lightning through the rolling smoke,
    The war was waked anew,
Three hundred cannon-mouths roar'd loud,
And from their throats, with flash and cloud,
    Their showers of iron threw.
Beneath their fire, in full career,
Rush'd on the ponderous cuirassier,
The lancer couch'd his ruthless spear,
And hurrying as to havock near,
    The Cohorts' eagles flew.
In one dark torrent broad and strong,
The advancing onset roll'd along,
Forth harbinger'd by fierce acclaim,
That from the shroud of smoke and flame,
Peal'd wildly the imperial name.

XII.

But on the British heart were lost
The terrors of the charging host;
For not an eye the storm that view'd
Changed its proud glance of fortitude,
Nor was one forward footstep staid,
As dropp'd the dying and the dead.
Fast as their ranks the thunders tear,
Fast they renew'd each serried square;
And on the wounded and the slain
Closed their diminish'd files again,
Till from their line scarce spears' lengths three,
Emerging from the smoke they see
Helmet and plume and panoply,—

Then waked their fire at once!
Each musketeer's revolving knell,
As fast, as regularly fell,
As when they practise to display
Their discipline on festal day.
    Then down went helm and lance,
Down were the eagle banners sent,
Down reeling steeds and riders went,
Corslets were pierced, and pennons rent;
    And to augment the fray,
Wheel'd full against their staggering flanks,
The English horsemen's foaming ranks
    Forced their resistless way.
Then to the musket-knell succeeds
The clash of swords—the neigh of steeds—
As plies the smith his clanging trade,
Against the cuirass rang the blade;
And while amid their close array
The well-served cannon rent their way,
And while amid their scatter'd band
Raged the fierce rider's bloody brand,
Recoil'd in common rout and fear,
Lancer and guard and cuirassier,
Horsemen and foot,—a mingled host,
Their leaders fallen, their standards lost.

XIII.

Then, WELLINGTON! thy piercing eye
This crisis caught of destiny—
    The British host had stood
That morn 'gainst charge of sword and lance
As their own ocean-rocks hold stance,

But when thy voice had said, 'Advance!'
    They were their ocean's flood.—
O Thou, whose inauspicious aim
Hath wrought thy host this hour of shame,
Think'st thou thy broken bands will bide
The terrors of yon rushing tide?
Or will thy Chosen brook to feel
The British shock of levell'd steel?
    Or dost thou turn thine eye
Where coming squadrons gleam afar,
And fresher thunders wake the war,
    And other standards fly?—
Think not that in yon columns, file
Thy conquering troops from distant Dyle—
    Is Blucher yet unknown?
Or dwells not in thy memory still,
(Heard frequent in thine hour of ill)
What notes of hate and vengeance thrill
    In Prussia's trumpet tone?—
What yet remains?—shall it be thine
To head the reliques of thy line
    In one dread effort more?—
The Roman lore thy leisure loved,
And thou can'st tell what fortune proved
   That Chieftain, who, of yore,
Ambition's dizzy paths essay'd,
And with the gladiators' aid
    For empire enterprized—
He stood the cast his rashness play'd,
Left not the victims he had made,
Dug his red grave with his own blade,
And on the field he lost was laid,

Abhorr'd—but not despised.

XIV.

But if revolves thy fainter thought
On safety—howsoever bought,
Then turn thy fearful rein and ride,
Though twice ten thousand men have died
    On this eventful day,
To gild the military fame
Which thou, for life, in traffic tame
    Wilt barter thus away.
Shall future ages tell this tale
Of inconsistence faint and frail?
And art thou He of Lodi's bridge,
Marengo's field, and Wagram's ridge!
    Or is thy soul like mountain-tide,
That, swell'd by winter storm and shower,
Rolls down in turbulence of power
    A torrent fierce and wide;
'Reft of these aids, a rill obscure,
Shrinking unnoticed, mean, and poor,
    Whose channel shows display'd
The wrecks of its impetuous course,
But not one symptom of the force
    By which these wrecks were made!

XV.

Spur on thy way!—since now thine ear
Has brook'd thy veterans' wish to hear,
    Who, as thy flight they eyed,
Exclaimed,—while tears of anguish came,
Wrung forth by pride and rage and shame,—

'Oh that he had but died!'
But yet, to sum this hour of ill,
Look, ere thou leav'st the fatal hill,
    Back on yon broken ranks—
Upon whose wild confusion gleams
The moon, as on the troubled streams
    When rivers break their banks,
And, to the ruin'd peasant's eye,
Objects half seen roll swiftly by,
    Down the dread current hurl'd—
So mingle banner, wain, and gun,
Where the tumultuous flight rolls on
Of warriors, who, when morn begun,
    Defied a banded world.

XVI.

List—frequent to the hurrying rout,
The stern pursuers' vengeful shout
Tells, that upon their broken rear
Rages the Prussian's bloody spear.
    So fell a shriek was none,
When Beresina's icy flood
Redden'd and thaw'd with flame and blood,
And, pressing on thy desperate way,
Raised oft and long their wild hurra,
    The children of the Don.
Thine ear no yell of horror cleft
So ominous, when, all bereft
Of aid, the valiant Polack left—
Aye, left by thee—found soldier's grave
In Leipsic's corpse-encumber'd wave.
Fate, in these various perils past,

Reserved thee still some future cast;—
On the dread die thou now hast thrown,
Hangs not a single field alone,
Nor one campaign—thy martial fame,
Thy empire, dynasty, and name,
    Have felt the final stroke;
And now, o'er thy devoted head
The last stern vial's wrath is shed,
    The last dread seal is broke.

XVII.

Since live thou wilt—refuse not now
Before these demagogues to bow,
Late objects of thy scorn and hate,
Who shall thy once imperial fate
Make wordy theme of vain debate—
Or shall we say, thou stoop'st less low
In seeking refuge from the foe,
Against whose heart, in prosperous life,
Thine hand hath ever held the knife?—
    Such homage hath been paid
By Roman and by Grecian voice,
And there were honour in the choice,
    If it were freely made.
Then safely come—in one so low,—
So lost,—we cannot own a foe;
Though dear experience bid us end,
In thee we ne'er can hail a friend.—
Come, howsoe'er—but do not hide
Close in thy heart that germ of pride,
Erewhile by gifted bard espied,
    That 'yet imperial hope;'

Think not that for a fresh rebound,
To raise ambition from the ground,
    We yield thee means or scope.
In safety come—but ne'er again
Hold type of independent reign;
    No islet calls thee lord,
We leave thee no confederate band,
No symbol of thy lost command,
To be a dagger in the hand
    From which we wrench'd the sword.

XVIII.

Yet, even in yon sequester'd spot,
May worthier conquest be thy lot
    Than yet thy life has known;
Conquest, unbought by blood or harm,
That needs nor foreign aid nor arm,
    A triumph all thine own.
Such waits thee when thou shalt controul
Those passions wild, that stubborn soul,
    That marr'd thy prosperous scene:—
Hear this—from no unmoved heart,
Which sighs, comparing what THOU ART
    With what thou MIGHT'ST HAVE BEEN!

XIX.

Thou, too, whose deeds of fame renew'd
Bankrupt a nation's gratitude,
To thine own noble heart must owe
More than the meed she can bestow.
For not a people's just acclaim,
Not the full hail of Europe's fame,

Thy prince's smiles, thy state's decree,
The ducal rank, the garter'd knee,
Not these such pure delight afford
As that, when, hanging up thy sword,
Well may'st thou think, 'This honest steel
Was ever drawn for public weal;
And, such was rightful Heaven's decree,
Ne'er sheathed unless with victory!'

XX.

Look forth, once more, with soften'd heart,
Ere from the field of fame we part;
Triumph and Sorrow border near,
And joy oft melts into a tear.
Alas! what links of love that morn
Has War's rude hand asunder torn!
For ne'er was field so sternly fought,
And ne'er was conquest dearer bought.
Here piled in common slaughter sleep
Those whom affection long shall weep;
Here rests the sire, that ne'er shall strain
His orphans to his heart again;
The son, whom, on his native shore,
The parent's voice shall bless no more;
The bridegroom, who has hardly press'd
His blushing consort to his breast;
The husband, whom through many a year
Long love and mutual faith endear.
Thou can'st not name one tender tie
But here dissolved its reliques lie!
O when thou see'st some mourner's veil,
Shroud her thin form and visage pale,

Or mark'st the Matron's bursting tears
Stream when the stricken drum she hears;
Or see'st how manlier grief, suppress'd,
Is labouring in a father's breast,—
With no enquiry vain pursue
The cause, but think on Waterloo!

XXI.

Period of honour as of woes,
What bright careers 'twas thine to close!—
Mark'd on thy roll of blood what names
To Britain's memory, and to Fame's,
Laid there their last immortal claims!
Thou saw'st in seas of gore expire
Redoubted PICTON's soul of fire—
Saw'st in the mingled carnage lie
All that of PONSONBY could die—
DE LANCY change Love's bridal-wreath,
For laurels from the hand of Death—
Saw'st gallant MILLER's failing eye
Still bent where Albion's banners fly,
And CAMERON, in the shock of steel,
Die like the offspring of Lochiel;
And generous GORDON, 'mid the strife,
Fall while he watch'd his leader's life.—
Ah! though her guardian angel's shield
Fenced Britain's hero through the field,
Fate not the less her power made known,
Through his friends' hearts to pierce his own!

XXII.

Forgive, brave Dead, the imperfect lay!

Who may your names, your numbers, say?
What high-strung harp, what lofty line,
To each the dear-earn'd praise assign,
From high-born chiefs of martial fame
To the poor soldier's lowlier name?
Lightly ye rose that dawning day,
From your cold couch of swamp and clay,
To fill, before the sun was low,
The bed that morning cannot know.—
Oft may the tear the green sod steep,
And sacred be the heroes' sleep,
  Till Time shall cease to run;
And ne'er beside their noble grave,
May Briton pass and fail to crave
A blessing on the fallen brave
  Who fought with Wellington!

XXIII.

Farewell, sad Field! whose blighted face
Wears desolation's withering trace;
Long shall my memory retain
Thy shatter'd huts and trampled grain,
With every mark of martial wrong,
That scathe thy towers, fair Hougomont!
Yet though thy garden's green arcade
The marksman's fatal post was made,
Though on thy shatter'd beeches fell
The blended rage of shot and shell,
Though from thy blacken'd portals torn
Their fall thy blighted fruit-trees mourn,
Has not such havock bought a name
Immortal in the rolls of fame?

Yes—Agincourt may be forgot,
And Cressy be an unknown spot,
    And Blenheim's name be new;
But still in story and in song,
For many an age remember'd long,
Shall live the towers of Hougomont,
    And fields of Waterloo.

CONCLUSION.

STERN tide of human Time! that know'st not rest,
    But, sweeping from the cradle to the tomb,
Bear'st ever downward on thy dusky breast
    Successive generations to their doom;
While thy capacious stream has equal room
    For the gay bark where Pleasure's streamers sport,
And for the prison-ship of guilt and gloom,
    The fisher-skiff, and barge that bears a court,
Still wafting onward all to one dark silent port.

Stern tide of Time! through what mysterious change
    Of hope and fear have our frail barks been driven!
For ne'er, before, vicissitude so strange
    Was to one race of Adam's offspring given.
And sure such varied change of sea and heaven,
    Such unexpected bursts of joy and woe,
Such fearful strife as that where we have striven,
    Succeeding ages ne'er again shall know,
Until the awful term when Thou shalt cease to flow.

Well hast thou stood, my Country!—the brave fight
    Hast well maintain'd through good report and ill;
In thy just cause and in thy native might,

And in Heaven's grace and justice constant still.
Whether the banded prowess, strength, and skill
    Of half the world against thee stood array'd,
Or when, with better views and freer will,
    Beside thee Europe's noblest drew the blade,
Each emulous in arms the Ocean Queen to aid.

Well art thou now repaid—though slowly rose,
    And struggled long with mists thy blaze of fame,
While like the dawn that in the orient glows
    On the broad wave its earlier lustre came;
Then eastern Egypt saw the growing flame,
    And Maida's myrtles gleam'd beneath its ray,
Where first the soldier, stung with generous shame,
    Rivall'd the heroes of the wat'ry way,
And wash'd in foemen's gore unjust reproach away.

Now, Island Empress, wave thy crest on high,
    And bid the banner of thy Patron flow,
Gallant Saint George, the flower of Chivalry!
    For thou hast faced, like him, a dragon foe,
And rescued innocence from overthrow,
    And trampled down, like him, tyrannic might,
And to the gazing world may'st proudly show
    The chosen emblem of thy sainted Knight,
Who quell'd devouring pride, and vindicated right.

Yet 'mid the confidence of just renown,
    Renown dear-bought, but dearest thus acquired,
Write, Britain, write the moral lesson down:
    'Tis not alone the heart with valour fired,
The discipline so dreaded and admired,

In many a field of bloody conquest known;
—Such may by fame be lured, by gold be hired—
'Tis constancy in the good cause alone,
Best justifies the meed thy valiant sons have won.

NOTES†

Note I.
The peasant, at his labour blithe,
Plies the hook'd staff and shorten'd scythe. [stanza II line 5]
The reaper in Flanders carries in his left hand a stick with
an iron hook, with which he collects as much grain as he
can cut at one sweep with a short scythe, which he holds in
his right hand. They carry on this double process with great
spirit and dexterity.

Note II.
Pale Brussels! then what thoughts were thine. [stanza IX line 1]
It was affirmed by the prisoners of war, that Buonaparte had
promised his army, in case of victory, twenty-four hours
plunder of the city of Brussels.

Note III.
'Confront the battery's jaws of flame!
Rush on the levell'd gun!' [stanza X line 2]
The characteristic obstinacy of Napoleon was never more
fully displayed than in what we may be permitted to hope
will prove the last of his fields. He would listen to no
advice, and allow of no obstacles. An eye-witness has given

---

†These are Walter Scott's original notes.

388

the following account of his demeanour towards the end of the action:—

'It was near seven o'clock; Buonaparte, who, till then, had remained upon the ridge of the hill whence he could best behold what passed, contemplated, with a stern countenance, the scene of this horrible slaughter. The more that obstacles seemed to multiply, the more his obstinacy seemed to increase. He became indignant at these unforeseen difficulties; and, far from fearing to push to extremities an army whose confidence in him was boundless, he ceased not to pour down fresh troops, and to give orders to march forward—to charge with the bayonet—to carry by storm. He was repeatedly informed, from different points, that the day went against him, and that the troops seemed to be disordered; to which he only replied,—*"En avant! en avant!"*

'One general sent to inform the Emperor that he was in a position which he could not maintain, because it was commanded by a battery, and requested to know, at the same time, in what way he should protect his division from the murderous fire of the English artillery. "Let him storm the battery," replied Buonaparte, and turned his back on the aid-de-camp who brought the message." '—*Relation de la Bataille de Mont-Saint-Jean. Par un Temoin Occulaire.* Paris, 1815, 8vo. p. 51.

Note IV.
The fate their leader shunn'd to share. [stanza X line 11]
It has been reported that Buonaparte charged at the head of his guards at the last period of this dreadful conflict. This, however, is not accurate. He came down, indeed, to a hollow part of the high road leading to Charleroi, within less than a quarter of a mile of the farm of La Haye

Sainte, one of the points most fiercely disputed. Here he harangued the guards, and informed them that his preceding operations had destroyed the British infantry and cavalry, and that they had only to support the fire of the artillery, which they were to attack with the bayonet. This exhortation was received with shouts of *Vive l'Empereur*, which were heard over all our line, and led to an idea that Napoleon was charging in person. But the guards were led on by Ney; nor did Buonaparte approach nearer the scene of action than the spot already mentioned, which the rising banks on each side rendered secure from all such balls as did not come in a straight line. He witnessed the earlier part of the battle from places yet more remote, particularly from an observatory which had been placed there by the king of the Netherlands, some weeks before, for the purpose of surveying the country.* It is not meant to infer from these particulars that Napoleon shewed, on that memorable occasion, the least deficiency in personal courage; on the contrary, he evinced the greatest composure and presence of mind during the whole action. But it is no less true that report has erred in ascribing to him any desperate efforts of valour for recovery of the battle; and it is remarkable, that during the whole carnage, none of his suite were either killed or wounded, whereas scarcely one of the Duke of Wellington's personal attendants escaped unhurt.

Note V.
England will tell the fight. [stanza X line 18]

---

* The mistakes concerning this observatory have been mutual. The English supposed it was erected for the use of Buonaparte; and a French writer affirms it was constructed by the Duke of Wellington.

In riding up to a regiment which was hard pressed, the Duke called to the men, 'Soldiers, we must never be beat,—what will they say in England?' It is needless to say how this appeal was answered.

Note VI.
As plies the smith his clanging trade,
Against the cuirass rang the blade. [stanza XII line 29]
A private soldier of the 95th regiment compared the sound which took place immediately upon the British cavalry mingling with those of the enemy, to *'a thousand tinkers at work mending pots and kettles.'*

Note VII.
Or will thy Chosen brook to feel
The British shock of levell'd steel. [stanza XIII line 12]
No persuasion or authority could prevail upon the French troops to stand the shock of the bayonet. The imperial guards, in particular, hardly stood till the British were within thirty yards of them, although the French author, already quoted, has put into their mouths the magnanimous sentiment, 'The guards never yield—they die.' The same author has covered the plateau, or eminence, of St Jean, which formed the British position, with redoubts and entrenchments which never had an existence. As the narrative, which is in many respects curious, was written by an eye-witness, he was probably deceived by the appearance of a road and ditch which runs along part of the hill. It may be also mentioned, in criticising this work, that the writer states the Chateau of Hougomont to have been carried by the French, although it was resolutely and successfully defended during the whole action. The enemy, indeed, possessed themselves

of the wood by which it is surrounded, and at length set fire to the house itself; but the British (a detachment of the Guards, under the command of Colonel Macdonnell, and afterwards of Colonel Home,) made good the garden, and thus preserved, by their desperate resistance, the post which covered the return of the Duke of Wellington's right flank.

THE END.

Notes to *The Field of Waterloo*

A majority of the following notes detail changes to the text of the poem suggested at proof stage by James, and sometimes by John, Ballantyne. They are taken from Lockhart's *Life* of Scott, volume V, pp. 91–4.

1   ***Though Valois... monarch bound***: see Mark Akenside (1721–1770), 'To the Country Gentlemen of England' (1758).

2   Stanza I line 1: **Fair Brussels, thou art far behind**: James Ballantyne wrote: 'I do not like this line. It is tame, and the phrase "far behind," has, to my feeling, some associated vulgarity.' Scott's reply was terse: 'Stet.'

3   Stanza II lines 12–13: originally **Let not the *stranger* with disdain, / *The* architecture view**. Ballantyne thought the repetition of the definite article 'cacophanous' and asked, 'Would not *its* do?' in the second case. Scott replied: 'Th. is a bad sound. Ts. a much worse. Read *their*.' Possibly to avoid a repetition in Stanza IV, 'gazer' was substituted for 'stranger'.

4   Stanza IV line 3: **A stranger might reply**: Ballantyne wrote, 'My objection to this is probably fantastical, and I state it only because, from the first moment to the last, it has always made me boggle. I don't like *a stranger* – Query, "The questioned" – The "spectator" – "gazer," etc.' Scott responded: '*Stranger* is appropriate – it means stranger to the circumstance.'

5   line 11: **Teniers**: the Flemish genre painter David Teniers the Younger (1610–1690) specialised in scenes of peasant life.

6   Stanza VI line 16: **Her garner-house profound**: Ballantyne thought this 'quite admirable' but Scott wanted the phrase altered to 'garner under ground', which Ballantyne thought 'quite otherways'. He took the liberty of not making the change and asked, 'Must I?' Scott replied: 'I acquiesce, but with doubts: *profound* sounds affected.'

7   Stanza VIII lines 5–8: **The deadly tug of war . . . Vain hope!**: Ballantyne took issue with the sense of these four lines. 'I must needs repeat, that the deadly tug *did* cease in the case supposed. It lasted long – very long; but, when the limits of resistance, of human strength, were past – that is, after they had fought for ten hours, then the deadly tug *did* cease. Therefore the "hope" was not "vain".' Scott explained, 'it did *not*, – because the observation relates to the strength of those actually engaged, and when *their* strength was exhausted, other squadrons were brought up.' He employed an analogy from the legal profession. 'Suppose you saw two lawyers scolding at the bar, you might say this must have an end – human lungs cannot hold out – but, if the debate were continued by the senior counsel, your

well-grounded expectations would be disappointed.'
He ended the discussion with a genial admonition
from *Richard III*, Act IV, Scene II: 'Cousin, thou wert
not wont to be so dull!'

8   line 19: originally **Nor ceased the *intermitted* shot**.
Ballantyne reported, 'Mr Erskine contends that
"intermitted" is redundant.' Scott agreed and made
the change as published.

9   Stanza X: originally contained the lines, **Never shall
our country say / We gave one inch of ground
away, / When battling for her right**. James
Ballantyne suggested '*In conflict*' for 'When battling'.
His brother John suggested '*Warring*', but conceded, 'I
am afraid *battling* must stand.' Scott replied, 'All worse
than the text', and excised the passage.

10   Stanza XI lines 13–14 and 18: Ballantyne had a number
of issues here. He suggested 'with diffidence' that
Peal'd wildly the imperial name, was 'a somewhat
tame conclusion to so very animated a stanza'. He
pointed out that Scott had no rhyme to the line that
read originally **The Cohort eagles *fly***, and he did not
like the original beginning of the following line, ***Thus
in a torrent***, suggesting 'In one broad torrent', as being
'more spirited'. Scott altered 'fly' to 'flew', substituted
'in one *dark* torrent broad and strong', but stipulated,
'The "imperial name" is *true*, therefore must stand.'

11   Stanza XII line 5: originally **Nor was one forward
footstep *stopped***. 'This staggering word was intended,
I presume,' wrote Ballantyne, 'but I don't like it.'
'Granted,' Scott replied. 'Read *staid*.'

12   lines 20–21: originally **Down were the eagle banners
sent, / Down, down the horse and horsemen**

went. Ballantyne thought it 'very spirited and very fine' but liable to the charge that Scott was repeating himself, having used a similar couplet in *The Lord of the Isles* earlier in the year: 'Down! Down! In headlong overthrow, / Horseman and horse, the foremost go.' Similarly, lines 29–30: 'As hammers on the anvils reel, / Against the cuirass clangs the steel', Ballantyne thought too close to a couplet in *The Lady of the Lake*, published five years earlier: 'I heard the broadswords' deadly clang, / As if an hundred anvils rang'. Scott made the necessary alterations but inserted a note (VI, p. 391) which justified the blacksmith analogy.

13 Stanza XIII line 5: **As their own ocean-rocks hold stance.** John Ballantyne objected, 'I do not know such an English word as *stance*.' Scott made a joke of it, playing on the phrase 'for the nonce', or for the moment: 'Then we'll make it one for the *nance*', and let it stand.

14 line 17: originally **And *newer* standards fly**. James Ballantyne did not like '*newer*' and it was changed to '*other*'.

15 lines 20–21: originally **Or can thy memory fail to *quote*, / Heard to thy cost the vengeful note**. James Ballantyne pleaded, 'Would to God you would alter this *quote*!' His brother agreed: 'Would to God *I* could! – I certainly should.' Scott offered alternatives: 'Or can thy memory fail to know, / Heard oft before in hour of wo', settling on 'Or dwells not in thy memory still, / Heard frequent in thine hour of ill'.

16 Stanza XV line 5: originally **Wrung forth by pride, *regret*, and shame**. James Ballantyne thought '*Regret* a faint epithet amidst such a combination of bitter

feelings', and suggested the line as published. Scott agreed.

17 lines 16–18: James Ballantyne objected to the lines as originally written: **So mingle banner, wain, and gun, / Where in one tide of horror run / The warriors**... 'In the first place, warriors *running* in a tide, is a clashing metaphor; in the second, the warriors *running* at all is a little homely. It is true, no doubt; but really running is little better than scampering. For these causes, one or both, I think the lines should be altered.' Scott pointed out that 'a tide is always said to *run*', but admitted he had not noticed the clash of meanings, and altered the line as published.

18 Stanza XVI line 13: **the valiant Polack**: Marshal Josef Antoni Poniatowski (1763–1813).

19 line 14: originally **found** *gallant* **grave**. Ballantyne thought this 'a singular epithet to a grave', but considered the whole stanza 'eminently fine; and, in particular, the conclusion'. Scott altered the line as published.

20 Stanza XXI line 7: Ballantyne objected to **Redoubted PICTON's soul of fire**. 'From long association, this epithet strikes me as conveying a semi-ludicrous idea.' Scott replied, 'It is here appropriate, and your objection seems merely personal to your own association.'

21 line 12: **MILLER**: mortally wounded at Quatre Bras, Colonel William Miller of the 1st Regiment of Foot Guards said: 'I should like to see the colours of the regiment before I quit them for ever.' They were brought to him. 'His countenance brightened, he smiled, declared himself well satisfied, and was carried from the field.' He died in Brussels three days later.

22   line 21: originally **Through his friend's heart to** *wound* **his own**. Ballantyne suggested '*Pierce*, or rather *stab – wound* is faint.' Scott replied, 'Pierce' and altered the line as published.

23   Stanza XXII lines 1–4: originally **Forgive brave** *fallen*... **To each** *appropriate* **praise**. Ballantyne: 'Don't like "brave fallen" at all; nor "appropriate praise", three lines after. The latter in particular is prosaic.' Scott agreed and altered as published.

'The Dance of Death'

Introduction

Its catalogue lists a substantial section of Walter Scott's library at Abbotsford as devoted to 'MISCELLANIES, INCLUDING BOOKS ON WITCHCRAFT, DEMONOLOGY, APPARITIONS, ASTROLOGY, AND THE OCCULT SCIENCES',[1] testifying to his enduring fascination with the subject. The scurrilous mockery aimed by the *Morning Chronicle* at his *Field of Waterloo* had made reference to this characteristic and recurring theme of Scott's earlier poetry: 'Such goblins! Such frights!' It was not surprising, therefore, that his visit to the recent battleground – a haunted place reeking with thousands of dead – should have inspired a ghost story. But although a tale of supernatural apparition, the setting of 'The Dance of Death' is rooted in circumstantial details of the Waterloo campaign.

Weather conditions described in the poem's opening

---

[1] *Catalogue of the Library at Abbotsford* (Edinburgh: 1838), p. 122.

verses – 'Tempest-clouds...thunder-clap and shower...sheets of levin-light' – are those that prevailed before the battle. The storm that broke over the Anglo-Allied army in the afternoon of 17 June 1815, and which continued throughout the night, was by all eyewitness accounts cataclysmic. 'Such torrents of rain,' wrote one British officer, 'and...such vivid lightning, accompanied with such tremendous peals of thunder, that, though long in a tropical climate, I never beheld or heard the like before.'[2] And a French veteran concurred: 'Never so cold as in Russia...never so wet as on the eve of Waterloo.'[3]

Scott chose to make his protagonist 'grey Allan' – blessed or cursed with the gift of second sight – an old soldier of the 1st Battalion, 92nd Highland Regiment of Foot. This battalion had fought on 16 June at Quatre Bras and been reduced – dead and wounded – from 700 men to 412. Their commanding officer, Lieutenant-Colonel John Cameron of Fassiefern, killed during that carnage, is referred to in both *The Field of Waterloo* and *Paul's Letters to His Kinsfolk*. The 1st Battalion would be further depleted on 18 June by twenty killed and ninety-nine wounded.

There is another accurate detail, albeit one in a fantastical context, that perhaps only a writer who had collected information about the condition of the ground before and after the fighting for his longer poem would have thought to include. The phantom dancers that grey Allan sees move above tall crops covering the land between the two armies: '...airy feet, / So light and fleet, / They do not bend the rye...' It was June, approaching harvest time, and after

---

[2] Lieutenant Pattison to Major General H.T. Siborne, *Waterloo Letters*, p. 337.

[3] Georges Barral, *L'épopée de Waterloo* (Paris: 1898), p. 112.

the day's fighting these crops would be flattened into 'A trampled paste / Of blackening mud and gore'.

Scott described 'The Dance of Death' as 'an odd wild sort of thing'[4] that had sprung out of his main poem. Perhaps it came as a tempting, supernatural fantasy interrupting composition of the more serious work. Or perhaps it was among his first thoughts. 'Each great painting has its original sketch,' he explained to Lady Louisa Stuart, calling this – in conscious recollection of the second witch's words in *Macbeth* – 'a hurly-burly sort of performance'.[5] His novel, *Guy Mannering*, subtitled *The Astrologer* – purportedly 'the work of six weeks at a Christmas'[6] and its first edition sold out on the day of publication – had a similar inspiration and conception but the occult element was all but abandoned after the early chapters.[7]

While they were still in Paris, in September 1815, the poet treated his companion, John Scott of Gala, to the opening of 'the wild and imaginative poem' that would be published in the *Edinburgh Annual Register* later in the year; a poem 'in which the fatal choosers of the slain are supposed to select their victims from the ranks of the combatants on the night before the battle'. Gala would 'never forget the tone and manner in which (with the low impressive voice he recited poetry) he began...'[8]

---

[4] Scott to J.B.S. Morritt Esq., 2 October 1815, quoted *Life* V, p. 90.

[5] *Letters* IV, p.114.

[6] *Life* V, p. 19.

[7] Scott's 'Introduction to *Guy Mannering*', *Introduction and Notes from the Magnum Opus*, ed. J. H. Alexander with P. D. Garside and Claire Lamont (Edinburgh: 2012), p. 108.

[8] *Journal*, p. 206.

ORIGINAL POETRY.

THE

DANCE OF DEATH.

'The Dance of Death'

I.

Night and morning were at meeting
  Over Waterloo;
Cocks had sung their earliest greeting,
  Faint and low they crew,
5 For no paly beam yet shone
  On the heights of Mount Saint John;
  Tempest-clouds prolong'd the sway
  Of timeless darkness over day;
  Whirlwind, thunder-clap, and shower,
10 Mark'd it a predestined hour.
  Broad and frequent through the night
  Flash'd the sheets of levin-light;
  Musquets, glancing lightnings back,
  Shew's the dreary bivouack
15   Where the soldier lay,
  Chill and stiff, and drench'd with rain,
  Wishing dawn of morn again
    Though death should come with day.

II.

'Tis at such a tide and hour,
20 Wizard, witch, and fiend have power,
  And ghastly forms through mist and shower

405

Gleam on the gifted ken;
And then the affrighted prophet's ear
Drinks whispers strange of fate and fear,
25   Presaging death and ruin near
      Among the sons of men—
Apart from Albyn's war-array,
'Twas then grey Allan sleepless lay;
Grey Allan, who, for many a day,
30   Had follow'd stout and stern
Where, through battle's rout and reel,
Storm of shot and hedge of steel,
Led the grandson of Lochiel,
      Valiant Fassiefern.

35   Through steel and shot he leads no more,
Low-laid 'mid friends' and foemen's gore—
But long his native lake's wild shore,
And Sunart rough, and high Ardgower,
      And Morven long shall tell,
40   And proud Bennevis hear with awe,
How, upon bloody Quatre-Bras,
Brave Cameron heard the wild hurra
      Of conquest as he fell.

III.

'Lone on the outskirts of the host,
45   The weary sentinel held post,
And heard, through darkness far aloof,
The frequent clang of courser's hoof,
Where held the cloak'd patrole their course,
And spurr'd 'gainst storm the swerving horse;
50   But there are sounds in Allan's ear,
Patrole nor sentinel may hear,

And sights before his eye aghast
Invisible to them have pass'd,
  When down the destined plain
55 'Twixt Britain and the bands of France,
Wild as marsh-borne meteors glance,
Strange phantoms wheel'd a revel dance,
  And doom'd the future slain.—
Such forms were seen, such sounds were heatd,
60 When Scotland's James his march prepared
  For Flodden's fatal plain;
Such, when he drew his ruthless sword,
As Chusers of the Slain, adored
  The yet unchristen'd Dane.
65 An indistinct and phantom band,
They wheel'd their ring-dance hand in hand,
  With gesture wild and dread;
The Seer, who watch'd them ride the storm,
Saw through their faint and shadowy form
70 The lightning's flash more red;
And still their ghastly roundelay
Was of the coming battle-fray
  And of the destined dead.

IV.
Song.

Wheel the wild dance
75 While lightnings glance,
  And thunders rattle loud,
And call the brave
To bloody grave,
  To sleep without a shroud

80   Our airy feet,
    So light and fleet,
      They do not bend the rye
  That sinks its head when whirlwinds rave,
  And swells again in eddying wave,
85   As each wild gust blows by;
  But still the corn,
  At dawn of morn
      Our fatal steps that bore,
  At eve lies waste
90 A trampled paste
      Of blackening mud and gore.

V.

  Wheel the wild dance
  While lightnings glance,
      And thunders rattle loud,
95 And call the brave
  To bloody grave,
      To sleep without a shroud

  Wheel the wild dance!
  Brave sons of France,
100   For you our ring makes room;
  Make space full wide
  For martial pride,
      For banner, spear, and plume.
  Approach, draw near,
105 Proud cuirassier!
      Room for the men of steel!
  Through crest and plate
  The broad-sword's weight

Both head and heart shall feel.

VI.

110 Wheel the wild dance
 While lightnings glance,
  And thunders rattle loud,
And call the brave
To bloody grave,
115   To sleep without a shroud

Sons of the spear!
You feel us near
  In many a ghastly dream;
With fancy's eye
120 Our forms you spy,
  And hear our fatal scream.
With clearer sight
Ere falls the night,
  Just when to weal or woe
125 Your disembodied souls take flight
On trembling wing—each startled sprite
  Our choir of death shall know.

VII.

Wheel the wild dance
While lightnings glance,
130 And thunders rattle loud,
And call the brave
To bloody grave,
  To sleep without a shroud

Burst ye clouds, in tempest showers,

135 Redder rain shall soon be ours—
    See the east grows wan—
Yield we place to sterner game,
Ere deadlier bolts and drearer flame
Shall the welkin's thunders shame;
140 Elemental rage is tame
    To the wrath of man.

VIII

At morn, grey Allan's mates with awe
Hear of the vision'd sights he saw,
    The legend heard him say;
145 But the seer's gifted eye was dim,
Deafen'd his ear, and stark his limb,
    Ere closed that bloody day—
He sleeps far from his highland heath,—
But often of the Dance of Death
145   His comrades tell the tale
On picquet-post, when ebbs the night,
And waning watch-fires glow less bright,
    And dawn is glimmering pale.

Abbotsford, October 1, 1815

Notes to 'The Dance of Death'

Stanza I line 12: **levin-light**: archaic term for lightning.

Stanza II line 33: **grandson of Lochiel...Fassiefern**: Lieutenant-Colonel John Cameron of Fassiefern was the great-grandson of John Cameron (died 1748), 18th Chief of the Clan Cameron and Lord Lochiel. See also p. 316, Letter VI, note 12 of *Paul's Letters* and Stanza XXI of *Field of Waterloo*.

Line 38: **Sunart**: an area south-west of Lochabar.

Line 38: **Ardgower**: derives from the Gaelic, *Ard Ghobhar*, meaning 'height of the goats'. The mountain is situated on the Ardamurchan Peninsula, on Loch Linnhe.

Line 39: **Morven**: the highest peak in the county of Caithness.

Line 40: **Bennevis**: or Ben Nevis, the highest mountain in the British Isles.

Stanza III line 60: **James...fatal plain**: James IV of Scotland was killed at Flodden, 9 September 1513, the last British monarch to die in battle.

Line 63: **Chusers...unchristen'd Dane**: every Viking warrior would wish to be taken from the battlefield to Valhalla by a *valkyrja* or 'chooser of the slain'.

THE HISTORY OF VINTAGE

The famous American publisher Alfred A. Knopf (1892–1984) founded Vintage Books in the United States in 1954 as a paperback home for the authors published by his company. Vintage was launched in the United Kingdom in 1990 and works independently from the American imprint although both are part of the international publishing group, Random House.

Vintage in the United Kingdom was initially created to publish paperback editions of books bought by the prestigious literary hardback imprints in the Random House Group such as Jonathan Cape, Chatto & Windus, Hutchinson and later William Heinemann, Secker & Warburg and The Harvill Press. There are many Booker and Nobel Prize-winning authors on the Vintage list and the imprint publishes a huge variety of fiction and non-fiction. Over the years Vintage has expanded and the list now includes great authors of the past – who are published under the Vintage Classics imprint – as well as many of the most influential authors of the present. In 2012 Vintage Children's Classics was launched to include the much-loved authors of our youth.

For a full list of the books Vintage publishes,
please visit our website
www.vintage-books.co.uk

For book details and other information about the classic authors we publish, please visit the Vintage Classics website
www.vintage-classics.info

www.vintage-classics.info